FEB 11

D1523445

HÜSKER DÜ

HÜSKER DÜ

THE STORY OF THE NOISE-POP PIONEERS

Andrew Earles

WHO LAUNCHED

MODERN ROCK

Voyageur Press

First published in 2010 by Voyageur Press, an imprint of MBI Publishing Company, 400 First Avenue North, Suite 300, Minneapolis, MN 55401 USA

Voyageur Press titles are also available at discounts in bulk quantity for industrial or sales-promotional use. For details write to Special Sales Manager at MBI Publishing Company, 400 First Avenue North, Suite 300, Minneapolis, MN 55401 USA.

To find out more about our books, visit us online at www.voyageurpress.com.

ISBN-13: 978-0-7603-3504-8

Library of Congress Cataloging-in-Publication Data

Earles, Andrew, 1973–
  Hüsker Dü : the story of the noise-pop pioneers who launched modern rock / Andrew Earles.
      p. cm.
  Includes index.
  ISBN 978-0-7603-3504-8 (plc)
  1. Hüsker Dü (Musical group) 2. Rock musicians–United States–Biography. I. Title.
  ML421.H86E27 2010
  782.42166092'2–dc22
  [B]
                                    2010026096

Design Manager: Katie Sonmor
Cover and Book Design: John Barnett / 4 Eyes Design
Layout: Elly Gosso

Printed in the United States of America

This book is dedicated to the memory of my father, Dennis A. Earles (1923-1993).

CONTENTS

INTRODUCTION

These introductions often find the author spinning some poignant tale about the first time he or she was introduced to the band that they are writing about. Usually, it's an incredibly boring and self-serving story, and the circumstances detailed are in no way unique but, in fact, shared by most fans of the band. I would never bore you with the story of my discovering this band. Having stated that, the music of Hüsker Dü is undoubtedly among the core works that massively impacted my taste and frame of reference. I do love this band's music; a fact that has remained unchanged since age sixteen.

But that's not why my name is on a book about Hüsker Dü.

When discussing music-based nonfiction, three goals pop to mind: criticism, telling a good story, and documenting the importance of an artist's work (to his or her contemporaries, to those who have followed, and to those who will make music in the future). Many books cover all three goals to some degree because it's impossible to address one without discussing the others, and this book is no exception. However, I have hopefully placed an obvious weight on the latter aspect. Hüsker Dü's body of work has not yet received its deserved exposure, nor is its influence on the past twenty-five years understood in the same way that the influences of, say, Black Flag, Sonic Youth, or Slayer are understood.

In the time since their breakup, Hüsker Dü's legacy has been grossly mishandled by the music press. As a result, the band's body of work has been transformed into something unapproachable. For a young music fan interested in learning about the band, being subjected to even a paragraph of tired, misguided speculation about the dynamic between Bob Mould and Grant Hart before getting to the goods (e.g., the best place to start, why the music is influential, what the musicians went through to make it, etc.) can confuse and perpetuate a continual game of Chinese telephone. There are more people carrying around salacious untruths about Hüsker Dü (in case conversation calls for them) than there are people who have actually *heard* Hüsker Dü. If this book shifts that trend in the right direction, even by a tiny degree, I will consider it a personal success.

So be warned: Readers of this book will be disappointed if they hope to be rewarded with the gritty details of any band member's drug use. In the beginning, Hüsker Dü did not play fast due to amphetamines. In the end, Grant Hart's drug use did not break up the band. About a year ago, I received an email that began with excitement over the fact that someone was writing a book about Hüsker Dü. Then the writer asked, "So I gotta know . . . did Grant and Bob get it on?" The fact is Hart's and Mould's sexuality has absolutely nothing to do with why this band is important.

I've also gotten email requests for "Just one story, man, come on!" And, of course, there are more than a few people, including one festival organizer, who believe I hold the definitive answer to the question "So, do you think they will reunite?" Despite all three members' continued denials, this last question is still occasionally fueled by the October 2004 appearance of Mould and Hart together onstage at a benefit for cancer-stricken friend Karl Mueller of Soul Asylum (they played "Never Talking to You Again" and "Hardly Getting Over It"). I can't predict the future, but I can tell readers with certainty that I hope they do not reunite onstage in front of thousands upon thousands of people (because I guarantee that's what the draw would be). What I do hope is that they reunite in a rented banquet room in a quiet Holiday Inn, in someone's living room, or over a good meal in a restaurant where no one will recognize them. From there, I hope they take the necessary measures to gain control of their back catalog so that a conscientious label can produce the lavish reissue jobs their music deserves. Then I hope each man can continue his life with a little less stress and a little more happiness. These idealistic, possibly naïve wishes are further delayed each time a certain type of Hüsker Dü coverage sees the light of day. Actually, this type of coverage isn't really a "type" because there really hasn't been an alternative. The acrimony between band members is as much a product of shoddy journalism as it is a product of any band member's mouth.

These are human beings who at one time, around a quarter-century ago, created a type of rock 'n' roll that is so important to the form's overall evolution that many bands we now take for granted would have never existed or would have sounded completely different without Hüsker Dü's influence: Nirvana, Foo Fighters, Superchunk, Pavement, Deftones, Pixies, My Bloody Valentine, Guided by Voices . . . the list goes on. Listen to side two of *Zen Arcade* or even just to Mould's "I'll Never Forget You." How similar does this sound to noise-rock of the '90s? Grant Hart's "Don't Want to Know If You Are Lonely" is the blueprint for a sizeable chunk of the indie- and alt-rock movements that would flip the music business on its ear just five years after the release of *Candy Apple Grey* in 1986.

Anyone who came up going to loud, sparsely attended shows in the '90s knows that many very, very loud bands blasted their noise-drenched melodies (or anti-melodies) into empty clubs. Hüsker Dü was one of a tiny handful of bands that invented that air-moving level of volume. Hüsker Dü also helped to create the network of clubs that still exists and was crucial in laying the groundwork that supports the wildly successful pop-punk movement led by Green Day, the Offspring, NOFX, second-act Bad Religion, the Epitaph and Fat Wreck Chords labels, and the Vans Warped Tour.

Going back even further to DIY trailblazing in the American hardcore movement of the early '80s, Hüsker Dü is every bit as important as Black Flag or Minor Threat. "Purists" ignore them because the band outgrew hardcore and went on to level a huge impact on more musically inclined movements. The band ran its own label from 1981 to 1985, releasing almost twenty titles that are essential to understanding this period of underground music in America. Hüsker Dü established the notion of the album as an item to sell on tour. At the same time, the band did not tour *behind* albums—they toured *in front* of them, releasing an album and selling copies at gigs but filling their set with songs from not only the next as-yet-unreleased album but from the album *after* the next album. This was progress, not disrespect for their audiences. The band's shows weren't sing-alongs filled with familiar material, but Hüsker Dü was so consistently mind-blowing as a live band it didn't matter if the set contained previously unheard songs. In fact, Hüsker Dü cared greatly for their audiences, and they knew it was their duty to give one hundred percent to ten people or to ten thousand people. They were always approachable and were unbelievably generous to new or less successful bands.

I am in my mid-thirties, which makes me too young to have seen the band perform. I have never even lived in Minneapolis or St. Paul, though they share the Mississippi River with the city in which I was born and raised, and currently reside. Some readers may be of the mindset that this book needs to be written by someone who was "part of the scene" or of a certain age. This logic is flawed. Despite my love for Hüsker Dü's music, my age and location provide a very important objective disconnect from the subject at hand. Writers who were "there" almost invariably get in the way of a good story by giving in to a personal angle of some sort.

I began work on this book at the end of 2007. It was my eleventh year writing about music, but it was my first as a full-time writer. The typical response to the statement "There's a Hüsker Dü book being written by Andrew Earles" has been "Who's that?" There were prospective sources, names that readers may or may not recognize, who declined to participate in this book. While I respect these decisions completely, I am inclined to feel they negate criticism from these same individuals. If you declined to participate in this book and read, for example, a particular sub-strand of the story that is not expounded upon to your liking, ask yourself how your participation might have produced a different outcome.

Luckily, I nabbed some wonderful and generous sources, but due to the dynamic between the band members, the status of their back catalog on SST, the refusal of the aforementioned sources to be interviewed, and difficulty confirming claims made by participating sources, there are some unavoidable holes in the tale. There are also intentional holes and the downplaying of subject matter that is unimportant to the principal goal of this book: to give the band proper credit for the music they made and practices they pioneered. Never was this book envisioned as a lurid tell-all. Somewhere at this very moment a band is breaking up for the same unspectacular reasons that Hüsker Dü broke up. Creative differences, friends getting sick of one another, pressure from a record label—these things happen all the time.

Though Bob Mould respectfully declined to participate in this book, great effort has been made to present his views through the years. Before I started writing this book, I had respect for Bob Mould. When I finished this book, after all of the research and all of the interviews absorbed into the wee hours of each night, the word *respect* doesn't do justice to my view of him. As of this writing, Bob Mould is preparing his own book for publication, and it is my wish that both texts will exist in a complementary manner.

Both Grant Hart and Greg Norton did participate in this book. Neither man knew who I was when I approached them, yet eventually placed their trust in me. And they did so separately of each other's influence. Not once did I forget this as work went forward. I am very fond of each man as a person with whom I now have a certain rapport that spans professional courtesy to friendship, depending on the context of our communication, and I hope this never changes.

In one particularly productive two-year span, Hüsker Dü wrote five albums and two 7-inch singles. All of them are untouchable. Sometimes such considerations get overlooked in the race to tell the world one band member's feelings about his former band mates. Sure, discontent is communicated in this book. It is, ultimately, an unhappy story. But it's also a very positive story about a band that was a major player in a crucially important period of music history. This book is not perfect. If you want that Hüsker Dü book, you may die waiting. This book does, however, come from the right place. ╪

SOMETHIN' TO DÜ

1

Located mostly within New York State's vast Adirondack Park, Franklin County sits hard against the state's border with Quebec. The county is home to potato and dairy farms and, not surprisingly, brutal winters. Franklin County is also notable for a number of correctional facilities brought to the area in an attempt to stabilize the economy. Two of these prisons are located in Malone, a dot a little more than ten miles south of the Canadian border comprising a town and a smaller village of the same name. In short, Franklin County is upstate of the upstate New York commonly known as a vacation destination.

Bob Mould spent the first seventeen years of his life in Malone. Born on October 16, 1961, his parents were literally the "mom and pop" who owned and operated the small local grocery store. Mould was introduced to music early on. His grandmother cared for a woman who had been struck by lightning and permanently disabled. Bob would tag along and was allowed to play the woman's piano while his grandmother worked. He eventually learned how to bang out songs that were familiar through hours of radio listening. Bob also spent a lot of time helping out around his parents' grocery. The store's cigarette distributor happened to stock jukeboxes as well, so Bob's father would purchase 45-rpm records for a penny apiece. During an installment of San Francisco's City Arts & Lectures in late 2007, Mould was asked to describe how he came to punk rock in such an isolated town:

> Well, the path, the way that I got into it, it was a circuitous route. You know in high school I was into KISS and Aerosmith and all that. My first concert was going to the Montreal Forum on a bus with a bunch of my drunk friends on a high school trip to go see Rush opening for Aerosmith and I would buy . . . a magazine that was published in the mid-'70s called

Rock Scene. . . . And they focused a lot on KISS and Aerosmith . . . but also they would always talk about these bands, like the Ramones and Television and Patti Smith and the whole CBGB scene at the time and I got sort of introduced to it that way. And, you know, I thought they looked sort of cool and I remember getting the first Ramones album when it came out and I put that on the stereo and I said, okay this is music, you know, this is what music is supposed to be. No offense to Aerosmith or any of the other groups, but when I heard that, everything sort of changed for me and I decided that I needed to make that kind of music.

That wasn't going to happen in Malone, especially for Bob Mould, who by that time was hit with the reality of his prospects in the tiny village:

I started applying for college in my sophomore year of high school. I took SATs very early. I had an exit strategy. I mean [Malone] was a great place. It was a very idyllic, you know, a quiet place to grow up. You are used to long winters; very harsh winters. I guess I was a little different than most kids. I had friends and did sports in high school, so I was engaged with other folks. But I knew that I really had to get away from that town as quickly as possible, partially because there were no jobs and partially because of my awareness as a homosexual. As a gay kid I knew that it wasn't the place to be. So yeah, I got accepted to Macalester College, I think at the end of my junior year, on an underprivileged scholarship. My parents were sort of poverty-line and I was lucky that they had a spot for me at the school. Macalester is a good school and I was very fortunate. And I also knew that there was punk rock in Minneapolis already.

The political leanings at Macalester, located in Minneapolis' "Twin City" of St. Paul, also attracted Mould, who liked the fact that in the 1960s the school gave college credits to students who protested for at least three hours a day (with official organizations, of course). And Mould liked that Macalester was notorious for having one of the historically worst teams in all of college football.

So in 1977, Mould, an intellectual punk rocker with an impressive knowledge of underground music, moved to the Twin Cities. In retrospect, considering their common interests and proximity, it would have seemed a freakish accident if Mould didn't eventually meet G. Vernon Hart.

Grant Hart was a friendly, outgoing, resourceful, underground-obsessed teen who was also fearless and inventive, especially when he wanted something. "I was a mall rat at the Signal Hills Mall in West St. Paul on Robert Street," he explains, going on to describe time spent in the mall's record store, Melody Lane. "I probably put in a thousand hours sitting on the radiator being turned onto new and different music by this employee named Mark Wheeler. Also on staff there was Sharon Boyd, a funky little fox that had more or less made lip service to me about the possibility of working there. I, of course, took this to be a job offer. Then one day I go up there and a new guy is working. I approached Sharon, asking her why she didn't call me about the job, and her response was, 'Grant, you're only fifteen.'"

That new employee was a lanky teen—one year older than Grant—named Greg Norton. Norton remembers his first encounter with Grant a short time later. "I was hired at Melody Lane in February of 1978, and I met Grant a month later," Norton says. "I'm walking through the mall and this kid comes up to me and says, 'Hey man, you took my job . . . Sharon said I could have a job at the store once I turned sixteen, but she went and hired you!'"

Norton attended Henry Sibley High School in West St. Paul. "I already knew how to roll a joint before I entered high school and that really helped hone my people skills once I was there," remembers Norton. "When I was fourteen, I worked in downtown St. Paul, when there was still an actual, vibrant downtown with lots of theaters, lots of cool things happening. Then, over the years, St. Paul literally died. They did some weird things with some malls, they tried to copy some things done elsewhere, but St. Paul culturally, more or less, died towards the end of the '70s, which was sad to see."

Hart attended South St. Paul High School. Like West St. Paul, South St. Paul is a separate municipality from St. Paul, and Hart remembers a certain issue with his high school experience: "I was marking time in high school. I took the art and music classes that I could, and I was in the band, but it was a weird situation at South St. Paul. The band had separated itself so much from the cheerleading activities but had won a couple of 'Best Instrumental Jazz Ensemble Awards' already. The school decided that the band needed to be more in line with the football and hockey activities, so they hired this guy who was really big on marching in uniform. Just marching and marching and marching and marching so much that it didn't take long for me and this man to alienate ourselves from one another, and he had the power to tell me not to sign up for my senior year."

While in high school, Hart had a cover band called Train. He was the keyboardist and owned a Farfisa organ. Train played out one time, at a bowling alley called The Cooler. "I suggested a Patti Smith song to be added to our cover repertoire," Hart recalls, "and the guitarist, who was in his early forties and was the biggest redneck to ever wear a ponytail, shot it down with 'Well, that's punk rock!'"

It wasn't that people were unaware of punk rock by 1977—it was that people hated punk rock, especially in places like South St. Paul, a noted blue-collar bastion whose economy was based in its stockyards. "Grant and I would go to parties with a knapsack full of records and eventually commandeer the turntable and just piss people off by playing the Ramones and Patti Smith," remembers Norton. "We cleared a few rooms."

In his high school art class, Hart made a T-shirt depicting Cleveland band Pere Ubu's logo in preparation for their upcoming show at what was then Minneapolis' premier punk rock club, the Longhorn Bar, in 1978. "We show up, and [the band] thought we had followed them from Cleveland," remembers Norton. Instead of wearing the shirt, Hart had made it as a gift so that he and Norton could meet the band. "They were really impressed," Norton adds.

Hart's and Norton's penchant for punk rock would also capture Mould's attention. "I had a practice PA that would fit into the back of my car, and I had a powered turntable," Hart continues. "We would go to the park and set up. . . . When I worked at Cheapo Records [near Macalester College], I would hook my PA up to the main system, put the speakers out in front of the store, and just blast punk rock out across and down Grand Avenue. And that's what got Bob Mould's attention. Plus, it was the only record store within walking distance of the dorm. I don't remember what quantity, but I was also moving a little weed at the time, and that might have played into the early contact we had with one another."

Hart may or may not have sold weed to Mould, but the common claim that it resulted in their meeting is a convenient yarn. A better and more poignant explanation of their meeting lies in their common interests. Punk rock had arrived in the Twin Cities, which, though culturally progressive, was still a moderately sized urban area, unlike New York or L.A.

"There were probably several ways that Bob and I got the attention of one another," Hart explains. "These were the days when there was no competition. We were both young homosexuals and we weren't destined to be two ships passing in the night—we were going to find one another somehow. Bob would bring in records [to Cheapo] that he had purchased up in Toronto or Montreal before he moved to St. Paul. Bob could also bring a record back to his dorm room and know how to play all of the guitar parts by the following morning."

By his late teens, Hart was musically formidable in his own right and could play multiple instruments. However, he was most proficient on the drums. His kit had been inherited from his older brother, who taught him to play along to "The Age of Aquarius." In 1971, Hart's brother was killed by a drunk driver when Grant was ten. His brother was just two years older.

Hart was still in high school when he and Norton formed the outfit that would morph into Hüsker Dü. "We hung out a lot in my basement on Pontiac Place," Norton says, referring to his mom's address in suburban Mendota Heights, an address that would later appear on most Reflex Records releases. "Also, in the year leading up to the band forming in March of 1979, Grant and I spent a lot of time at the Longhorn. We went to a lot of shows, and Grant was underage. The funniest thing was, on his eighteenth birthday, when he was finally legal, they carded him for the first time and he'd left his ID at home. They wouldn't let him in."

Hart goes on to recall the band's first gig. "A bunch of us were at a friend's house one night and things got weird, so part of the party, including myself and a guy we knew named Charlie Pine, went up to Ron's Randolph Inn [a few miles from Macalester] because it was in the neighborhood," he explains. "When Charlie was getting a pitcher of beer, he asked the guy managing that night, 'So you have bands here?' The guy's response was, 'Yeah, you got a band?' to which Charlie replied, 'Yeah, we're called Buddy and the Returnables.' The bartender said, 'Good, you're booked on the 30th and 31st of this month.' Buddy and the Returnables was something that Charlie had just pulled out of his ass right at that moment."

"Charlie came back to the table," Norton continues. "'Grant! Grant! We've got to put a band together. I just booked us here on March 30th and 31st. Who else can we get to play?' And Grant said,

'Well, I know this guy that's really good on guitar." The next day, Grant and I picked Bob up and we went to my mom's basement and jammed out a bunch of Ramones tunes, essentially. Then we practiced with Charlie in his kitchen for the actual gigs. We put together three sets of cover songs."

In Michael Azerrad's *Our Band Could Be Your Life*, Greg Norton is quoted describing his and Hart's first impression of Mould: "Bob was this dorky kid in a leather jacket with long hair and a Flying V like the Ramones."

Norton was probably misheard, as Johnny Ramone didn't play a Flying V, and certainly Norton, a dedicated Ramones fan, wouldn't associate a Flying V with the band, especially seeing as how Ramone famously played a white Mosrite Ventures II. Norton likely was referring to a purple Mosrite that Mould used sporadically throughout '79 and '80 (it can be heard on a couple of their first demo tracks), though Mould *did* own a "Flying V" of sorts. Often wrongly identified as a Gibson Flying V, the guitar was a 1975 Ibanez Rocket Roll, and it would become Mould's mainstay and as much a band icon as the umlauts in their name and Norton's handlebar moustache.

During the first explosion of copy guitars in the early '70s, the Japanese company Ibanez went perhaps overboard, producing its own versions of Gibson's Flying V, among many other models. (The company even made a copy of Ampeg's Dan Armstrong model, the transparent Plexiglas guitar that became Greg Ginn's signature instrument throughout Black Flag's history.) In 1977, Gibson's parent company brought a copyright infringement case against Ibanez, and a certain stigma became attached to copy guitars, regardless of their quality.

"I never knew him without it," Hart says of Mould and his Ibanez.

"That was the guitar that Bob brought with him from Malone," Norton remembers. "That was *the* guitar."

In a 1981 *City Pages* interview (just the second piece of local Hüsker coverage), Mould told the writer, "I use the Flying V [*sic*] partly because I don't want an angular sound. I just go for a real flat signal. Greg's bass is the same way; it's a real antagonizing sound."

It was at the first practice sessions in Pine's kitchen that Hart yelled out "Hüsker Dü!" during an improvised section of a cover song. It means "Do You Remember?" in Danish but most likely popped into Hart's head because it was also the name of a popular board game from his childhood.

The practice sessions in Pine's kitchen not only yielded a name but eventually would result in a final lineup too. "After the first night at Ron's," Norton continues, "the three of us—Grant, Bob, and myself—said 'Well, this seems to be working out, we like playing together.' And that was based on the previous times we jammed in my basement. So the three of us got to the gig really early the next night, and the guys that worked there took us downstairs to smoke some weed. Once Charlie showed up, it was clear that we weren't going to be playing with him for long."

Pine's tenure with the band wasn't quite over, however. "At that point, Charlie Pine calls up and says, 'Hey, I've got another gig for us.' It was playing SpringFest at Macalester. It was a yearly festival and we were the headlining band." After Bob, Greg, Grant, and Charlie had played everything they knew from the Ron's Randolph Inn gig, they were informed that fifteen to twenty minutes remained in the set, so Bob, Grant, and Greg launched into some of the original songs from their practice sessions in Norton's basement.

Though justifiably taken off guard, Pine made a game attempt to play along with the songs he'd never practiced.

"His organ was one of those older, hard-wired pieces," Hart recalls. "It had a series of wires coming out of it. A friend of ours, Steven 'Balls' Migitowski, had given the thumbs-up to Bob, Greg and I, while giving the thumbs-down to Charlie, literally, and he had also disabled Charlie's organ."

Officially a three-piece after the SpringFest incident, the band was ready to take on the city's top punk rock stage. "The third time we played out was our very first gig at the Longhorn," Hart says, referring to the former downtown steakhouse turned pillar of punk rock, both for local and touring bands. "We probably spent a little while practicing and developing new material, because this was like playing the Apollo for us."

"It was us, then Wilma and the Wilbers, and I want to say the Testers," Norton remembers. "We got paid twenty bucks for that gig."

In order to play the Longhorn, local bands had to first schedule a weekday audition. These auditions were held during what was called "the businessmen's lunch," though it was unclear what criteria had to be met for a band to be invited back for the elusive nighttime gig.

"The way I remember it, Grant told us that we had an audition at the Longhorn, when there was no audition," Norton says. "We hauled all of our gear down there on a Tuesday, in the middle of the day. We set up and started playing. A few minutes later, the guy who ran the Longhorn—his name was Hartley Frank—showed up screaming, 'Stop! Stop! Okay! Okay! You can play here. You got the gig!' The thing is, we never had an audition. It was a completely balls-out move on Grant's part. We just went in there and set up, played, and the purpose of the whole thing was to keep Bob in town for the summer."

"Bob was prepared to go back to Malone for the summer because we had no other gigs lined up," Hart confirms.

"Not only did we get that gig," says Norton, "but we got a lot of gigs. I remember all summer, the only way we knew if we were playing an upcoming Friday or Saturday was by looking at the Longhorn ad in the paper. We'd open it up each week and it was 'Look! We're playing this Friday!'"

▮   ▮   ▮

After the 1979 school year, Mould did indeed fly home to Malone, but only for a short stay—the Longhorn ploy to keep him in the Twin Cities for the summer worked. "That was the summer that Bob lived at my folks' house until the fall semester started up," remembers Hart.

Also by the summer of '79, Hart and Norton were working at Northern Lights, a legendary but now defunct record store owned by John Carnahan on University Avenue in St. Paul. "My boss made us an offer: If we cleaned out the basement of the store, we could start practicing down there," Norton says. "We practiced every night. We would just mess around, each bringing in ideas, until we had a decent amount of original material. The store would close, everybody would be kicked out. There was a Montgomery Ward across the street and another shopping center next door, [so] there wasn't anyone to complain about noise. We would practice every single night at nine o'clock. We'd start writing music and we'd just keep writing music. And we wrote a lot of crap—tons of crap. We kept this practicing schedule up for almost six months."

The Twin Cities underground music scene was growing at a rapid rate. Most of the growth was taking place in Minneapolis, and Hüsker

Dü was a St. Paul band. The location of the Longhorn and other music hubs like Oar Folkjokeopus record store across the Mississippi in Minneapolis allegedly caused some problems for the band, but all three members would remain in St. Paul until early to mid-1982. Hart was the driver during this period, and his station wagon did a fine job of getting everyone to gigs and parties as needed.

"As for base differences, St. Paul is the government center, it's the capital," Norton explains. "Minneapolis, it could be argued, is the cultural center. You've got the Guthrie Theater, you've got the Walker Art Center, you've got the Minneapolis Institute of Art. When the band first started, we were from St. Paul. 'Where are you from?' [Assumes proud tone] 'We're from St. Paul.' We just kept doing what we wanted to do . . . we didn't really give a shit what everyone in Minneapolis thought. Every once in a while, we'd say, 'Oh, you know, it's that "St. Paul Sound"' . . . we were making music for us." A mix of powerpop and straightforward punk rock is the best way to describe the earliest incarnation of Hüsker Dü's three-piece lineup, the lineup that would remain static for the full run of the band.

Such a sonic amalgamation would have come as no surprise to anyone who was paying attention. After all, the Twin Cities scene didn't pop up out of nowhere in 1979. In fact, it could be argued that a forward-thinking music community emerged in Minneapolis at the same time, if not before, things took off for New York City's storied and much-chronicled scene. What's inarguable, however, is that a small collective of Twin Cities thinkers and doers was responsible for this avant activity on the edge of the northern prairies, and within that tiny group, one man can be credited with steering the ship. In retrospect, it's incredibly bizarre that Chris Osgood and his cohorts—people like Peter Jesperson, Paul Stark, Terry Katzman, and others—haven't garnered more historical coverage in the pantheon of journalism documenting the first wave of U.S. proto-punk/punk/avant-underground activity in the mid-'70s. Osgood and this group were crucial to the movement that Hüsker Dü would soon be co-leading as the '80s commenced.

Osgood's punk rock band, the Suicide Commandos (with bassist/vocalist Steve Almaas and drummer/vocalist Dave Ahl), could very well have been the first U.S. punk rock band to tour the country in a do-it-yourself manner, and even though the group's self-released singles on P.S. Records came out in 1976 and 1977, respectively, the band was active as far back as 1974. There is a commonly traded anecdote about the first Ramones record hitting the racks and those in the Minneapolis scene responding with glee that another band sounded like the Suicide Commandos. Also notable is that the Ramones had little to do with the DIY aesthetic or ethic, having been scooped up by Seymour Stein's major label, Sire Records, which also secured debuts from Television, DMZ, Talking Heads, Blondie, and several others. These bands toured in buses if they toured at all, and they hit major markets.

"We did two singles on P.S. Records, and a lot of people think that stands for 'Paul Stark' because we recorded them in Paul Stark's studio," remembers Osgood. "P.S. Records was the band's label, and it was in fact the precursor to Twin/Tone."

The Commandos would land a major-label deal, but before they did, they got in the van. Osgood recalls touring before there was any semblance of a circuit:

> We knew we wanted to play at Max's Kansas City and CBGB, and we had no way to get there, so we tried to find places to play on the way there and back. Our model for doing it was to try and find the cool record store in town, call them up, and ask, 'Is there a cool club to play there?' I worked for K-Tel, the company that did those compilation LPs like *Goofy Greats* and *Wacky Westerns*, and they had an office in [suburban] Hopkins. My job was to sit on a WATS line and call every Osco Drug store in Oklahoma and get them to restock our records. I was rack-jobbing long distance. I had a really nice sales manager who allowed me to use the last fifteen minutes of each day to call anywhere in the country. A WATS line was a phone line with unlimited long distance for a price. My manager said, "Yeah, just use that time to call your grandma," so I booked two tours that way, just trial and error. After we had been out a few times, other people started doing the same thing and a little route got established. We couldn't have played New York if we didn't have the Pirate's Cove to play in Cleveland, and that was thanks to Pere Ubu. We made friends with those guys, and we loved Pere Ubu's singles at the time.

> We lived in a farmhouse at the time, called Utopia House, and there was no running water or heat. We lived there for three years, because we wanted to play and have very little overhead. We paid thirty bucks a month, collectively, for rent. We were able to go out on these tours that were pretty long, and if it's the middle of winter and your house has no heat, you're not going to be in a hurry to get home.

Back home, Osgood became one of the three principals behind the formation of Twin/Tone Records in 1977. The other two were studio engineer Paul Stark and Charlie Hallman, a sportswriter for St. Paul's daily paper, the *Pioneer Press*. When Osgood's Commandos signed with Mercury for their one and only full-length studio album, 1978's *The Suicide Commandos Make a Record*, he no longer had time to focus on Twin/Tone, and his position was filled by Peter Jesperson. As the money guy, Hallman's tastes often ran more traditional than those of Jesperson and Stark.

Jesperson managed Oar Folkjokeopus—*the* record store on the scene since 1973. (The name was a combination of owner Vern Sanden's two favorite psychedelic folk albums: Moby Grape guitarist Skip Spence's solo record, *Oar*, and Roy Harper's *Folkjokeopus*.) Jesperson was also a DJ and show-booker at the Longhorn. "My principal work at Twin/Tone was in the A&R and distribution channels," he explains. "The Longhorn opened up in '77, and that was *the* place—the only place a band could play from '77 through when the [7th Street] Entry opened up in 1980. I booked shows and was a DJ there until Halloween of 1981."

As for Osgood and the Suicide Commandos, Jesperson enthuses, "If you go back to the Suicide Commandos, they really forged their own path. They went out and talked their way into rooms that didn't know what the hell the band was about. The importance of the Suicide Commandos cannot be overstated: They were the granddaddies of the whole scene and DIY before I'd ever heard the term DIY . . . they were such innovators and groundbreakers and found relative success in weird pockets."

I   I   I

Sometime in the summer or fall of 1979, Hüsker Dü met the man who would wear many band-related hats in the coming years. Terry Katzman was an employee at Oar Folk and a writer for an alternative weekly paper in Minneapolis known as *Sweet Potato*.

"A couple of friends told me about this band I should see because they did Johnny Thunders songs," Katzman begins. "That was my initial reason behind seeing them the first time. I think they did two sets, and at some point I met Grant out by the bar, and we talked for a while. I told him I worked at Oar Folk and we talked about some of the Twin/Tone bands. He suggested I meet Bob, so we went in the back and that's when I met Bob for the first time. Then I met Greg outside smoking, I think. . . . They had been together, I want to say, around four months at that point, and their name was just starting to pop up around town. As '79 went into '80, that's when my efforts to see them play intensified, and when I started to get bowled over by them as a live act."

Katzman was soon the band's biggest booster and an unflinchingly loyal friend and employee. Hüsker Dü, along with another up-and-coming Minneapolis band called the Replacements, would be Terry Katzman's ticket to many a gig running sound and archiving performance recordings as the '70s turned into the '80s.

The Suicide Commandos' time on a major label proved to be short-lived. As with many of these situations at the time, the record didn't sell according to the label's needs, so the band was promptly dropped and then split up. In 1979, Twin/Tone released an album of the Commandos' farewell gig, *The Commandos Commit Suicide Dance Concert.*

For a brief time after that, Osgood became a guitar instructor. "I gave lessons out of my apartment, and I called it The New Wave Academy of Applied Guitar Sciences," he explains. "Bob of course knew who the Commandos were, and he started taking lessons from me. What I remember is Bob coming over for about four or five lessons, and me telling him, 'Well, you have the gist of it.' I lived in the service quarters of a mansion, on the third floor, and Bob would get off the bus from Macalester and lug his guitar all the way up those stairs and plug in. Even from the first day I met him, I could tell he knew exactly what he wanted to do."

When it came time to record Hüsker Dü's first demo, the band asked Osgood if he would accompany them. "They invited me over to one of their first recording sessions in the choir room of Macalester College. In fact, Grant said it was their very first recording session," says Osgood. "I was sort of being the producer. They just wanted my input as to what was going on. I'm not claiming I produced it, but I was there."

Actually, the producer role for this recording was officially played by a former co-worker of Hart's, Bill Bruce, who explains:

> Grant and I worked together at Hot Licks, a record store/head shop. I lived in Arden Hills at the time and had set up a small recording studio in the

basement of the house that I rented. Grant approached me about recording the band in the auditorium at Macalester College. I brought my gear and was assisted by Chris Osgood. He was someone that both the band and I looked up to. The Commandos are a legend in Minneapolis. We did some vocal overdubs back at my studio that were pretty wild. I remember them doing the vocals for a song called "Do the Bee." They were all rolling on the ground while we were recording, doing a dance called the "Bee." It reminded me of the Beatles in *A Hard Day's Night* because they were so happy and full of energy. I really thought right then that they had a chance, but I, of course, had no idea how far they would go or the impact that they would have. After the recording I spent a couple of days mixing down the tracks on a Revox 2 tape machine. I gave the tape to Grant and that's the last I ever saw of it. I greatly regret not making a backup of the master because of how great it was for an early recording.

The five recordings completed for the demo—"Nuclear Nightmare," "Do the Bee," "Uncle Ron," "Don't Try to Call," "Sex Dolls," and "MTC"—have never surfaced as bootlegs or among tape traders. The same can't be said for the band's next demos.

In October 1979, Hüsker Dü did the first of three sessions with Colin Mansfield producing. Mansfield was also a Twin Cities notable, since his band, Fine Art, had self-released a full-length album earlier in the year. Fine Art, who was getting a little local radio play at the time, had its own label called Good Records, which would end up releasing material by bands that didn't want to work with Twin/Tone or simply didn't fit with the label's angle. Mansfield worked with Norton and Hart at Northern Lights. Hailing from England, he came to the States in 1971 and in the mid-'70s played improv guitar for some theater productions and worked as the import buyer for the locally based Pickwick Records before moving on to Northern Lights. He recalls working with the Hüskers for the first time:

The recordings for those demos were all done in the basement of Northern Lights. John Carnahan had hired me to create Twin Cities Imports, which would supply import records locally in competition with Pickwick. I was dissatisfied with the big corporation, as was he for different reasons, and he had this basement that was doing nothing at the time. Greg worked in the record store and head shop [and] was in charge of pipes and screens and stuff full time. Grant worked there part time. John generously let them use half the basement for rehearsals.

[Norton and Hart] asked me if I'd record some demos for them with my four-track recorder. We worked fairly quickly as I recall, maybe a couple of nights for basic tracks, a few overdubs, and that was that. I mixed some cassettes for them and gave them the masters so they could mix them elsewhere if they wanted. There were no copies made of the master tapes. It was disappointing to find they lost them soon after. I didn't have a dub for myself.

These sessions yielded "Picture of You," "Can't See You Any More," "The Truth Hurts," "Do You Remember?," "Sore Eyes," "All Tensed Up," "Writer's Cramp," and "All I Got to Lose Is You."

"There was an untitled track or two, if I remember correctly," Mansfield adds, "and I suggested the title 'Everything Falls Apart.' They didn't like it."

These recordings commonly surface under the names "Savage Young Dü" and "The Northern Lights Demos" (usually the former). At least four of the tracks, especially "Picture of You" and "Sore Eyes," show a serious knack for pop hooks and fall into the category of powerpop, if a little punkish. Also, the entire set could pass for a compilation of Midwestern DIY or private-label bands. Such compilations were omnipresent at the time if you looked hard enough, but they were way under the radar of mainstream radio and most music retailers. Independent record labels were not known as such in the late '70s because major labels had yet to achieve the bogeyman status that they would acquire once hardcore punk took hold. That's when labels became far more obviously independent from the big guys and when the shortened slang of *indie*, imported from the UK, first surfaced.

Looking at these early Hüsker Dü demo track listings, one can't help but ponder the lack of cover songs. In the late 1970s it was very unique for a band not even a year old to have this many originals. Also, a future Hüsker Dü trend is apparent when the Bill Bruce demos are compared with the later Mansfield tapes: The band had written several new songs in a small handful of months, many of which, such as "Nuclear Nightmare" and "Sex Doll," would forever leave the band's repertoire even more quickly. The truth was, as Hüsker Dü played its last gigs of 1979 at the Longhorn, it had amassed more than twenty original compositions that they felt were worthy of playing live. Not bad for a band that was eight months old. ╪

REAL WORLD

2

The flyer for the Hüskers' first shows at 7th Street Entry on March 26 and 27, 1980, featured multiple pairs of binoculars, all different sizes and no doubt clipped from different magazines or catalogs, pasted around a prominent Hüsker Dü logo. Tiny directions ("Under Uncle Sam's") were printed beneath the already-small name of the opening band ("Wilma and the Wilbers"). Over the next twelve months, Hüsker Dü would play the Entry between twenty and twenty-five times.

The first musician to play on the stage of the much larger "main room" adjoining the Entry was Joe Cocker on April 3, 1970. The downtown club was called The Depot at the time, a reference to the building's original status as Minneapolis' Greyhound bus depot (opened in 1937). In 1968, Allan Fingerhut, the twenty-five-year-old heir to the Fingerhut catalog fortune, chose the location to be Minneapolis' first venue to serve alcohol and feature live music (an urban rarity in the 1970s).

In 1972, The Depot's name was changed to Uncle Sam's. For a spell, rock gave way to disco before both met a happy middle ground with the "rock disco" trend of the late '70s and early '80s. Rock discos featured local or touring rock bands until eleven o'clock or midnight, when the club would abruptly transform into a discotheque. The more the merrier as far as club owners were concerned, and rock audiences were rarely afforded the time to vacate the premises before the stage and dance floor filled with late-night revelers.

"Uncle Sam's was actually part of a disco chain and then they opened the Entry in the spring of 1980 and started booking bands," remembers Terry Katzman. Many midsized clubs around the country tried to adapt to the new wave craze by dedicating a smaller section of their venues to up-and-coming locals or smaller touring bands. A stone's throw from First Avenue was Goofy's, a strip club that in

1982 opened its Upper Deck room to host punk bands. Minneapolis' legendary Longhorn, located just a few blocks from Uncle Sam's and the Upper Deck, hosted local stalwarts as well as touring bands like the Ramones, Blondie, and Talking Heads. "The Longhorn was going through its final phases. They started a different room upstairs, called Zoogie's Lounge, which was behind the idea that they were going to split up the new local new wave and punk rock upstairs and reserve the downstairs for the Iggy Pops and such, but it never really worked out," says Katzman. "Between the Longhorn with Zoogies upstairs and Uncle Sam's with the 7th Street Entry, it was pretty clear which club was going to be the one. Less and less people went to the Longhorn/Zoogies and the transformation was soon complete."

The 7th Street Entry came about shortly after two longtime friends, Steve McClellan and Jack Myers, took over Uncle Sam's around the turn of the decade. "It was basically the room where they stored the bus parts," continues Katzman. "It could be entered on 7th Street, hence the name, so that maintenance people didn't have to haul things through the main lobby of the depot. The Entry was pretty much the Hüskers' home until they graduated to playing the main room," says Katzman, referring to the larger room that in 1981 underwent another name change, becoming First Avenue.

Hüsker Dü also played sporadic gigs at Duffy's, an out-of-the-way venue run by a married couple. This husband-and-wife team was not exactly overburdened with a love for punk rock, but the couple did pay good money for gigs. Duffy's was located on the edge of a residential neighborhood and just around the corner from Sound 80, made famous as the room Bob Dylan used to record parts of *Blood on the Tracks* in 1974. Prince also recorded demos at Sound 80 in 1977, and the Suicide Commandos recorded their debut LP, *The Suicide Commandos Make a Record*, there. "The other clubs were within five blocks of one another—Duffy's was in the more southeast part of town. It was definitely a haul, a lot harder to get to for people that didn't have cars," explains Jesperson. "You could take the bus to those other three venues, but not to Duffy's. It was a place that bands played because they paid the money; nobody really liked the place itself."

Venues amenable to local underground talent and up-and-coming artists with mainstream aspirations fueled the Minneapolis scene. Still, Uncle Sam's/First Avenue/7th Street Entry, the Longhorn, Duffy's, and Goofy's Upper Deck did not completely distinguish the Minneapolis scene of the late '70s and very early '80s from scenes in other like-sized U.S. cities. This would be achieved by Twin/ Tone, the independent record label that perpetually peopled the Entry stage with bands and provided warm-up acts for the nationally touring bands playing in the main room.

Twin/Tone finished out 1980 with a catalog comprising five full-length LPs, a compilation LP, and twelve 7-inch singles or EPs. The label's discography would grow dramatically in the next couple of years. One of those full-length LPs in the Twin/Tone catalog in 1980 was the Suicide Commandos' swan song, the live *The Commandos Commit Suicide Dance Concert*, released in 1979. The label had no trouble filling the vacated flagship spot and did so with not one but two locally popular entities, Curtiss A and the Suburbs. The latter started out as a more funk-informed, more accessible answer to Cleveland's Pere Ubu, releasing two 7-inches with Twin/Tone before the label issued the excellent debut full-length, *In Combo*, in 1980. The five members of the Suburbs—a lineup that would remain static throughout the band's long and fleetingly prosperous journey through the '80s—were essentially introduced to one another in 1977 by Chris Osgood. Curtis Almstead, a.k.a. Curtiss A, was a founding member of the pre-Twin/Tone rock band Thumbs Up!, one of the only local bands of the early and mid-'70s to perform original material. Almstead debuted on Twin/Tone in 1978 with a 7-inch by his band, the Spooks, which also counted Slim Dunlap, later of the Replacements, among its members. By the end of 1980, Twin/Tone had released three 7-inches and two full-length LPs by Almstead.

The label's roster was filled out by the Pistons (rootsy powerpop), Fingerprints, the Jets, and the Hypstrz. The latter made their mark by appropriating R&B and '60s garage classics and infusing them with punk rock energy. By far the strangest album ever released on Twin/Tone was Orchid Spangiafora's *Flee Past's Ape Elf* (1979), an amazing tape-collage/musique concrète/drone experiment by Rob Carey, who was Chris Osgood's roommate and the Commandos' roadie/tour manager.

Regionally, 1979's *Big Hits from Mid-America, Volume Three* compilation LP (the title was a nod to Volumes One and Two of the same name put out in the mid-1960s by Twin Cities label Soma Records) yielded moderate radio airplay around the upper Midwest. "The Suburbs' *In Combo* in 1980 was a huge local deal," remembers Jesperson. "Everybody thought that they were the best band in Minneapolis at the time."

So how did Hüsker Dü fit into all of this? They did, and they didn't. Hüsker Dü, along with their right-hand man, Terry Katzman, and an inner sanctum of friends/fans (who would soon coalesce into something more defined), were unavoidably headed in a different direction than the Twin/Tone camp. By the time Twin/Tone rejected Hüsker Dü's latest demo recordings in the fall of 1980, Jesperson had signed the Replacements to the label. Magazine articles and biographical writings of a more thorough, non-periodical format, most of them appearing since the breakups of both bands, gravitate toward an oil-and-water oversimplification of the relationship between the two factions. But it's convenient to use loaded terminology like "local rivals" or "arch nemeses." Jesperson sheds some light on the Replacements end of this often misunderstood issue:

> I remember very clearly—in fact, I can almost see this taking place at the Longhorn—when Bob got wind of the fact that Twin/Tone was getting involved with the Replacements, he looked at me, and said with a slight sneer, something like, "Well, I suspect that the red carpet is going to roll out for these guys." For better or worse, I was very connected at the time, I was a good person to give a tape to, and when I liked something, I've always been the type of person that screamed at the top of my lungs about bands that I was crazy about, whether they were on Twin/Tone or not. So I think that there was a little resentment, not horrible, nasty, "we hate you" type of resentment, but I think it's safe to say that there was some resentment there. I think it's important to establish that Hüsker Dü preceded the Replacements and had quite a good, tight, small following, and Hüsker Dü was part of what was happening as a national scene, which was the hardcore movement.

In Twin Cities music journalist Jim Walsh's 2007 oral history, *The Replacements: All Over but the Shouting*, Mould is quoted as saying, "I think there was a rivalry; I like to think it was a healthy one. I think at the end of the day, everybody helped each other out. It wasn't like anyone was trying to sabotage each other. From the Hüsker camp, there was a bit of a snub that Twin/Tone, which was the prevailing label at the time, wasn't that interested in the Hüskers. But the Replacements, on one gig, got an album [deal]. It was sort of like, 'Hmm.'"

The demo that was rejected by Twin/Tone was a result of the Hüskers' first foray into a real studio. Mould, Hart, and Norton once again enlisted the help of Colin Mansfield. It had been almost a year since the recordings in the basement of Northern Lights. In the time that elapsed, Hart, Norton, and Colin had all been terminated, separately, from their jobs at the store. Mansfield recalls, "They were getting faster and faster, and they were playing a lot! They were also writing a lot of songs. Mostly Grant and Bob, but maybe Greg had a couple too. On stage, they were moving around a lot more—well, Greg was—and Bob moved back and forth from the mic to his amp. And as happens, everything got faster."

"John Carnahan let me go from Northern Lights as the band was just starting to get going," recalls Norton. "He said I was too distracted with the band and that I needed to be focused on the record store, which was okay. Mainly it meant that we lost our practice space. That's why we started practicing in my mom's basement at Pontiac Place."

"It's a little foggy, but the Blackberry Way sessions in 1980, the first ones to happen since I had started recording the shows, were the ones that everyone initially wanted to be a 10-inch release," remembers Katzman. "Everybody knew that it wasn't going to be feasible. It was just an idea. Too cumbersome, too expensive. It was ridiculous to think about doing a 10-inch as your self-released debut."

Named after a song by Jeff Lynne's pre-E.L.O. outfit, the Move, Blackberry Way Studios was located in Minneapolis' famous Dinkytown area near the University of Minnesota, where today it is run by Neil Weir as the Old Blackberry Way Recording Studio.

Hüsker Dü's August 1980 sessions were engineered by Steve Fjelsted, Twin/Tone's go-to engineer for many of the label's studio recordings, a relationship that may have partially resulted from Fjelsted partnering with Twin/Tone's Paul Stark to maintain the studio. The sessions yielded four usable tracks, plus a phantom fifth track, whose identity no one can agree upon. Out of this, the band chose three songs for the demo that was given to Twin/Tone.

Norton remembers, "We went into Blackberry Way and recorded the 'Statues' single, along with a couple other tracks. We put together a three-song demo for Twin/Tone. At that time, Twin/Tone had three principals: Paul Stark, Peter Jesperson and Charlie Hallman. Each one of them liked only one of the songs. So they didn't want to put any money behind us. Then we said, 'Screw it. Let's put it out ourselves.' We named our label Reflex because we were like, 'If Twin/Tone doesn't want to put our record out, then this is our reflex to that: We will put it out ourselves.' In 1980, do-it-yourself was a mantra."

But who can blame Twin/Tone for passing on the material? "Statues" did boast an uncanny resemblance to a certain strain of rhythm-happy post-punk that would overwhelm underground music fans of 1980 and 1981. It was a rough-around-the-edges, slightly crooked interpretation of PiL's *Metal Box/Second Edition*, A Certain Ratio's early recordings, much of the Clash's *Sandinista!*, and pretty much anything issued up to that point by the UK's Factory Records, especially Joy Division and Crispy Ambulance.

Another of the Blackberry tracks, "Writer's Cramp," is of a style that probably dominated the mountain of cassette demos that Stark and Jesperson had to clear out of the way in order to find their respective desks each morning. "Writer's Cramp" is paint-by-numbers powerpop of a distinctly Midwestern flavor—and for some reason, the Midwest had produced hundreds upon hundreds of 45s that sounded identical to or better than "Writer's Cramp." Used-record bins overflowed with terminally regional bands that self-released black-and-white-sleeved 45s adorned with a photocopied picture of the band members wearing skinny ties and standing against a brick wall (usually smoking). Anyone with a decent head on their shoulders and a label to run would hit the fast-forward button after the first twenty seconds of "Writer's Cramp."

This may have been the fate of "Let's Go Die" as well but for a different reason. The more traditional and roots-enthused factions at Twin/Tone would have vetoed this one right off the bat despite its great big hook and mostly melodic vocals (two qualities that would soon disappear altogether from a large portion of the Hüsker set). It was just too fast and could have been a Zero Boys or very early Black Flag outtake. But if anyone wanted to keep up with Hüsker Dü from this point onward, they better have had an affinity for fast because it wasn't long before the band was making music that made this version of "Let's Go Die" sound like Philip Glass.

"I believe the plan was for a 7-inch EP, up to four tracks," says Mansfield. "Once everything was mixed it was pretty obvious that 'Statues' was going to be on it, but it was a long track and took up a full side. The boys insisted that 'Amusement' be on the other side and I think we all agreed that one studio and one live side felt right. They did a good job with the other tracks, but they were already changing their direction from the more 'pop' sound of them."

"'Amusement' was a total afterthought, written as a reaction to Twin/Tone's rejection of our demo," says Hart.

"We recorded some stuff at Duffy's and they liked that version of 'Amusement' so much that we ended up using that as the B-side," states Katzman. "I gave the tape to Bob, and they went over [to Blackberry] that night and Steve [Fjelsted] transferred it to the two-track, snipped it, and spooled it. I was never really in the studio with them. Something you have to understand is that not too many people were in the studio with them."

Mansfield offers some technical insight into the extremely low-fidelity endeavor that was to be the B-side of the band's debut release. "Well, it was recorded to a cassette tape and I think it was taken off the mixing board at the gig," he says. "It was also recorded in a fairly small hall, so a lot of what the audience heard of the bass, drums, and guitar actually came off the stage and there wasn't much going through the mixer to the PA, so we had to recover what we could of the instruments and balance them against the vocals. We also had to deal with the limited bandwidth and fidelity of the cassette medium. The tape itself was recorded fairly hot, so levels weren't a problem, and luckily any distortion was minimal or masked."

All in all, the Hüskers spent a total of four or five days at Blackberry Way. The first half of that would have been consumed by laying down the basic tracks, then a day for overdubs, then the extra day needed for the last-minute inclusion of "Amusement." At this point the Hüskers would have gotten a slight break on Blackberry's going rate of $25 to $30 per hour. "I didn't ask to be paid . . . my thing was helping people, not making a living off of them," says Mansfield. "We put the final mix to tape, Steve Fjelstad edited the songs together, and as far as I know, that was the master."

According to Hart, before Twin/Tone rejected the demo, "It was a done deal in Bob's mind." Did the band sulk away with heads lowered, only to settle on a worst-case scenario of self-releasing the material? "Bob realized pretty quickly that [Twin/Tone] were not in line with what we were doing, so we just decided to put it out on our own," according to Katzman. "They knew they were doing something outside of the Twin/Tone mode, and that was almost a feeble attempt just to see what would happen. I don't think any of us actually expected Twin/Tone to put it out. There might have been a fleeting moment when they thought there might be a chance, but that was it. . . . With the holidays coming up, Bob didn't want to screw around anymore, so it turned into 'We've got to get this thing out.'"

For almost a year Katzman was the band's biggest (and earliest) supporter, as well as a close friend, but beginning in the summer of 1980, he found himself the Hüskers' sole soundman, performance archivist, and general right-hand man.

"My real 'coming out' gig, so to speak, was the Gang War show in July of '80," he recalls. "And from then on it was known that I did sound for the Hüskers at the Entry. The Hüskers and the Replacements, those are the two bands behind which I apprenticed at the Entry, as all of the other soundmen were too afraid to deal with that stuff, especially the Hüskers. Plus, when they were playing, the Hüskers didn't want anyone behind the soundboard but me because they were very cautious about recordings circulating and from the very beginning, we had an agreement that I would never trade or swap."

Landing an opening slot for a touring band was crucial during this stage of Hüsker Dü's development. Landing an opening slot for musicians they were big fans of (Gang War featured Johnny Thunders and Wayne Kramer), well, that was icing on the cake. They worked very hard to secure the opening set at the aforementioned Gang War at Uncle Sam's.

Peter Davis, editor and publisher of *Young Flesh*, one of the longest-running 'zines to come out of the American underground, witnessed their opening set and implies that Hüsker Dü had adopted a menacing stage presence by this point in their development. "They really made a positive impact on me," he says. "Not just because they were completely different than anything else I'd seen or heard, but even more so by their unbridled aggressiveness—their obvious attitude and open hostility toward the extremely sparse and unappreciative, nonresponsive audience. Short of breaking chairs over people's heads, this was about as clear a case of contempt I'd ever seen a band show to a crowd and they were deadpan serious."

"They had a way of playing together that was very different from what I was used to in the Commandos," Osgood observes. "I don't know what they cued off of, but they certainly developed their sound and were tight in a different way. Different from virtually every other band . . . I think I can say that."

It was through later shows, opening for bands that were closer contemporaries instead of simply idols, that Mould began flexing his networking muscle and laying the groundwork for the Hüskers to play outside of Minneapolis when they were ready. "We opened for quite a few bands that came through and played at the

Entry," recalls Norton. "D.O.A. came through, we opened for them. The Subhumans came through and we hooked up with them. Ken Lester, the manager of the Subhumans, he gave us a bunch of places to play in Canada."

In November 1980, Mission of Burma came through to play the Entry. This was a band that all three members could agree on. Norton remembers, "It was [future Hüsker roadie and member of local Hüsker fan circle, the "veggies"] Mike Madden that went out to Boston, probably early summer 1980, and he comes back and he says 'Oh my god, I saw this band out there that is just incredible.' So when Burma came to town, we made sure we opened for them. They dug what we were doing, and we were totally into them, so we became friends and ended up playing a bunch of shows with them later on, when we made it to Boston, but it must have been at the very end, as they broke up right after that."

For the Burma show, the band decided to lean heavily on the angular, post-punk end of their live repertoire. Burma bassist Clint Conley recalls, "We had an opening band with a funny name and funny looks, sorta overweight and non-rock. We were not unpleased because we'd had a string of gigs with what, in retrospect, could be termed 'new wave' bands with synths and horizontal stripes and eye make-up, which were a dominant cultural strain at the time. Hüsker Dü was friendly, as was the local custom—Minni [Minneapolis] was always a notably congenial place. We really dug their set, which was, I recall, PiL-ish—it's possible 'Statues' is affecting my recall—long-ish single-chord riff-rants."

Mission of Burma stuck around for a couple of days, since the band was on their infamous "Tour of America's Airports" in which they actually toured the country by taking advantage of an economical airline special that required them to fly to every destination out of Atlanta. Conley continues: "We were crashing at a loft of one of the [members of the] Suburbs, and we went to a party where one cute scenester pulled me aside and said, 'It's too bad you were playing with those guys, otherwise more people would've come—no one likes them.' I was surprised and said we liked them a lot. I remember Grant coming to pick us up the next day to take us to a used-record store. A gracious host, showing us around his city. We really appreciated it, as we were in a semipermanent state of alienation. Some months later, their single came into Newbury Comics, the hip record store in Boston. The clerk, radio DJ Tammi Heidi was having herself a great time making sport of their name. We played their single a lot at the Burma house in Brighton."

As Conley indicates, the Hüskers were not without their local detractors as they steadily hammered out a distinctive take on punk rock and trimmed their live set of blatantly derivative fare. Like many bands that eventually achieved legendary status, Hüsker Dü was working through the identity crisis that often precedes the discovery of an inspired style. In the Hüskers' case, they would discover more than one inspired style, but first, they had to transform the locals into the room-packing throngs who would be eating out of their hands in less than a year.

But as they slogged through 1980, the signs of support were slow to come. One uplifting moment came by way of a feature written in *Sweet Potato*, the precursor to Minneapolis' long-running alt-weekly *City Pages*. Written by none other than Terry Katzman, it made a (not surprisingly) convincing case for checking out their live show. "Unless there was something written in another city, I'm pretty sure it was the first piece of Hüsker coverage," says Katzman. "I just kept talking up the band. My editor asked if I'd seen them live and I told him I'd seen them several times so they asked me to scramble up seven hundred words and they'd see how it turned out. I wrote it over a weekend, they liked it, and that was my first foray into covering the Minneapolis music scene." Katzman's *Sweet Potato* piece also documented the fact that by November 1980, Hüsker Dü was drawing a respectable local following:

> Ultra-fast song delivery is a major component of any live Hüsker performance. Songs will invariably end and begin within the same breath or chord. With an impressive catalog boasting 50 or more originals, the music of Hüsker Dü speaks of a harsh world confused with inner anxieties, a society dealing with its own nightmarish realities.
>
> Live, the band has a stage presence quite unlike any other local band. Grant Hart's ferocious drumming, coupled with the electro-shock quiver of bassist Greg Norton and the Flying V bombast of Mould along with the aid of Hüsker "veggies" (loyal followers) usually turn the stage and the dance floor into a throng of quivering and uncontrollably sweaty bodies. Recently the band has begun to move away from their hundred-mile-an-hour head-banging delivery, though they still remain the undisputed kings of speed (a total of 20 songs were once delivered in under a half-hour). Newer material shows the band moving into a more contemplative phase

while still adhering to the grim topics of everyday existence: the love song "Dianne" [*sic*]; a near love song, "Gravity"; and the superbly dismal masterpiece "Private Hell."

Undeniably, the band puts their stamp on the original material. A familiar guitar hook or riff occasionally surfaces, but before you place it, it disappears. The band exists on the sheer strength of their music, nothing else.

As of this writing, plans are being made for a West Coast tour after the first of the year. The band's strength as a front act (Johnny Thunders, Nash the Slash, Skafish) as well as headliners has prompted a much overdue out-of-town trip. In addition, the members of Hüsker Dü have formed their own Reflex Records, which will release the first single, "Statues/Amusement," sometime after Christmas.

"Statues" b/w "Amusement" was officially released in January 1981. For the cover art, Grant had used the copy machine at the teachers' credit union where his mother was employed. This was also the financial establishment in which $2,000 was added to an existing loan, then used to cover the pressing and recording costs the band had accumulated.

When folded open and flipped over, the cut-and-paste job reveals that Grant already had "Fake Name Graphx" for his design imprint. The band's temporary address was listed as "PO Box 4596 St. Paul, MN 55104." The post office box was purchased shortly before the release of the record, yet the next vinyl release on Reflex would carry the Mendota Heights address where Greg lived with his mom. The only band credits given are:

BOB MOULD: GUITAR, VOCALS
GREG NORTON: BASS, VOCALS
GRANT HART: DRUMS, VOCALS

The Reflex logo was a generic all-caps font and not yet the efficient razor-blade design found on future releases. The single had two front covers, one for each song, instead of the traditional top-to-bottom, inverted layout design seen on most fold-over 7-inch sleeves. The "Amusement" side displays a group of clip-art kids being "amused" by a television, a corkboard to-do list, a handgun, and, in the case of the lonely looking little girl against the brick wall, nothing.

The "Statues" side is a photograph of a factory manufacturing small bust statues of Chairman Mao. "As far as samples or promos,

I think they might have sent three or four off to some labels like Slash, but it wasn't fifty or any large number, because we'd already spent all of our loan getting the thing recorded, pressed, and printed up," says Katzman. "They were running on empty out of the gate, but were geniuses at figuring out a way to make everything work. The Hüskers correlated touring with having a release to sell and push while they were out. There was more of a purpose behind 'Statues' in that they knew they had something special going on . . . at that point they had fourteen or fifteen original songs of differing tempos, whereas most bands had three or four of the same type. 'Statues' was just one type of Hüsker Dü song, even that early. It was their way of saying, 'Okay, here we are and we're not going away that easily or quickly.' [The record] used to skip sometimes. When Bob screams it would actually throw the needle on some turntables, it was recorded so hot."

In fact, Hüsker Dü almost single-handedly set a new standard for live volume. The Hüskers were possibly *the* first band to explore air-moving, heart-stopping volume. Pure noise was an important component of early industrial music pioneers, mainly Throbbing Gristle, and it was a genre in and of itself with artists like the Whitehouse (also in the UK) and Boyd Rice's Non (a stateside example). These performers were most assuredly informed by Lou Reed's *Metal Machine Music*, a double album of freeform noise that inadvertently became one of the ultimate punk rock statements.

In 1980, an important component of the band's volume was Mould's small Fender Twin amplifier, which he never stopped feeding back between songs. As the resulting Hüsker sound became bigger and less-defined, the band increased the velocity of their attack and focused on brevity while writing new material. "At one point in '80, we decided we wanted to play faster than the Dickies. We were also very influenced by Stiff Little Fingers," Norton remembers.

Today, even the most casual listener can pick out Mould's guitar sound, which is one of the most unique in rock history. The first commercially released studio track in which his tone can be heard as a fully formed sonic calling card is the title track to the three-song EP *In a Free Land*, released in May 1982. Clearly, Mould knew exactly what he wanted from a guitar rig. Chris Osgood remembers:

All of the pieces of what eventually coalesced into what would become "the Hüsker sound" were there very early on. Bob's famous thing about playing with light picks and light strings, and still getting a big sound?

That was going on at that time. And at that time, Bob was getting a much fuzzier sound than the rest of us. . . . Unlike the Replacements, who just chewed up gear and they'd have different rigs every time you saw them, Bob was pretty steady with what he used. Bob has always been a very methodical guy. The feedback you were hearing was very much within the realm of Bob's control. He wasn't like a Bob Stinson, in which there was a 50/50 chance his amp was going to last the night. With Bob Mould, there was a one hundred percent chance that the amp was going to last three years. Then there was the thickness of tone that Bob would go for. It might sound funny to say, but I think Bob would agree with me that it's thickness of tone and thinness of pick, so that the very, very tightly accentuated downbeat didn't happen; it was much thicker than that. He was always playing just slightly behind the beat, but it didn't matter, because he was laying down what was very much a wall of sound.

A 'zine out of Xenia, Ohio, reviewing "Statues" b/w "Amusement" offered a glimpse into the immediate future: "I found this much looked-for single down at Another Record Shop in Cincinnati (along with Kirk Brandon's Pack E.P. and the Avengers' Dangerhouse single. Great store!). This single was recorded way back in 1980 before Hüsker Dü 'went hard-core' and is very raw progressive rock, in the same vein as hmm . . . letsee . . . maybe Clock DVA or Birthday Party, although they sound nothing like either of those bands. Anyways, this is a good single, if not a collector's item."

Systematic Record Distribution and Rough Trade picked up the debut for distribution. Colin Mansfield concludes, "I knew they would last to at least one more record. They had the drive and incentive to make a go of it, and they weren't afraid to work it hard. I also knew they had a lot of songs to draw on. Even if they went dry the next week, they could still make records. Bob was still at Macalester, neither Greg nor Grant had long-term jobs, so they were quite flexible. Being a three-piece band helped—the more people you have involved, the harder schedules become. I was glad to offer my services in the hope of getting them to the next step and I believed they would do that." ‡

NEW ALLIANCES

3

By the early spring of 1981, Hüsker Dü had logged upward of fifty local gigs in Minneapolis/St. Paul when they left to play Chicago on March 21 and 22. The industrious trio pulled off two major hat tricks for their first out-of-town gig. First, through a connection of some sort, Grant Hart went into a car dealership in South St. Paul and left driving a brand-new station wagon after convincing a salesperson that he was interested in purchasing the vehicle and needed to "test drive" it for the entire weekend. The second hustle came by way of a bartender at First Avenue. "Her brother worked for Radisson, and she actually got us rooms," explains Norton. "So, for our first trip to Chicago, we stayed at a swanky hotel."

Punk rock history is littered with infamous dumps that served each regional scene supporting more than a trace of underground activity. While Goofy's Upper Deck could qualify as Minneapolis' entry into the pantheon, the Oz would be Chicago's contender. "The Oz was this legendary, decrepit hole in the wall that had actually been moved around a couple of times because the cops kept shutting it down," says Norton. "The place was a shithole. They were selling amyl-nitrate behind the bar."

On March 23, the night after the Hüskers' second gig at the Oz, Black Flag was scheduled to play across town at the Space Place. Having also booked the Flag show, Oz owner Dem Hopkins asked Hüsker Dü to play a Black Flag after-party in the wee hours following the Space Place gig. Of course, the trio went down to the Space Place to catch Black Flag and spread the word about the after-party. "Strike Under and the Effigies opened, then Black Flag played, and it was Henry's [Rollins] first tour with the band," Norton remembers. "I don't even think he'd been to L.A. yet, they'd just picked him up and they were on their way to L.A. He had one tattoo, and it was the four bars. Dez was also singing and playing guitar, it was intense. Black Flag was a very intense band.

"We were pretty intense ourselves already," Norton adds. "We played really fast, jumped around a lot. It was right before and on this trip to Chicago that it got to be rapid fire one after the other. We didn't really have anything to say to the audience—we were very tight very early on."

As the Hüskers had hoped, Black Flag and their entourage showed up at the gig and witnessed a very antagonistic side of the trio that would forever be remembered as the "blue paint show." After playing an impressive set that the sparse audience enjoyed, Hart capped off the band's third evening in town with a classic bit of rock 'n' roll chaos that has largely been blamed on audience heckling. "The blue paint incident was definitely after the Black Flag show," explains Hopkins. "I remember Grant throwing the bucket of blue paint all over the place after the band finished but it wasn't because of any heckling. The crowd liked them a lot. He was just fucked up and was looking for a big finish."

Norton offers his own take on the spectacle: "Somehow a paint can got tipped over, and it was blue paint. This woman dressed from head to toe in leather started scooping up the paint from the floor with one of Grant's cymbals. This did not go over well—he inherited that drum kit from his older brother, who was killed by a drunk driver when Grant was ten. So Grant comes up to this woman and pushes her straight down so that she sits in the paint. Then he and Dez take turns picking her up and bouncing her off of the wall, butt-first, so that it made all of these blue butt prints down the wall."

Having used up their stay at the Radisson, the band found accommodations more appropriate to their finances. "We stayed two nights at the Radisson, and the night of the Black Flag after-party we stayed in a bad area of Chicago," says Norton, "at a Ho-Jo that had bullet holes in the glass."

Madison, Dayton, Milwaukee, Indianapolis, and Detroit, along with Chicago, provided good weekend out-of-towners, given the Twin Cities' central location and Bob's school schedule. "And in Madison, we met Robin Davies, who became our good friend. His band, the Tar Babies, became our allies there. His brother was in Mecht Mensch."

By the summer of 1981, Hüsker Dü had been a band for two and a half years. The pieces were in place for a pivotal career move, one that would strengthen the commitment of the three members.

The trio had cemented a firm local reputation and provided floors and gigs to any like-minded bands visiting the Twin Cities. "So leading up to the first big tour, the Children's Crusade tour, we had opened for quite a few bands that came through and played at the Entry," Norton explains. "D.O.A. came through, we opened for them, the Subhumans came through and we hooked up with them. Ken Lester, the manager of the Subhumans, he gave us a bunch of places to play in Canada."

"When Hüsker Dü did it, they had that circuit, which was an advantage of being a hardcore band, they were able to plug into some sort of network, be it fledging, but it was there," states Peter Jesperson.

The popular belief that Hüsker Dü was the first Twin Cities band to extensively tour the country is incorrect. The Suicide Commandos stand as one of the only lower-profile first-wave American punk rock bands to do so. "The importance of the Suicide Commandos cannot be overstated," says Jesperson. "They were the granddaddies of the whole scene and DIY before I'd ever heard the term DIY."

Though the Commandos' label, Twin/Tone, was the region's primary indie, most of its new-wave, post-punk, and roots-rock bands were not interested in living out of a van for weeks, sleeping on strangers' floors, or walking into ominous rooms with no turnout or expectation of a financial return. Not that the Twin/Tone bands were devoid of careerist aspirations; the majority just seemed content with local popularity, which is precisely why these bands fizzled while acts that later capitalized on the fruits of hardcore labor, like the Replacements (who didn't go on a tour of any note until early 1983) and Soul Asylum, went on to prominence.

Hüsker Dü's Children's Crusade tour presented its biggest challenges before the first note of live music was played. Norton recalls:

> We started that tour with a weeklong stint in Calgary at the Calgarian Hotel. So we're getting ready to head out on the road, and Grant had lined up the van. It was an older Ford Econoline, and the thing threw a rod or something serious happened to the engine and we couldn't leave. I had a friend that worked at a Ford dealership, and we worked out a deal where we actually rented a brand-new Ford Econoline window van. So we took off on our way to Calgary. We drove all night to the Canadian

border to cross into Manitoba, go up to Winnipeg, and head west from there. We get to the border at about five in the morning. It's Pembina, North Dakota, and Canadian customs is in Emerson, Manitoba. We have to hang out for a while, then we make it into Canadian customs at Emerson to get our work permits and the customs official was kind enough to explain that our papers hadn't been sent to Emerson . . . for some reason they were sent to Coutts, Alberta. He told us we were more than welcome to come into Canada on a visitor's permit, but we would have to drive two or three hours south of Calgary to Coutts before we were able to play. He said that we'd probably just want to drive through the States, so we turn around and get back over to the U.S. side, and I'm trying to explain this to the U.S. customs officer and he's just shaking his head, saying "Nope. Not going to have any part of this. They wouldn't let you into Canada, there's got to be a reason for it. Park the van over here. Everybody inside."

In fact, the band had cleaned themselves up for the Canadian customs officials, hiding any visual "punk rock" cues that might cause alarm with the border authorities. Before arriving at the American customs checkpoint, they had reverted to their normal dress. Norton continues:

Grant unzipped his leather jacket and had no shirt on. Then he takes off his hat and he's got this big shock of dyed white hair in the middle of his head. I'm sure we were quite the sight to the customs official. They drag us into the office, they interview each one of us individually, they're going through all of our things, and at some point, one of the agents asks, "Who's the driver of this van?" and I told him I was and he said, "In my office right now."

He had this thing on his desk, it was huge, and he claimed that it was a marijuana seed, and that they'd found several of them. I don't know what it was, but it definitely wasn't a marijuana seed. I said there's no way, we're clean, the van is clean, if there's anything in that van, it's not ours, and I told him this was a load of crap, that we were just trying to get to Calgary to play, and I sort of went off on the guy. He said, "Let me see the papers for the van." So I showed him those, and he said, "You're lucky that the van is rented, otherwise you and your friends would have been detained a lot longer."

So there we are, back in the U.S., and we take Highway 1 through North Dakota to Shelby, Montana, where we spent the night. . . . We got our papers fine and got up to the Calgarian.

A rickety, five-story relic in the skid-row area of the already-isolated Calgary, the Calgarian had hosted a limited number of punk rock shows by touring bands, but the scene was tight-knit and supportive.

"Part of our pay was a room, so we had one room," says Norton. "It was not a nice part of town, so I'm sure there were all sorts of things going on. And you had, basically, cowboys and Indians hanging out at the bar. Calgary was a big cattle town. Actually, they had a pretty sophisticated scene. We stayed there for a week and ended up making friends, hanging out with them, and going to parties. It was really bizarre, because at nine, when the music started, all the punks showed up. It would go from being a redneck bar to a punker bar."

"What people fail to remember in the first place is that Canada was part of the British Empire," explains Hart. "We hadn't done any British gigs at that point to compare it to, but it was as if we were playing on another continent, not just in another country. If nothing else, it was the equivalent of the Upper Deck; not a whole lot of touring bands playing there, but I would imagine that anyone on the way to Vancouver, an important gig, would want to fill in some days off."

Hart also goes on to somewhat dispel the "into the unknown" nature of the Calgary trip. "There's been a little bit of exaggeration in regards to how 'Wild West' it was," he says. "We had rooms upstairs to escape to. As a matter of fact, we had a huge suite that all of us stayed in. And, as I recall, the bedroom situation was pretty private. The Calgarian was operating as a hotel, though quite a bit of it might have been residential, but I don't remember seeing a lot of whores around."

The six-day residency at the Calgarian was a vital step in the Children's Crusade tour and in Hüsker Dü's confidence as a live act. "At the time we didn't realize what playing twenty-four sets was going to do for us, as far as giving us confidence," Hart remembers. "When we stepped on the stage for the first set, we were essentially scared shitless. Then by the end of the last set of the last night, we were looking for reasons to keep playing."

Hüsker Dü had an actual tour manager for the Children's Crusade tour. A longtime friend of the band, Mike Madden had emerged from the "veggies" fan circle and left Minneapolis with Hüsker Dü as their tour manager; his brother, Richard, assumed the role for the second half of the tour, joining the band in Seattle. "Mike brought his bike with him," Norton recalls. "We dropped him off in Vancouver and he rode his bike all the way back to Minneapolis."

According to Hart, Mould's heavy hand in band operations began to show itself as early as this tour. Mike Madden either didn't care or didn't realize that this dynamic existed. "Mike was functioning on 'Hey, this is the time of our lives!' and was well-traveled, whereas Bob might have taken the Greyhound to New York City a couple of times," Hart says. "Bob's ability to travel in a group was not great at that point." Hart also remembers a particular incident in Calgary:

> I remember Mike putting his foot down. One case in particular, Mike wanted to attend a party thrown for us as we were leaving town. Mike pretty much grabbed the steering wheel and the idea was "If you move this car, it's going to go in whatever direction I'm holding the wheel." So we were at this party in our honor, and me and this local punker girl were swapping some spit on the couch. It was obvious that it wasn't going to go anywhere because we *were*, and later in the van, Mould starts this, "I don't want to be in a band where there's a girl in every city for everybody, blah, blah, blah." The funny thing is he wouldn't have ended up meeting any of his lovers had it not been for the fact that he was traveling in a band.
>
> Mike's departure in Seattle might not have been planned. He was very hard working without being wide eyed about things. Richard . . . was not tall where Mike was tall [and] rather quiet, and because he would automatically back down a lot, that's why he prospered on the rest of the tour.

The handwritten flyer for the weekend portion of the Calgarian residency lists the bands as SFY "from The Manor" (which is believed to be the hotel itself), the Office "from Edmonton," and Hüsker Dü "from U.S.A." The word "maybe" is written next to "U.S.A." A small box in the bottom right-hand corner announces "pictures and autographs at 10:00." Hart remembers, "Those sets contained anything at all that we had learned up to that point, and probably thirty songs that never made it to record."

"When we were done with our week stint in Calgary, it was a long drive to Vancouver. It was the first day of July, and we actually saw snow," explains Norton. "We get to Vancouver and we play Victoria Day on July 1. . . . That was a real good crowd. In Vancouver, we were basically put up by D.O.A., and we stayed with [guitarist] Dave Gregg. He had a funky little house in an area near a lot of warehouses for fresh fruit. So they'd go dumpster diving . . . I remember it was a lot of kiwis."

D.O.A. and the Subhumans were two of Canada's better-known and earliest punk rock bands. Formed in the late '70s, D.O.A. was, at its core, a simple, fast street-punk band until their legendary *Hardcore '81* unveiled a sped-up, two-guitar makeover that the scene embraced with open arms. The LP also helped popularize the term and is sometimes considered the point that *hardcore* started to signify a more specific form of punk rock, rather than serving as a catchall for a wide range of weirder, faster, or noisier post-punk/ punk/art-punk.

With D.O.A. calling ahead to secure some gigs and rumors spreading on the hardcore circuit that Hüsker Dü were ripping people apart with their live show, Seattle turned out the tour's best crowds yet. With nothing to offer but the largely unheard and somewhat unrepresentative "Statues" b/w "Amusement" single, Hüsker Dü was blowing minds on impact, in no small part due to the many months spent sharpening their edge at the 7th Street Entry and the further transformation that began with the strenuous nightly schedules in Canada. The 'zine *Desperate Times* had this to say when the band played Seattle's WREX on July 11:

> Bob Mould rarely stood still; he would edge to the front of the stage and grimace with emotion, then suddenly jump and crash into the wall. Greg Norton became more and more active, and at the end of the second set he was never still, always jumping into the air, doing a cool war-dance, jerking his body all over. Grant Hart was furious as he pounded his drums, getting these great looks on his face. His vocals were the most impressive to me, at times sung in a clear voice, at times growled and spat out, dripping with feeling. These three men keep the music coming without breaking between songs. I've seldom seen such energy in a band. I loved it when Greg and Bob jumped into the air at the same time, and after the set Grant pushed the drums out of his way and stalked off stage. After the set, the audience was smiling, their eyes were wide, and they were soaking with sweat and spilt beer.

"We spent a week in Seattle, and that's where we met Jello Biafra," says Norton. "In Seattle, we got added to the Dead Kennedys gig at the Showbox. The local band the Fartz [featuring future Guns N' Roses bassist Duff McKagan on drums], they helped get us on that bill. There were four hundred, five hundred people at the Showbox. At this point, we didn't have any gigs lined up after

Seattle, besides Portland, so Biafra put us on the two Kennedys gigs at [San Francisco's] Mabuhay Gardens."

Peter Davis, a Seattle scene stalwart and future friend to the band who had met Hüsker Dü on a visit to Minneapolis the previous year, has a slightly different take on their stay in Seattle and credit for the Showbox gigs. His story begins with the trip to Minneapolis:

> Long story short, I chatted with the band a spell, hit it off well, and upon parting gave them my contact info, assuring them that if they bothered to include Seattle in their touring plans, they'd not only have a place to stay but my roommates and I could definitely set a show or two up for them, too, which would more than likely be worth their while. A number of months later, they came out and my roommate Dennis White [of *Desperate Times*] got them slotted on a Dead Kennedys bill at the Showbox and the fortunes and rise in popularity on a national level from there is pretty much known history, though a definite part of accurate history, for one reason or another, is completely glossed over by both the band and historians' irresponsibility to date. Something in all honesty I still resent.

Farther down the coast, Portland was a bust. "It was twelve people and we're up on stage saying, 'Uh, we're looking for a place to stay tonight,'" says Norton.

Hart remembers a frightening road story from this juncture in the tour. "Going through Grants Pass, Oregon, I caught a glimpse of Richard's head bobbing up and down while he was driving, so I let out a bit of a yelp, 'What's the matter, what's the matter!'" says Hart. "I told the rest of the band that I was just checking on Dick, because if I had revealed that he was falling asleep, it would have been a lot more drama than it was worth. It would have meant that Richard would have never driven again on the tour."

Compared to the Portland gig, San Francisco was another story. In addition to the two opening slots for the Kennedys at Mabuhay Gardens, Hüsker Dü got on two additional, albeit smaller, bills at the same venue. Joe Carducci, an underground jack-of-all-trades who would go on to pen the exhaustive *Rock and the Pop Narcotic*, arguably one of the all-time greatest nonfiction rock books, recalls his first Hüsker Dü gig:

> I saw them play at the Mabuhay on July 31 . . . and [legendary San Francisco promoter] Dirk Dirksen introduces them as "aggro-punk." They

each sang their own songs, including Greg. I liked about half their fast stuff where you could hear they could write songs and play them well, but I especially liked the closing track, "Data Control," and told them that. I preferred slower music generally and Flipper was my favorite band of those days.

Hüskers weren't a big attraction then but the Mab had its usual punk crowd and people in the know and they loved them. . . . At one point Greg says, "We'll come back and play after these assholes are off the stage," so they had some punks interfering with them, getting to their mic stands. I don't remember it being unusually raucous. Bob also says at the end of the set, "Let me ask you something. We're from Minneapolis. Is beating up your friends supposed to be fun? I don't think so." They come back for an encore, which is "Data Control," and Bob says, "This one's for them," which I took to mean [the punks] wouldn't like it as it was slower. Grant sang it.

After the Mabuhay shows, Hüsker Dü hung around San Francisco for almost three weeks, trying to drum up gigs in other towns. "Biafra was kind enough to extend an invitation to sleep on his floor," says Norton. "He actually forged a rent receipt for me, and I went down and got food stamps for the band. It was a five-dollar per diem, sometimes less than that, and of course, we all smoked, so a lot of times it was, 'Do I want to eat or do I want a pack of smokes?' and sometimes you'd have money left over for a beer at the bar."

The band was unable to get any gigs in L.A. Allegedly, there was a ban on hardcore shows, since bands and fans had attracted such negative attention from the LAPD that the heat was at its peak. SST Records, founded by Greg Ginn of Black Flag, often found itself the victim of surveillance, and at one point the police were convinced the label was a drug-smuggling ring. Norton remembers a slightly less dramatic situation. "We were making phone calls to [the Minutemen's] Mike Watt trying to get gigs lined up in L.A.," he says. "Nothing was really panning out. As I recall, it was more a matter of there not being any real set venues, especially for bands that were on the road that no one had ever heard of. And Mike Watt had never seen us, this was before *Land Speed Record*, and he was basically a contact number I had gotten. He was trying to figure out what bands we would match up with [on a bill]. I remember him talking about putting us on a bill with a band called the Chiefs, but that never happened."

The band finally left San Francisco and took I-80 straight through to Chicago, then played Madison before returning home to Minneapolis. "There was a real strong support network between Chicago, Minneapolis, and Madison," says Norton. "Madison was always a really great crowd. They had a great scene, and it could be argued that Madison had a better scene than Chicago did. One of the things about Chicago, there was so much diversity in venues and genres and aesthetics that it was real splintered and scattered all over the place."

The Children's Crusade tour would prove one of the most important moves in Hüsker Dü's career. It gave the band a heightened level of confidence and proved to them and others the irrefutable value of touring. Bands all over the Midwest followed Hüsker Dü's lead, and the hardcore touring circuit began to explode. "This was the first independent adult traveling that any of us did," explains Hart. "We may not have been on everyone's tongues when we got there, but when we left, we were. We weren't that cocky about it, but we'd kind of leave towns thinking, 'Well that was easy.'"

"They came back three times faster than when they left. It was so fast that it was slow . . . it had sort of gone around the other side," says Terry Katzman.

Once the band returned home, they took a week to spread the word and to put the final organizational touches on an August 15 gig at the 7th Street Entry. The evening would be split into an early and a late set (see sidebar), the former of which became the band's full-length debut. The trio had hatched the idea to record their homecoming show while on tour. The black-and-white paste-job flyer for the Entry shows is quintessentially hardcore, stating "Hüsker Dü Returns Home" around a random photo of government

CHILDREN'S CRUSADE TOUR HOMECOMING SET LISTS
7th Street Entry, Minneapolis
August 15, 1981

EARLY SET
All Tensed Up
Don't Try to Call
I'm Not Interested
Guns at My School
Push the Button
Gilligan's Island
MTC
Don't Have a Life
Bricklayer
Tired of Doing Things
You're Naive
Strange Week
Do the Bee
Big Sky
Ultracore
Let's Go Die
Data Control

LATE SET
Won't Say a Word
Wheels
Don't Try It
Private Hell
Diane
In a Free Land
Sex Dolls
Statues
It's Not Fair

officials exiting a plane. Both sets were packed to the Entry's 250-person capacity, and both sets ("slow" and "fast") were recorded to two-track without a sound check. "They just launched right into it," remembers Katzman. "My head was basically underneath Grant's drum riser. We had to check the levels as they played."

Initially planned as the second Reflex release, it was soon apparent that Hüsker Dü would not be able to pull the funds together for what by now had the working title of *Land Speed Record*. The band sent the tapes to SST. Carducci, who was working at SST by the time the tapes arrived, recalls, "We were trying to find the cash to release the Stains album and Overkill 45 . . . and trying to keep the Black Flag 45s and Jealous Again 12-inches in print. I had come down with a few thousand dollars which went to the pressing plant to get the Minutemen's *The Punch Line* and Saccharine Trust's *Paganicons* pressed."

SST passed the tape along to Mike Watt, who, along with Minutemen bandmate D. Boon, had formed New Alliance at the turn of the decade as a sort of sister label to SST. "New Alliance was a label that me and D. Boon had," says Watt. "We were motivated by Black Flag and SST." Watt informed Hüsker Dü that New Alliance would be able to release *Land Speed Record.*

"Hüsker Dü gave that tape to Black Flag after they had recorded it. The Flag guys [SST] couldn't put it out, but they handed it off to us," remembers Watt. "We heard it, and really dug it, we thought it was like really, really fast Blue Öyster Cult. So that ended up being the first New Alliance full album. We thought that people should hear this."

It was the beginning of the New Alliance/Reflex/SST/Hüsker Dü relationship that would last for years to come.

❚   ❚   ❚

Sticking around Chicago an extra day on March 23, 1981, to play a Black Flag after-show may have been the most important decision Hüsker Dü ever made.

Greg Ginn, Black Flag's guitarist and primary songwriter, was also the founder of SST Records. In this case "SST" stood for "Solid State Tuners," a mail-order business for ham radio operators that Ginn founded when he was in his teens. Ginn's stoic nature and off-the-charts intelligence, qualities he shared with his brother, artist

Raymond Pettibon, tended to alienate prospective band mates. So did his insistence that Black Flag practice up to seven hours per day. The band's debut was the *Nervous Breakdown* EP, released in 1978 as SST 001.

The Chicago gigs at the Oz marked the beginning of Hüsker Dü's rapport with Black Flag, and as such, the other bands in the SST orbit. Hüsker Dü's punk rock was reaching an unprecedented velocity by this time, and the band was clearly striving to be a top-shelf hardcore unit—not mid-tempo "Class of '77" enthusiasts, not a buzzsaw power-pop or pop-punk band á la the Buzzcocks, and not a jagged art-punk band like Pere Ubu or PiL (all styles that they had already proved adept at). Volume, speed, and brevity inspired Hüsker Dü's exploratory impulses at this time, just as those qualities had inspired Black Flag around 1979 and 1980.

Critic Ira Robbins (cofounder of *Trouser Press*) stated that "for all intents and purposes, Black Flag was America's first hardcore band," because the outfit played at ferocity level that was new to rock 'n' roll. This was especially true for the lineup whose tour blew through the Midwest in March 1981. Beginning in New York City, this string of dates was the first ever for the band's fourth vocalist, Henry Garfield, who would soon change his surname to Rollins and end Black Flag's vocalist turnover issue for good. The singer for Washington, D.C., band S.O.A., Garfield had requested Black Flag's "Clocked In" at a 1981 gig in that city, which Black Flag invited him to sing. Impressed with Garfield's performance and looking for a vocalist anyway (vocalist/guitarist Dez Cadena was dropping his singing role due to a ruined voice), the band called down to D.C. from a subsequent New York City show and invited Garfield up mid-tour to start learning the songs. The change was crucial: Black Flag with two guitarists and a dedicated vocalist became hands-down the most powerful lineup the band ever had. Rollins was still in the training stages when the band made it to Chicago in March.

Hüsker Dü's desire to be on SST has been cited as the reason they decided to stay in Chicago to play a Black Flag after-show. SST's March 1981 discography, however, calls this theory into question. SST was not yet the operation it would be just one year later. In early '81, those operating SST were either in Black Flag or traveling along as crew (e.g., Spot, their in-house engineer). In fact, the only non–Black Flag release on the label was the Minutemen's *Joy* EP. The same band's full-length debut, *The Punch Line*, would see release later that year, as would Saccharine Trust's *Paganicons*. Add two Black Flag titles by year's end—*Six Pack* (an EP with Cadena on vocals) and *Damaged* (the legendary and cursed full-length debut that marked Rollins' first studio appearance with the band)—and SST would greet 1982 with only seven titles under its belt. No, Hüsker Dü's desire to impress Black Flag was just that: a desire to impress Black Flag, a band whose recordings reached iconic status almost immediately and whose reputation as the ultimate live band in American punk rock preceded them. In 1982, SST would branch out and become a known quantity among American independent labels.

Once Hüsker Dü became comfortable at the 7th Street Entry back in Minneapolis, those paying attention began to notice a steady increase in speed and a slight darkening of the band's mood and material as the band found themselves at the beginning of 1981 with some weekend jaunts booked for the future and a summer tour to continue booking. Hüsker Dü was changing into a hardcore band, and not just any hardcore band, but one with the velocity and volume that only a small handful of contemporaries could match or exceed. This can be partially attributed to Mould's almost inhuman drive not only to survive but to survive on superior terms—if Hüsker Dü was going to get caught up in what was happening all over the country, they were going to be the best of the bunch.

The first wave of punk rockers spent the late '70s and very early '80s in a decidedly different mindset from that which fueled their creativity from 1975 to 1977. Some took newfound loves of early-'70s Krautrock, topical disco, funk, dub reggae, or early industrial music and adapted them into the next underground movement of note: "post-punk." Because most practitioners of post-punk were first-wave punkers themselves, the always restless demographic just a few years younger dialed up some of punk rock's signature qualities, in some cases to such a drastic extent that a fair amount of criticism came not from new wavers or arena rockers but from the makers of post-punk who were punk rockers just a few years younger. "The first punkers, the ones that aligned themselves with all of the Sire punk bands, a lot of those people were really hostile towards us and definitely towards the bands that really were hardcore," says Minutemen bassist Mike Watt.

Hüsker Dü was not alone in entering the fray as a bona fide hardcore band in 1981, though they were locally and (almost) nationally peerless when it came to precisely the type of hardcore band they became. This was hardcore's banner year, with bands, band-operated imprints, and "scenes" gaining footholds in Washington, D.C., Los Angeles, San Francisco, Seattle, Chicago, Vancouver, Boston, Detroit, Denver, Minneapolis/St. Paul, and pretty much any city with a large college.

As of this writing, the definitive history of American hardcore has yet to be written. Of the thirteen bands profiled in Michael Azerrad's *Our Band Could Be Your Life*, one is unquestionably responsible for shaping the hardcore movement (Minor Threat); one was not hardcore in sound or appearance but will always be lumped in with hardcore due to their location, label, and only somewhat similar qualities (Minutemen); and two began as hardcore bands that morphed into more complex and influential incarnations (Black Flag and Hüsker Dü). But Azerrad never claims to be writing a history of hardcore; the majority of the book profiles bands with stronger if not all-encompassing ties to the "indie underground" mentioned in the subtitle. The curious are left with a selection of books that look at slices of the hardcore scene. Henry Rollins' *Get in the Van* is the most comprehensive, fascinating, and sometimes uncomfortably personal telling of the Black Flag story. This tome was born of Rollins slightly massaging his journal entries into an addictively entertaining linear story line. Stevie Chick's *Spray Paint the Walls: The Black Flag Story* is a less personal examination of SST by way of Black Flag, with no shortage of information on non-SST bands that Black Flag influenced and contemporaries who shared their time frame. Finally, George Hurchella's *Going Underground*, while also a personal telling of the author's journey through the American hardcore underground of the early to mid-'80s, is nonetheless an exhaustive, honest, unpretentious, and highly recommended text on the subject.

Despite the lack of a single comprehensive text on the hardcore genre, one thing is for certain: The word "hardcore" did not enter the American punk rock lexicon in until mid-1982. Until then, the music and culture were simply "American punk rock" because the States hadn't really experienced anything comparable to the UK's 1976–1977 explosion, American "punk rock" bands of that period emerged as fully formed post-punk bands (e.g., Television, Talking Heads, Pere Ubu) or as somewhat advanced proto-punk bands (e.g., the Ramones, DMZ, Suicide Commandos). When it came time for the stateside kids to sonically strip down and speed up, it was really a reaction to the aforementioned American and UK punk rock movements, rather than a reaction to the bloated AOR (album-oriented rock) and progressive rock that dominated the airwaves. The result was faster, tougher, and generally more musically nihilistic than anything that had come before it. At the turn of the decade, the UK was already giving punk rock a great big dose of metal with Mötörhead, the Exploited, and Discharge, which would in turn prove a big influence on the American punk rock that was developing during the same period.

The most important thing to note about the American punk rock that would become known as "hardcore" was yet another first in the stateside underground: It was the first widespread embrace of the DIY (Do It Yourself) ethic. It's important to note that DIY had always been around, especially in the States, with examples like John Fahey's Tacoma label and the ESP avant-jazz label of the late '60s and early '70s. Even the 'zine movement that paralleled hardcore had years of precedence with underground comics, sci-fi fanzines, and even "gentlemen's magazines" (Hugh Hefner produced the first issues of *Playboy* in his kitchen in the 1950s). But the term wouldn't gain a foothold until the late '70s and early '80's, in the UK (with a certain strain of post-punk) and hardcore, respectively.

Black Flag wasn't the only "hardcore" band to precede Hüsker Dü, of course. There existed a tiny handful of slightly faster bands than Hüsker Dü at their fastest, D.C.'s Bad Brains being an obvious example. Nor was SST developing into a "hardcore" label, at least not if judged by the sonic quality of what was released in 1982. The Meat Puppets were as fast, if not faster, than Hüsker Dü, but the Arizona trio's *In a Car* EP and self-titled debut (both released in 1982) were far too weird and drug-damaged to be accepted by garden-variety hardcore fans and participants, which is another notable, though unfortunate, attribute of hardcore: 1981 into 1982 may have witnessed the first opening of the hardcore floodgates, but mediocrity and strict, laughable doctrines were instituted shortly after. Because the Hüskers made a lasting connection with Black Flag and the SST camp at the infamous "blue paint" gig in Chicago, the label was a no-brainer, even in 1981. Plus, SST was obviously peopled with open-minded elitist outsiders—they released records that were different, that flirted with hardcore ideals, but, more importantly, were judged to be of the highest quality and coming from the right places for the right reasons (i.e, not serving some sort of rule-heavy scene).

The same month that Hüsker Dü returned from their Children's Crusade tour to record what would be their debut full-length, the Replacements' own debut album, *Sorry Ma, Forgot to Take Out the Trash*, finally hit stores some thirteen months after the first sessions. Rumors of a rivalry between the two bands were frequently overblown by uninformed word of mouth. In many ways, the two bands couldn't have been more dissimilar.

Hüsker Dü had been toiling in the trenches since March 1979. The band was beginning to put a premium on getting the job done in the most extreme DIY fashion and wanted nothing more than to release a debut album but could not financially do so. They had toiled across the country as virtual nobodies and chose their home-coming show as the basis for a debut album not just because they realized that their fine-tuned live attack needed to be documented but because it was the quickest and cheapest way to produce a debut. It must have been a little irritating to be trumped by the 'Mats, a band that, at times, couldn't seem to care less if they had a debut album at all, could barely be troubled to engage in the recording sessions being paid for by their label, and often drunkenly fell apart on stage. Had it not been for the guidance of Jesperson and Twin/Tone, *Sorry Ma* could have ended up as recordings unearthed some twenty years later, capturing a band that barely happened.

The Replacements' lackadaisical, bratty, and unpredictable qualities worked to develop an anticipatory air around *Sorry Ma*; though insiders knew of its greatness, others expected a train wreck, curious as to exactly how big a mess the album would be. Defying logic, the album silenced all doubters and remains one of the greatest albums of America's second major punk rock movement. Much of *Sorry Ma* is discernable as hardcore (e.g., "Customer," "Careless," "Otto," "Somethin' to Dü," "I Bought a Headache"), but like D.O.A.'s *Hardcore '81*, it's hardcore that rocks.

Supposedly penned as a good-natured salute to the other up-and-coming band in town, "Somethin' to Dü" has long been regarded as a jab at the Hüskers. As is often the case in these situations, opinions differ on the intentions behind the song's title and lyrics. The song closes with the lines, "Somethin' to Hüsker" and "Break the mold" in a classic bit of Paul Westerberg wordplay.

Peter Jesperson sees the song as a testament to the bored, frustrated youth stance "shared" by Westerberg and Mould. "It was a nod to our friends that we were supportive . . . there was no read-between-the-lines swipe there," Jesperson explains. "There was some competitive or rivalry issues at different points, but that was not one of them. I think that song really was based on Paul having been a bored teen-ager [more] than it was a catchphrase with a play on words."

Though the competitive juices may have been heated, Hüsker Dü had enough on their plates and enough of a local following that the energy was directed positively toward their own ends and support of the fledging Minneapolis hardcore scene. Hüsker Dü lacked no support locally. A few of the band's unofficial inner sanctum of fans, the "veg-gies," branched off into Man Sized Action. Rifle Sport sprouted out of the scene as well, and Hüsker fan and friend Peter Davis had moved to Minneapolis and started work on what would be one of the longest running underground 'zines in America, *Your Flesh*. Davis recalls:

> That was fall of 1981. Bob had a small hand in the formation of *Your Flesh*. Predominantly, outside of one or two written contributions for the first and maybe the second issues, his role was largely and purely that of a friend and mentor. Typical of the time and other music scenes throughout the country, we basically took it upon ourselves to fill the void that the established local press was plainly—and, as we felt, wrongly—ignoring. It was just one of those things where, sitting around, drinking beers, hanging out and bouncing ideas around, getting a handle on what the focus would be and how to go about it that we came about it all. In the larger context of things, this wasn't necessarily groundbreaking, really. The original progenitors were, along with myself, fellow expatriated Cali-fornian Ron Clark, Dave Roth—probably best known for his Ferret Comix contributions and video direction work in the early '90s—and Bob.

Released in January 1982, *Land Speed Record* captures the live version of Hüsker Dü that had just left jaws scraping floors in Madison and Chicago, up and down the West Coast, and across western Canada. This is the most likely reason the band chose to release the evening's "fast set" as opposed to the later, slower set, or even a mix of the two. "Bob knew they would only do one record like that, like *Land Speed*," says Katzman. "There was hardcore on other [Hüsker Dü] records, but nothing like that *Metal Machine Music*–meets–punk rock of *Land Speed*, that extremely ferocious thing."

If the set had been played with the same velocity and recorded in a studio, with even minimal fidelity, the album would be considered a hardcore classic and discussed in the same breath as Black Flag's *Damaged*, Minor Threat's *Out of Step*, the early Negative Approach singles, the Circle Jerks' *Group Sex*, Flipper's *Generic*, and Bad Brains' ROIR cassette. As it stands, *Land Speed Record* is too idiosyncratic to be commonly referenced when the history of American hardcore is mapped out in a cursory fashion (as it was in the documentary film version of Stephen Blush's book, *American Hardcore*).

With fidelity that's on the lower end of the spectrum reserved for bootleg recordings, *Land Speed*'s sound quality is inexcusably bad, especially for a recording that was planned ahead of time, let alone planned as a debut full-length. In fact, some bootleg recordings from the period actually have a superior sound. Its total cost, including the mastering session at Blackberry Way, came to around $300.

One theory about *Land Speed*'s sound quality is that Hüsker Dü was so loud that a dynamic live recording would have been impossible without an elaborate technical setup. And that was one of the unique qualities of Hüsker Dü circa 1981 that *Land Speed Record* translates properly: The band was unbelievably noisy. Mould punctuates the rare seconds between tracks with sheets of guitar distortion. As Watt recalls, "Bob used a weird thing on his guitar, a delayed chorus, so that his guitar would never stop . . . it was always going."

The noisy nature of *Land Speed Record* would ensure that some future critical assessments of the album would guess at an experimental, avant-garde, or free-form sense of purpose. The album burns hot, blurry, and noisy enough to create the perpetual, albeit very harsh, feeling of ambient music, hence Terry Katzman's comparison to *Metal Machine Music*, Lou Reed's 1975 *musique concrète* prank on his record label.

Another unique attribute of Hüsker Dü during this period is exhibited on *Land Speed Record*. Rare was it to find an American hardcore band in the early '80s in which all members sang (or screamed). Hüsker Dü had a "sing what you write" rule, and all three were writing songs at this point, but it's especially surprising to hear all three sometimes singing on the same track ("All Tensed Up"). This approach was not just rare for the genre but was virtually unheard of.

Then there was Mould's soloing. Soloing was seen as a red flag in hardcore, but Mould's blink-and-miss-it Johnny

Thunders–style lines push *Land Speed Record* further into the realm of not-just-another-hardcore-album. "I took the way Bob opened up his guitar sound on the slower, longer tunes or how Greg played chords or circling patterns as them incorporating psychedelia into their sound, which I was always partial to, and was somewhat rare in punk," remembers Joe Carducci. "I don't mean psychedelia as in retro bands' affected Sixties-isms, but as in coloring and bending sound beyond just some stock distortion setting."

With all of this in mind, *Land Speed*'s cover art didn't confuse any store clerks as to where the album should be filed. Black and white and brazenly political, the art would not have been out of place on a Discharge album released the same year. "That was the first advisers that were killed and shipped back from the Vietnam War, back before the days of public domain," Hart says of the sleeve photo. "I just took it and the folks at World Book Encyclopedia didn't notice."

Off with a bang, *Land Speed Record* starts with a split second of applause before Norton's three bass chords introduce Mould's "All Tensed Up." It's not hard to envision the patrons in the low-ceilinged 7th Street Entry simultaneously retreating three feet at the blunt force trauma of the new and improved Hüsker Dü. At just over two minutes, "All Tensed Up" is stretched out enough so that listeners don't have to strain to hear important qualities lost in the whirlwind of the shorter numbers. Not wholly unmelodic, Norton and Hart back up Mould's ode to the pros and cons of amphetamine use. This song, combined with the album title and the band's claim that they took speed on the road to suppress their appetites, would lead to many misconceptions about the band's actual drug intake.

"It was more recreational, it's not like they got up and took a bunch of speed every day," says Katzman. "It wasn't even real speed; it was just crap, like caffeine tablets. It was right around the time that prescription speed became pretty scarce. I think that it's been pretty overblown. It was one of those things that burned brightly for a while then receded into the background. With them playing the way they did and touring, you're never going to make it that way. I'm sure that they were drinking enough to offset it, anyway. I don't think that it made any impact on what they did or who they were. I mean, we all took drugs back then. I don't think it hurt them and I don't think it helped them."

Land Speed's second and third tracks, "Don't Try to Call" (Mould) and "I'm Not Interested" (Hart), are typical of the album's pounding, thrashing, extreme overtone. Both clock in at one minute, thirty seconds, and both beat the listener into complete submission. The same could be said for Mould's "Guns at My School" and Hart's "Push the Button" (tracks four and five), with the obvious difference being a shift from the personal politics expressed in the former two numbers to governmental/social politics.

"Gilligan's Island" (Hart's arrangement) is the first recorded instance of Hüsker Dü covering a song, as well as the first and last time they would cover a song in the spirit of comedic irony. The interpretation of the popular TV show theme song also marks the second point on *Land Speed* (after the opening track) where melody can be heard poking through the cacophony.

Norton's "MTC" and "Don't Have a Life" close out side one, mixing the bass player's personal and public politics, the former being a lamentation on the Twin Cities' public transportation system, the latter being another longer, relatively stretched-out attempt at hardcore (at least for *Land Speed*).

Kicking off side two is Mould's "Bricklayer," which would turn up in an even more abbreviated studio form a year later on *Everything Falls Apart*. The not-ready-for-college-radio lyrics were indecipherable on the live version.

Six hardcore blasts averaging under a minute a piece form the meat of side two: "Tired of Doing Things" (Hart), "You're Naïve" (Mould), "Strange Week" (Hart), "Do the Bee" (Hart), "Big Sky" (Mould), "Ultracore" (Mould), and "Let's Go Die" (Norton) blow by in such a blur that repeated inspection is required to pick out the subtleties. Not surprisingly, most of these songs would not be long for the Hüsker live set.

The album ends with Hart's "Data Control," a thick, slower break from the madness. One of the earliest amalgamations of thrashy, underground metal influences and hardcore, the song clocks in at more than five minutes and points to a distinctly experimental influence of the day: San Francisco's sludge masters, Flipper.

Hüsker Dü's debut album showed a bit of the forward thinking for which the band would later become notorious. Compared to the "Statues" b/w "Amusement" single, *Land Speed* was not so much a progression as it was a reflection of a completely different band. But compared to the live sets played in January 1982, as *Land Speed* was hitting the bins and mailboxes, attentive fans might have noticed that a new batch of songs had crept into the set. Mould's "First of the Last Calls," the highpoint of an album that wouldn't be released for almost two years (*Metal Circus*), was popping up about a third of the way into the set, which it should be noted was now starting to transform into a single, long succession of songs rather than two distinct "fast" and "slow" blocks. "First of the Last Calls" was also one of the first archetypal mid-period Hüsker Dü songs and the perfect distillation of Mould's much-heralded songwriting style that would eventually emerge in full. In January 1982, despite serving as a window to the future of Hüsker Dü, the song's frantically melodic pop-punk stood out of place in a set still ruled by songs like "Bricklayer" and "Ultracore." If "First of the Last Calls" popped up in the set, then other new additions like "Blah, Blah, Blah," "M.I.C.," "Obnoxious," "Target," and "What Do I Want?" spoke a hardcore language exponentially more accelerated, noisier, more airtight, and more developed than anything on *Land Speed Record*.

Throughout their early development as a musical unit, the band remained very opinionated, and their political concerns remained quite evident. In March 1982, Mould voiced some related critical viewpoints to the Macalester College newspaper, the *Mac Weekly* (he had since dropped out to focus on the band): "We get criticized sometimes for thinking too much. It's not like we contrive these songs out of thin air. We sit around and talk politics, as well as business and pleasure and music. We've got something to say, and it does piss us off." He continues with an assessment of the world's biggest "punk" band and a possible solution to political/social apathy: "After their first album, the Clash had absolutely nothing to say. Their politics are so timely now, and they're so contradictory. They say, 'We hate the system, we hate the government, blah, blah, blah' and look where they are—on fuckin' CBS, a huge corporate structure. Things can be changed by just making a few people wake up. One way to do that is to kick 'em in the face, like we try to do with our music. If they feel threatened enough, they'll respond. The only way modern politics keeps forging ahead is by groups threatening the established order."

In February, the band did a hit-and-run session at Blackberry Way, where *Land Speed* was mastered, finishing five songs in two days: Mould's "In a Free Land," "Target," "Signals from Above," and "M.I.C.," along with Hart's "What Do I Want?" The intention was to record enough material for a 7-inch and return to the Minutemen's New Alliance for its release. Moved by the need to stay prolific and have an additional record to sell on tour (they had started to plan a major undertaking for the summer), Hüsker Dü also wanted to document some of the newer tracks that had made it into the live set and then concentrate on another summer plan: the recording of their first studio long-player.

The result of the February Blackberry Way sessions was the *In a Free Land* EP. "[*In a Free Land*] was all done extremely quickly—a day to record and a day to mix it, very immediate, and they just wanted to put a couple of more thrashers on the back," explains Katzman. "It was just supposed to be a quick, quote-unquote 'hit' single, in punk rock sort of terms."

Though it surfaced as early as the Children's Crusade tour, "In a Free Land," the song for which the EP was named, is unquestionably one of the greatest hardcore songs of 1982 (and maybe the entire era). The band had since situated the song as their set opener, and months of playing and practicing the monster are definitely evident in the version that made it to the recording. Mould's backbone riff is unforgettable, his sophisticated but efficient soloing miles ahead of most genre colleagues. When Hart's backup vocals fly out in the song's final moment, "In a Free Land" proves that Hüsker Dü had mastered the underground sound of the times.

The song also marked the apex of the trio's short-lived political aesthetic, with the duality of Mould's lyrics serving as a harsh criticism of government practices at large, as well as the paint-by-numbers dogma of the hardcore elite and their followers. "It said a little bit more than some of the stuff on *Land Speed*. It was pretty much as political as they ever got," states Katzman. "There were hints of it later, but that was the most blatant example of it, I'd say. It showed what they didn't have in common with hardcore bands and what they did [have in common]—and the 'didn't' won out."

Of the five February 1982 Blackberry tracks, "M.I.C." and "What Do I Want?" made it onto the *In a Free Land* B-side. Appropriately penned by the least hardcore, most avant-leaning member of the band, "What Do I Want?" is a hidden classic straight out of left field. More than a decade before the term "spazzcore" would be applied to a subgenre of hardcore noted for exactly what it implies, Hart's one minute and sixteen seconds of cathartic insanity is in some ways terrifying. "I was never able to satisfy a search for a voice in that medium," Hart says of his relationship to hardcore. "'What Do I Want?' is the closest thing that I could do with hardcore."

Hüsker Dü opened for Bad Brains at Duffy's in mid-April 1982, two weeks before the May 1 release of the *In a Free Land* EP on New Alliance. Compared to the *Land Speed* sets of eight months prior, their set list from that evening gives a good idea of the Hüskers' song-writing pace in late 1981 and early 1982 (see sidebar). The length of the set might have been due to the importance of the gig, seeing that the trio was booked with one of the leading (and fastest) hardcore bands of the day.

On a short, several-day tour following the release of *In a Free Land*, Hart and Norton were subjected to an early run-in with the difficult side of Mould. "Bob had a gray military hoodie type of thing, and he put the hood up over his face for the entirety of the tour. This fucker is seeth-ing," remembers Hart, "because I had purchased a package of safety pins, and Bob found it and exclaimed, 'What the fuck is this?'

He would look for things so that he could continue to be this dark thing . . . we had to put up with this creature from his own lyrics, you know, 'It doesn't get along with the outside word.' Isolation is one thing, but the waiting for him to say something and the fact that he got away with it . . . that guy could chill an outhouse." ǂ

THE REFLEX RECORDS STORY

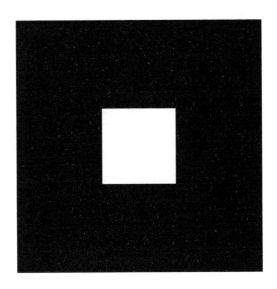

4

I t may be hard to imagine today, but by 1993, Sugar had brought Bob Mould a fan base that dwarfed even what came out of the 1986–1987 peak of Hüsker Dü's exposure. Much of this can be attributed to a post-*Nevermind* musical landscape that suited Sugar quite well. Though the trio never nabbed a flat-out alternative radio smash, there was radio airplay and a segment of Sugar fans who had no idea what Hüsker Dü was.

Because of the legal chokehold on the SST material, those with eyes on the reissue prize were limited to the Warners albums—1986's *Candy Apple Grey* and 1987's *Warehouse Songs and Stories*—live recordings, and a CD worth of pre-SST content released on New Alliance (1982's *In a Free Land* 7-inch EP) and the band's own Reflex Records.

The two Warners albums were still in print in 1993, so Rhino Records scooped up the pre-SST days and blindsided casual Hüsker Dü and curious Sugar fans. Up to eighty percent of *Everything Falls Apart and More* was culled from releases that originally carried the Reflex imprint. Who knows how many Hüsker fans had enough mental cobwebs cleared by the Rhino release to ask, "Hey, didn't Reflex release records by some other bands?"

Indeed they did. On paper, Reflex Records mirrors any number of micro-indies that popped up in the early '80s and fizzled out by mid-decade. In reality, Reflex documented a fascinating and wildly prescient Twin Cities scene that had bubbled beneath the more visible scene showcased by the domineering Twin/Tone Records.

Reflex launched in January 1981 with Hüsker Dü's debut release, the "Statues" b/w "Amusement" 7-inch. The record carries the impact of post-punk's first wave: the trademark angularity of Joy Division, some of New York's 99 Records roster, slower numbers by Wire and Gang of Four, and the urban/industrial-hellholes-put-to-music by Pere Ubu.

Reflex was set in motion when Twin/Tone was given a demo of the "Statues" sessions and each of the three label heads liked a different song. The label thought it sounded too much like PiL, though, and according to bassist Greg Norton, local response among the small but growing Twin Cities underground was 50/50, with one half siding with the Twin/Tone assessment. "A lot of people liked it, and a lot of people thought it was a Public Image rip-off," Norton recalls.

When "Statues" b/w "Amusement" was released, Twin/Tone entered its fourth year armed with twelve 7-inches, five full-length LPs, and a compilation LP—an almost fifty percent increase in frontlist catalog compared to 1980. The *Credit in Heaven* two-LP benchmark release by Minneapolis favorites the Suburbs, and more importantly, the recorded debut of Hüsker Dü's rivals, the Replacements, appeared in 1981. In fact, the 'Mats first 7-inch ("I'm in Trouble" b/w "If Only You Were Lonely") was released the same month as "Statues." Later that August, the full-length *Sorry Ma, Forgot to Take Out the Trash* introduced the Replacements at an early and sublime punk rock/hardcore hybrid moment (aggressively abandoned from that moment on); the album quickly demoted the Suburbs to Twin/Tone's number-two priority.

Twin/Tone should be credited for having the collective nerve to form in 1977, a dark void in the history of American indie labels amid Seymour Stein's punk campaign at Sire (Ramones, Blondie, Television, Dead Boys, Talking Heads, etc.) and other big-label concerns like Mercury Records' fake indie, Blank Records (Pere Ubu). Twin/Tone circa 1977–1980 cultivated a roots-based/powerpop/new-wave/punkish bar-rock scene that came together around, and in the wake of, criminally overlooked punk rock trailblazers the Suicide Commandos. It's not hard to imagine the Knack, Wall of Voodoo, or the Vapors having releases on Twin/Tone if they had been from Minneapolis/St. Paul.

Leading up to and including 1980, the still-tiny world of American independent labels was dominated by the L.A. model, courtesy of Bomp! and Slash, labels that often undertook thinly veiled (and sometimes unapologetic) attempts to farm bands out to the majors. Twin/Tone's interest in this particular agenda is unclear. "By 1982, Twin/Tone was four years old, and in my mind at the time, an aficionado of the Minneapolis music scene," explains Peter Jesperson, "We were pretty well established, certainly on a local level, but we were starting to get real national attention."

"At first, I don't think that anyone thought that someone was trying to make a viable business out of Twin/Tone," says then writer/Big Black founder Steve Albini, "It took some time for Twin/Tone to be taken seriously. The Hypstrz record, the Suicide Commandos record—these were incredible records that didn't make it out of Minneapolis. Twin/Tone was interesting because it documented a period before the explosion of independent labels, but it didn't take advantage of all of the talent that was available in Minneapolis. They had a few of the bands, like the Suburbs. . . ."

While the "do-it-yourself" mantra, as applied to record-making, prospered as a virtual punk rock/post-punk subgenre across the pond (Postcard, Rough Trade, Cherry Red), it took a year or so longer to catch on in America. From 1981 to 1983, Hüsker Dü's Reflex Records came to exemplify a purer and more vibrant indie-label ideal. Responsively enthusiastic artist-run micro-labels erected a middle finger at larger contemporaries like Twin/Tone, Bomp!, and Slash. Some of the earliest micro-indies were Blank/Plan 9 (founded in 1977 by the Misfits/Glenn Danzig, who sold the Blank name to Mercury), SST (founded by Greg Ginn of Black Flag in 1978), and Sudden Death (founded by Joey "Shithead" Keithley of D.O.A. in 1978). Alternative Tentacles was established by the Dead Kennedys in 1979, and Dischord was launched in 1980 by Ian MacKaye and Jeff Nelson, then of Teen Idles.

Reflex was not alone as the floodgates opened in 1981 and 1982. Mike Watt and D. Boon founded New Alliance Records as an alternate outlet for Minutemen releases, then released material by the Descendents and provided a pre-SST home for the Hüskers (the *Land Speed Record* LP and *In a Free Land* 7-inch EP, both 1982). In East Lansing, Michigan, Tesco Vee of the Meatmen turned the *Touch and Go* fanzine (established 1979) into a label with 7-inch debuts by the Necros, Negative Approach, and the Fix (Necros bassist Corey Rusk would eventually take over at Touch and Go). Ruthless Records (no relation to the future rap label) was strictly a Chicago concern run by the Effigies until the mid-1980s, when it was handed over to Steve Albini.

"Reflex was symptomatic of what was happening in a lot of towns at that time," Albini recalls. "Where there was no indigenous infrastructure for putting out records, the local hero band would start a record label, and that label would put out that band's records and all of their friends' bands records. It was a nice healthy development;

these little labels popping up all over. Their main focus was one band. Once that one band's needs were satisfied, other bands could get their records out."

At some point in Reflex's dormant stage between January 1981 and spring 1982, Hüsker Dü and longtime associate and friend Terry Katzman made plans to expose local talent they felt deserving. Opinions differ as to whether Reflex was originally seen as a vehicle for extraneous recordings or if it was intended to be used by Hüsker Dü alone until they arrived at greener pastures. Aside from being a local statement issued from David to Goliath, there was practical reasoning behind the Reflex imprint: it gave self-released titles the illusion of label affiliation. A label imprint made 7-inch records by total unknowns look a tad more attractive and "official" to an important stateside distribution presence like Rough Trade, which did, in fact, distribute the "Statues" release. This was a netherworld where it was common to see bands form, release one 7-inch single or EP or record a demo, and dissolve into obscurity after their music was met with a deafening silence. To today's post-Internet mindset, such a musical void probably seems distant and primitive.

Instead of focusing on 7-inch releases for one or two artists, Reflex's next move was on the cheap and quick: a cassette-only compilation with an accompanying staple-job 'zine of liner notes. Released in late spring 1982, *Barefoot & Pregnant* has all the trappings of guaranteed obscurity. Only two hundred copies were made; one hundred twenty-five sold, and the remaining copies were given to the bands. "Bands just sent us tapes. It was like an audition—we put up some posters and put an ad in one of the papers. . . . We probably put an ad in *Your Flesh*," Katzman explains. "We were just doing it for the fun of it."

Listened to today, *Barefoot* betrays Katzman's modesty. Thoughtfully reissued by Katzman on his Garage D'or label in 1998, the comp is by and large a holy grail of post-punk, punk rock, and hardcore gold representative of a 1981–1982 sub-Twin/Tone underground that naturally coalesced during this banner year for American hardcore (and satellite styles carrying an inaccurate "hardcore" tag). Minneapolis had a handful of viable venues, the Hüskers/ Replacements/Suburbs triple whammy looming over everything, coverage in the alt-weekly *Sweet Potato*, and immediate exposure via Peter Davis' *Your Flesh* 'zine. Though it would grow considerably and enjoy much greater influence later that decade, the Twin Cities scene had all the makings of a major player. Greg Norton remembers, "The scene back then . . . it was a good scene. We were at a club every night, there was always something going on. There was the Longhorn, Duffy's, the Entry . . . there were places to play and good bands coming through. Everybody would come out to support it. There were great house parties after shows."

Barefoot & Pregnant's high ratio of groundbreaking or enigmatic acts and future legends (in some cases, all of these rolled into one) puts it in an upper echelon commonly reserved for Alternative Tentacles' *Let Them Eat Jellybeans* and SST's *Blasting Concept* compilations.

Loud Fast Rules opens things with the neither loud nor especially fast "Black and Blue" and "Propaganda." The bouncy, sloppy bar-rock disguised as punk rock is malformed, a little unremarkable, and indicative of the band's very young age. But this is not just any quartet of eighteen- and nineteen-year-olds. When it came time for Loud Fast Rules to release their debut album in 1984, they changed their name to Soul Asylum.

Loud Fast Rules is followed by Hüsker Dü's "Targets" and "Signals from Above," two outtakes from the then recent *In a Free Land* sessions—soon to be redone that summer during the recording of what would be the band's first studio album, *Everything Falls Apart*. The four Man Sized Action tracks on *Barefoot* are primitive post-punk touched with hardcore, barely hinting at what the band recorded in the next three years. The same goes for the ultimately better-known Rifle Sport, also represented by four tracks, though the band's vision is a little more solidified here. The Replacements' barnstorming live obliteration of Mötörhead's "Ace of Spades" appears as less of a curio when followed by Minneapolis stalwart Mitch Griffin's one-off supergroup of Bob Mould, the 'Mats' Tommy Stinson, and the Suicide Commandos' Chris Osgood (with Griffin on drums), billed as Tulsa Jacks for the pub-rocking "Let's Lie."

Elsewhere, Mecht Mensch's five slots illustrate Reflex's early motive to work with the Madison, Wisconsin, band. Friends since 1980, when the Hüskers started booking short weekend tours around the region (carrying with them the promise of Minneapolis gigs for Madison bands), Mecht Mensch was allegedly a knockout live. "Those kids would part your hair in the middle. It was pretty astonishing," remembers Katzman. "The singer had this insane voice, and he was just this little stick of a kid. The biggest mistake by Reflex was to not make a full album with that band." The sparse Mecht Mensch discography ended up on Bone-Air Records, Madison's version of Reflex. Bone-Air was founded by Bucky Pope of the Tar Babies and survived to release that band's pre-SST material, along with the 1984 debut LP by notorious noise-rock wiseacres, Killdozer.

Barefoot & Pregnant was released around the same time as the Hüskers' *In a Free Land* EP. "A lot of the reasoning behind *Barefoot* was to use it as a tool to get the Hüskers gigs. That was certainly one of the intentions. Because they had their tracks on there too, it was justifiably a Hüsker release. . . . We wanted to capitalize on that," says Katzman. "It all came together in a month or less once we got all of the tapes. I've always wished that we could have [pressed] records for *Barefoot*. It would have made a great vinyl compilation."

With a new Hüskers album (*Everything Falls Apart*) recorded and in the can by summer's end, Reflex secured some financial help from Twin Cities Distribution, the distribution arm of Twin/Tone. "They just helped with the cost of pressing the first run," explains Katzman. "I don't remember them helping with any of the later releases. All of that came from band and label money until the [1983] deal with Dutch East."

"[Joe] Carducci didn't feel that *Land Speed Record* was the Hüsker Dü record to put out on SST at that point," says Norton, "and when we ended up in L.A. to record *Everything Falls Apart*, we were hoping they were going to put out that record, too, but Carducci was still 'Eh . . . maybe the next one,' so we decided that we would put out *Everything Falls Apart* on our own."

In late 1982, the Reflex "office" was, as Grant Hart puts it, "Bob's living room, Terry's living room, the checkout counter at Oar Folk. . . . The office was wherever the business was conducted, really."

"Basically, Reflex was a fairly loose organization until we actually had an office. Terry and Bob lived in Minneapolis, so we did a lot of things there," says Norton. "We used the copy machines at the Minnesota State Teacher's Credit Union where Grant's mom worked, which is also where we got the loan to help with *Everything Falls Apart*."

The "Statues" b/w "Amusement" single has a post office box as the Reflex address, but most subsequent releases list 2231 Pontiac Place Drive in Mendota Heights as Reflex HQ. This was Norton's childhood home and the residence that he shared with his mother during much of Reflex's history, as well as the first few years of Hüsker

Dü activity. "The P.O. box was at a post office a couple of blocks from Northern Lights [record store on University Avenue in St. Paul], which is where we rehearsed at the time of the single's release," Norton explains. "Then, when I was fired from Northern Lights, we had to get everything out of their basement, so we used my mom's place as the Reflex address and as a rehearsal space."

At Goofy's Upper Deck, a two-night extravaganza was booked for October 8 and 9. Billed as a benefit for Reflex Records, the proceeds went to releasing a cassette compilation that would document the shows. The result, *Kitten*, is as DIY as it gets. Katzman brought his home-stereo speakers to serve as monitors; cable "snakes" were run from the stage to one of the rooms behind it. Like *Barefoot*, the sound quality on a lot of *Kitten* requires patience on the part of the listener.

Two to six songs were chosen from each band's set, with brevity as the apparent criteria for the final number. The compilation has its fair share of greatness. Billed as "Proud Crass Fools," Loud Fast Rules covers Creedence Clearwater Revival's "Bad Moon Rising" (with the requisite curse words added) and delivers a raging, sublime original, "Happy." There are four songs by Todlachen, a better-than-average, short-lived hardcore band featuring future Halo of Flies and Amphetamine Reptile Records founder Tom Hazelmyer. Both Rifle Sport and Man Sized Action offer some sonic development, and a whopping six numbers introduce the frenetic Ground Zero, a Minutemen-esque art-core band.

"That was more like a jazz thing, capturing the moment," says Katzman. "But I remember actually calling an organized meeting with all of the bands about it." Five tracks were awarded Willful Neglect, comically fast Twin Cities thrashers with two full-length albums on their own Neglected Records label by 1983. *Kitten* also features the only known recordings of the X-inspired Radio for Teens, a short-lived band fronted by Polly Alexander, also the leader of Tetes Noires, widely considered to be Minneapolis' first all-girl rock band. (An accountant for many local bands, Alexander passed away in 2005.) Hüsker Dü headlined the second evening, and their epic (at almost six minutes) and rare "It's Not Fair" closes the compilation.

Hazelmyer, who helped organize the *Kitten* comp, "rounding up graphics, tapes, and such," recalls a third Reflex compilation that was recorded in his mom's kitchen and basement. "The kitchen recordings were actually for a different comp that was to be called *First Strike* that was supposed to [include] Man Sized Action, Todlachen,

Ground Zero, and Rifle Sport," Hazelmyer says of the aborted comp, which was intended to be released as a 12-inch. "Those tapes went missing long ago, and to my knowledge have never resurfaced or been released."

Hazelmyer also describes the early atmosphere surrounding Reflex: "My impression was that it was a very loose collective. Folks just pitched in as needed when something was happening. It never struck me in hindsight as being a label in the sense that there was a hardcore structure set up, or an overall game plan. Granted, those are the impressions made on a teenager, and I certainly have no claim to know the inner workings. But on the projects I had anything to do with, it was a pretty laissez faire operation. This was in '82–'83. I think they knuckled down a bit more by the time they started doing 12-inches, but I wasn't around then."

Over the first half of 1983, three releases charted Reflex's transformation from cassette imprint to viable indie label: *Everything Falls Apart*, Rifle Sport's *Voice of Reason*, and Man Sized Action's *Claustrophobia*. (Reflex releases carried alpha rather than numeric catalog numbers, thus these albums were Reflex D, E, and F, respectively.) "I took Rifle Sport under my wing, and Man Sized was Bob's department, for the first two records," says Katzman.

Rifle Sport's *Voice of Reason* is a skeletal prediction of where one type of post-punk would be taken a few years down the road. Traces of Mission of Burma and Wire's *154* can be heard. A garage-y Birthday Party or Scientists vibe also crops up every now and then, but mostly this is the sound of late-'80s and early-'90s post-punk, a crystal ball gazing at Fugazi and Circus Lupus, albeit with a much lower recording budget. Hardcore it is not.

Claustrophobia, Man Sized Action's debut, jerks along on its own mixture of invention and influence (like *Voice of Reason*). Imagine the *Nuggets* box set being covered by a great '90s indie-rock band with an ear for poppy Scottish post-punk à la Josef K.

The occasional misconception that all Reflex releases sounded like Hüsker Dü is exemplified by John Leland's early-'80s *Trouser Press* review of *Claustrophobia*: "To be the coolest band in Minneapolis nowadays you need a little more vision and talent than the gallant Man Sized Action could muster. But to be a cool band anywhere, all you need is this unpretentious lot's commitment to a few good ideas. Man Sized Action opened up punk structures with distorted, ringing guitar, some off-kilter rhythms and emotionally sung lyrics. Like Hüsker Dü, they applied a Neanderthal, propulsive attack to fundamentally poppy songs."

Hazelmyer, who was seventeen when he first got involved with the Reflex crew, helping them stuff cassette cases with inserts and generally lending a hand where needed, has his own view on the subject: "The word 'influenced' often bleeds over to folks thinking in strict terms of music. [Hüsker Dü] were hugely influential to all of us around in how they approached the whole undertaking of being in a band and getting things done. Most everyone around at that point was far too independent-minded and prideful to steal licks as it were [laughs]. I can't cite a band of that era that was heavily lifting the Hüsker sound per se. But it certainly showed up in later-era bands, even ones around initially, like Soul Asylum, who I think would have been far more heavy and less pop-oriented without the direct influence."

Also in the pages of *Trouser Press*, Byron Coley (of the excellent *Forced Exposure* 'zine), offered this summation of Rifle Sport and Reflex circa 1983: "Rifle Sport are central members of Minneapolis/ St. Paul's 'third wave.' After the Suicide Commandos/Suburbs in the mid-'70s, and the Hüskers/Replacements at the beginning of the '80s, along came bands like Soul Asylum, Man Sized Action and Otto's Chemical Lounge. These combos bloomed roughly around the time of the worldwide hardcore explosion, but none of them were the least bit doctrinaire. Rifle Sport drew on some of the 'post-punk' Angloisms that colored the sound of certain Chicago groups emerging in the same period, and the band has always valued structural tension over compositional speed."

When Hüsker Dü was interviewed by *Smash!* in 1983, Bob Mould explained to writer Jed Hresko what he found attractive about the music scenes in midsized American cities: "The scenes that don't get a lot of attention seem to be a lot more honest, in general, and they're a lot more earnest. Smaller cities like your Tulsas and your Dallases and Norman, Oklahoma. Stuff like that. Cincinnati. They just seem to be into it really for the music. Like, Boston, DC, LA, and San Francisco are, like, you know, everyone seems to know what happened in each one, and stuff. And you know, I think some people try to live up to it in a way."

Following the Man Sized and Rifle Sport LPs, debut recordings by Otto's Chemical Lounge and Final Conflict simultaneously finished the Reflex release schedule of 1983. Both were self-titled, four-song 7-inch EPs (Reflex G and H).

Otto's Chemical Lounge rose from the demise of Todlachen. "Me and Paul Osby started Otto's right after our previous band, Todlachen, fell apart," remembers Hazelmyer. "Can't recall if it was late '82 or early '83. Our first show with the new outfit was with the Hüskers, and as I had been involved in some Reflex activities I think it was just assumed by all that we would put it out via Reflex. I don't recall any pivotal moment where we asked them, or were asked by them."

Otto's dynamic psych-funk had tinges of hardcore but, in retrospect, was years ahead of its time. Dale Nelson, singer for Otto's Chemical Lounge and, later, the Blue Hippos, is a Twin Cities music luminary who had been embedded in the scene long before punk rock or hardcore came along. "Dale Nelson is someone who's really knowledgeable about '60s stuff, everything really, and all types of Minneapolis/St. Paul music," Katzman says. "He had his own record store for a while. He's someone that's been on the scene for a long time. He's fifteen or twenty years older than anyone else that was in Otto's. Dale was kind of the smarts behind the band, and Paul Osby was the technique."

Final Conflict was the absolute flip side of the coin. Fronted by a vocalist calling himself "Boneman," the quartet was a perpetual opening act at Goofy's and, in a way, the bar's mascot band. "They were just some kids from Minneapolis/St. Paul that started a punk band. There's no mystique behind it, it's fairly straight-ahead hardcore," Katzman remembers. After opening a few shows for the Hüskers, Final Conflict entered Blackberry Way with Mould at the controls and left with four finished songs: "In the Family," "The Lines Have Faded," "Your," and "Self-Defeated"—in one day. "They just wanted to bash out some songs. It's the only quote-unquote 'hardcore' release that Reflex did," adds Katzman.

Ground Zero's self-titled 12-inch debut (Reflex I) was the first title the label released in 1984. The Mould-produced album beautifully expounded upon the skeletal but punchy art-punk exhibited by the band's six tracks on *Kitten*. Other strange, not-so-punk-rock influences on the undeniably quirky Ground Zero sound were Zappa and '70s prog-rock. "The Ground Zero guys were friends of ours and contemporaries," says Katzman. "They were basically another opening band for Hüsker Dü at first. Taras [Ostroushko, guitar and vocals] comes from a very well-respected musical family here in Minnesota." (Taras regularly plays with Minneapolis' stalwart encyclopedia of pop music, Terry Eason, while his brother,

Peter, frequently appears on NPR's *A Prairie Home Companion* and is said to have played uncredited mandolin parts on Bob Dylan's *Blood on the Tracks*.)

Reflex had struck up a manufacturing and distribution (M&D) deal with Long Island's Dutch East India Trading Company, a fortuitous ally if you were a small indie in the 1980s. Gerard Cosloy remembers:

> Sam Berger, who was the founder of Homestead and the domestic buyer for Dutch East, he'd already talked with a number of different American indies about M&D deals. He made the original approach to Albini about the Ruthless label, and he was the one that talked to Bob and Terry before I got involved. I started in the fall of 1984. . . . Sam had contracted a lot of these original deals, but as far as getting everything together and putting it into the production process, then dealing with whatever marketing we were going to do . . . all of that kind of fell on my shoulders. I was hired to take over Homestead from Sam and be the domestic buyer for Dutch East, which was the only thing at the time that was generating any revenue. I was the de facto product manager for a couple of other labels at the same time. It wasn't until a couple of years later that I was able to give that up and run Homestead full time.

Then publisher of the 'zine *Conflict* and previously a show promoter in the Boston/Cambridge area, Cosloy was barely twenty years old when he dropped out of college to accept a position at Dutch East in late 1984. Earlier that year, Cosloy released the *Bands That Could Be God* LP compilation of Boston-area post-punk and hardcore. The LP's label, Radiobeat, was founded by future Hüsker Dü soundman Lou Giordano.

An M&D deal with Dutch East allowed a small label to take advantage of the distributor's huge footprint in the realm of independent and chain record stores, removing the often frustrating obstacle of distribution, as well as the financial strain that pressing and printing had previously exacted. Magazine and 'zine advertising also increased, since Dutch East often placed ads framing the release schedules of their manufactured and distributed labels.

"I always dealt with Bob or Terry, but I already knew the band," continues Cosloy. "The first couple of Boston shows were shows I promoted. I made a lot of connections through [*Conflict*], and the transition from being a guy that did a 'zine to running Homestead was in many ways a seamless one. Sam had already established relationships with people that I knew, so most of the labels were run by people I got along with."

"[Gerard] had heard and liked the earlier Reflex releases, and was a big fan of the first Ground Zero," remembers Terry Katzman. "Gerard was great to us; it was a great relationship while it lasted."

But Dutch East didn't go after small labels based on the quality of their roster, something label owners may or may not have known. "There was no such thing as a record that draws Dutch East to the table," Cosloy explains. "Ownership couldn't tell the difference between Articles of Faith and the E Street Band—not that there was a big difference to begin with—but there wasn't really anything there on Reflex or any other label that ownership gave two shits about. They were looking for products in a particular niche so they could open up accounts for exclusive distribution. This was a period of time when most of the indie distributors had exclusive deals with regional labels, so whatever repertoire you could get was key to opening these accounts. Having Homestead was helpful in that regard. Dutch East had a whole succession of M&D deals and ownerships."

The first Reflex title of the Dutch East deal was also the only Reflex release by a band from outside the Twin Cities. By mid-1984, Chicago's Articles of Faith was already making a name for itself as a force in hardcore, despite humble beginnings as a bar-rock band with political overtones. Chicago was the post-punk and hardcore hub of the Midwest—like the Minneapolis scene but older and blown out ten times over in variety and size. Articles of Faith was one of the scene's integral players, along with Strike Under, Naked Raygun, Big Black, the Effigies, and, very early on, Silver Abuse. "As much of a 'punk' label as they got, they were kind of a regular rock band early on, but obviously they got pulled along with the deluge like everybody else. . . . It was pretty hard to resist," explains Katzman. "With some of the Chicago bands, there was a completely different feel than with what we were doing, but we were so close geographi-cally and shared a working-class sort of thing with certain parts of the Chicago scene." Tracks like "In Your Suit" and "Five O'Clock" leave little room for misinterpretation, though singer Vic Bondi was (and continues to be) one of the most intelligent hardcore lifers the genre ever spawned.

"I met a couple of bands when they played out East, but there were rarely any occasions when I'd be talking to a band on Reflex about how a record was doing, or where it got pressed, et cetera," says Cosloy. "Probably the closest to that would be Vic Bondi . . . who was a little more organized than people in the other bands, as far as calling up and asking questions. He was a rarity . . . the only one that did that. The interesting thing about the Articles of Faith record is that I was also working closely with Albini, who had a very, very bad relationship with Vic Bondi, so there was a little friction."

Articles of Faith may have appeared doctrinaire on paper, but the band (especially on *Give Thanks*) was far from garden-variety hardcore—a fierce, pummeling rock machine that toyed with outside influences as varied as funk, folk, and dub reggae. Once *Give Thanks* was released, the band had sliced its own all-ages, hardcore-devoted chunk out of the Chicago scene.

By this time, Reflex was run by a band pointed in the opposite direction from Articles of Faith. The just-released *Zen Arcade* was, among other things, Hüsker Dü's classic hardcore signoff. Perhaps Articles of Faith releasing an album on Reflex reflected the band's standing as the cream of the hardcore crop. "Articles of Faith and the Hüskers played together a lot in Chicago and Minneapolis," Katzman recalls. "That's how the Hüskers got introduced to all of the bands in Madison and Chicago, because for a while, that's all they would do, weekend tours of the cities that were close by, and that's what those bands did as well. It was very beneficial; everybody was getting shows for everybody else."

In 1984, Man Sized Action returned a different beast with the addition of Brian Paulson as second guitarist. Paulson, who had contributod layout help and artwork for previous Reflex releases, would go on to a successful career as a producer (Uncle Tupelo, Beck, Dinosaur Jr, Superchunk, Babes in Toyland), namely after he recorded Slint's 1991 masterpiece, *Spiderland*, in four days. Man Sized Action's *Five Story Garage* (Reflex K) scarcely sounds like the same band responsible for the previous year's *Claustrophobia*. Whereas the earlier release was charming in its minimal, tinny delivery, *Five Story Garage* is thick and loud, with Paulson wonderfully spreading another layer of guitar across the jumpy noise-pop. "The new record is a large thing," drummer Tony Pucci told Steve Albini in *Matter*, "it's very much a sizeable, big, large record, as opposed to *Claustrophobia*, which was a teeny thing, a small thing. We've got more of everything this time." Albini went on to note, "It's different for MSA now. They can play. Like motherfuckers. Dig Paulson's guitar part to '57' (named for its position on the MSA Master Song List of History and Achievement): a rapid-fire sequence of chiming harmonics that would make [Gang of Four's] Andy Gill hang himself in jealousy."

This time, instead of Mould, Terry Katzman and Paulson produced the album, which was engineered by Steve Fjelstad, the longtime Hüsker associate based at Blackberry Way. No longer a pet project of Mould's, Man Sized Action was now a self-sufficient force that would nonetheless fracture in the coming year. "Bob really wasn't interested in doing the second Man Sized album," says Katzman. "He didn't have time; it was sort of my thing. We got a shimmering quality to it that Bob didn't on the first album."

During its final year and a half of operations, Reflex was no "reflex" against Twin/Tone. "It was more of a coming together," says Katzman. "The [labels'] offices were next door to one another and there was a lot of interaction. Everyone was trying to make it work together by then. Plus, [the Replacements'] *Let It Be* was that year, too, and nothing ever sold as much on Twin/Tone proper."

Twin/Tone also released the debut by Soul Asylum in August 1984. *Say What You Will, Clarence . . . Karl Sold the Truck* featured a young band finding its footing before going on to greater things. The opener, "Draggin' Me Down," however, is one of the more impressive direct hits of post-hardcore the Twin Cities scene had to offer, and the rest of the album is not without merit. "That could have been a Reflex project, but they had a big champion at Twin/Tone, so they ended up going with them and not Reflex," says Katzman. "It really would have fit on Reflex had it happened that way, but Twin/Tone was very nurturing of their development. They were Loud Fast Rules right up until that record came out, then I think they didn't really want to have that name. They thought it was too identifiable as a punk band."

Reflex's first release of 1985 was the Minutemen's *Tour Spiel* EP (Reflex L), somewhat of a gesture of thanks to Mike Watt and D. Boon for releasing *Land Speed Record* and *In a Free Land* on New Alliance. Also, the Minutemen were at the top of their game, having matched the Hüskers' double-album challenge with the simultaneously released (also by SST) *Double Nickels on the Dime.*

"In the winter of 1984, Bob said he wanted to put something out by us," recalls Watt. "We had this Tucson gig set up during our Campaign Tour of '84. Instead of getting paid, they gave us a tape of the show, which was actually a radio broadcast of the gig."

The Minutemen picked four songs from the Tucson recording and gave a tape to Mould. All were covers originally performed by artists that the Minutemen held in very high regard. The EP begins with the trio's forty-second version of Van Halen's "Ain't Talkin' 'Bout Love." This live version is the lesser of the Minutemen's three recordings of the song. *Double Nickels* and SST's *Blasting Concept II* (1985) compilation each feature a slightly altered studio take. Michael T. Fournier, in his 33 1/3 (Continuum Books) volume on *Double Nickels*, states that Van Halen and the Minutemen shared some "econo" habits, such as a no-overdubs rule in the studio and the occasional inclusion of mistakes in the recordings. The members of Van Halen, Fournier writes, "generally conducted themselves in a focused manner that was more similar to the Minutemen's attitude than that of the excess-laden Sunset Strip scene of the time." Boon, Watt, and Hurley were Van Halen fans, just as they were fans of the other artists covered on *Tour Spiel*: the Meat Puppets ("Lost"), Blue Öyster Cult ("The Red and the Black"), and Creedence Clearwater Revival ("Green River"). Like much of the SST crew, the Minutemen were not too cool to admit a deep love for classic rock.

When the Tucson DJ who provided the Minutemen with the original tape received his copies of the *Tour Spiel* EP, he was incensed that his name (credited as "Jonathan L") and acknowledgment was the same size and in the same proximity as the thanks given to Dave-O (Dave Markey, the roadie for that tour). "The radio DJ, we thank him on the cover, you know?" Watt remembers. "His name was Jonathan L. This guy says, 'I was thanked like a roadie' and thinks that we ripped him off in some way, and he goes and bootlegs the gig—he put out a fuckin' album of the whole gig. What a prick. The guy called me up to tell me about it! I was sick with a fever and just started ranting at him. But [Joe] Carducci had to go buy all of the fuckin' records from this guy. What a fucking asshole. The guy kept saying we treated him like a roadie and didn't give him a big enough thanks on the cover. We thanked him, and he thought it was too little of a 'thank you.' So that pisses him off royally and gives him the right to bootleg us?"

On the rare occasion that the Reflex discography is discussed online or in print, the *Tour Spiel* EP is flip-flopped with Ground Zero's sophomore long player, the Mould-produced *Pink* (Reflex M). The confusion may be a result of both records being the only two Reflex titles manufactured in Europe. A bizarre and obscenely infectious cluster of skate punk, Dead Milkmen–like whimsy and humor, jazz fusion, obligatory post-punk nods to the Pop Group/PiL, plus

Minutemen and Zappa/prog-rock salutations, *Pink* is a lost treasure of American '80s underground post-hardcore.

Then, in mid-1985, with a whimper, Reflex Records was no more. "It couldn't have lasted any longer because the Hüskers were way too busy by that time to work with other bands," explains Katzman. "That's really the essence of it. Gerard [Cosloy] was great to us; it was a great relationship while it lasted. We thought it would last a little longer than it did, but that relationship only lasted, what, about a year?"

Katzman continues: "This was unfortunate for me, because I still wanted to do it, but I had no choice. I wasn't going to run the thing by myself, and there was another band I was sort of working with at the time, the Blue Hippos . . . I really wanted to produce and do a record with them. That was sort of my first outro from Reflex. Also in '85, around that time, I was busy opening Garage D'or, the record store I would own for the next seventeen years. The fire at Oar Folk had occurred, and I was busy opening my own store, and we were open by the second or third week of October '85, so I went from one record store that I worked at to one that I owned."

"As far as Reflex releases, I was friends with Man Sized Action and Rifle Sport and I thought those records were awesome," says Steve Albini, "though they didn't really deliver 100 percent of what those bands were capable of live. But Otto's Chemical Lounge was sort of a revivalism that I wasn't into."

In summer 2008, Grant Hart brought back the Reflex imprint for the release of *Live Featuring J.C.*, a three-song CD EP of previously unreleased live material with friend John Clegg accompanying the band on saxophone. Clegg passed away from cancer in February 2008, though the CD had been planned before Clegg's departure. The CD features "What's Going On" and two versions of "Drug Party," all recorded live in 1982 and 1983.

Outside of the Hüsker material reissued by Rhino in 1993, the only Reflex re-releases have been the *Barefoot & Pregnant* and *Kitten* compilations (Katzman issued thoughtful CD versions on his Garage D'or label in 1998). Since the mid-'90s, a fanatical collector mentality has emerged around America's DIY movement of the late '70s and early to mid-80s, making it perplexing that neither Garage D'or reissue has garnered the same exposure as, say, the countless compilation CDs in the *Hyped 2 Death* series, or the hipster cache of the *Bloodstains* and *Killed by Death* compilations. Reissues of proper albums, EPs, and 7-inches—or a box set of the entire Reflex discography—would make for a spectacular reissue project and an important history lesson.

"I would, in hindsight, say [Reflex was] one of the biggest influences by far," says Hazlemyer. "They showed me and others that you just fucking roll up your sleeves and do it. Seems simple enough from the outside, but it has an impact I can't sum up in words . . . that watching your friends muddle through and figure out for themselves how to record, do graphics, manufacture, and distribute their own releases with little to no help or hope from outside sources, that indeed it can be done, and done well, was an incredible eye opener. What can't be understated is that, in that time period, there was no 'independent music industry' scene to speak of—it was just being born with clubs, record stores, fanzines, labels just starting to network and create ties between regions. So it was ten times the daunting task that those only familiar with the recent landscape can imagine." ‡

WHAT DO I WANT?

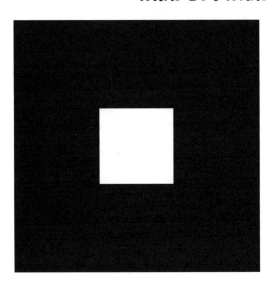

5

n spring 1982, the *In a Free Land* EP was barely on the shelves when plans were made to record the first full-length studio album. It would carry the iconic, prophetic, and generally "Hüsker Dü-esque" title of E*verything Falls Apart.*

In a Free Land introduced a particular tunefulness into the Hüsker Dü sound—a tunefulness that wasn't apparent on *Land Speed Record*. Mission of Burma bassist Clint Conley remembers: "*In a Free Land* was another surprising shift—this time, I was completely on board from first listen. The Hüskers had obviously been working really hard, and had somehow come to a place where they'd produced something big, with a beautiful gravity and weight distribution. And they had a new weapon: melody. Melody and power and speed—hmmm, I wonder why it had such instant appeal to me? It probably occurred to me around then that this wasn't any longer a 'little band that could'—Hüsker Dü was the real thing."

This grasp of melody would be embraced further during the *Everything Falls Apart* sessions in summer 1982. *Everything Falls Apart* is widely regarded as the first Hüsker Dü album to contain undeniably poppy moments mixed in with a blurry chaos, alluding to the style that would rule Hüsker Dü's future and break significant ground in America's hardcore, punk, and indie/college scenes.

The trio booked three days at Total Access Studios with Spot (SST's quasi-in-house producer) behind the controls. "The thing that hits me over the head the most is probably a desire to keep part of our business out of the Minneapolis loop," remembers Grant Hart. Like their growing touring agenda, the decision to record in California sent a message home: We support the scene, but we don't need the scene to survive. "The first time I saw them play in '79, '80, I knew then that they weren't going to be Minneapolis' for long," says Terry Katzman.

Fellow Twin Cities resident Peter Davis, publisher of *Your Flesh*, recalls the Hüskers' decision to record outside Minneapolis/St. Paul: "Outside of the band's immediate social circle, I don't recall there being that much chatter about it. For a lot of obvious reasons, it made logical sense for them to record with Spot. He had something of a name at that time, which couldn't have hurt, and he could provide the facilitation at an economical rate . . . and being at a remove from local distractions was probably a big help in a lot of ways, too."

In 1982, future Halo of Flies founder/Amphetamine Reptile Records proprietor Tom Hazelmyer was a member of the Hüsker Dü inner circle (one of the youngest, at age seventeen). "This was all good as far as the folks hanging out were concerned," he recalls of the band's decision to record in California. "It's not like back then there was a proliferation of affordable recording studios in the Twin Cities, let alone any that understood the sonics and dynamics of hardcore. It sounds hokey to say now, but back then it felt like we were all on the same team, and the fact that some of our own were getting opportunities and acknowledgment outside of our insular small world was a victory for everyone."

Unbelievably, studio time in Los Angeles was cheaper than in Minneapolis. The music business at large had weathered several damaging missteps in the late '70s and early '80s: a new and embarrassing round of payola scandals, a frenzy of overindulgence leading to lots of nameless AOR (album-oriented rock) bands signed by majors, as well as too much financial faith being placed in albums like Fleetwood Mac's *Tusk*. One account suggests that the June 1982 sessions for *Everything Falls Apart* lasted three days and cost $400. In reality, the fee was $1,200 for three days.

"They wanted to try out a different studio environment, number one, and number two, they wanted to make sure that everything was heard," says Katzman. "Bob wanted to get out of the scope of going to Blackberry Way. And he wanted to get out of the scope of recording here in Minneapolis and see what they could do in another place. I think that the Total Access situation helped them do that, and helped them get a perspective from a different producer."

Hart speculates that part of the reason for choosing Spot and Total Access might be found in Mould's listening habits at the time. "The Spot thing, I think, was Mould's love of Black Flag," Hart recalls. "I remember *Damaged* being Bob's album of the year, without a doubt. Maybe not with every song [on *EFA*], but you see the influence of

Damaged, that sensibility, the Greg Ginn guitar style. Not talking about skills so much, but the heavy approach, the real thick, dissonant chords. Guitar players are afraid to say, or at least this one [Mould] is afraid to say, that they're searching for a sound, or still hunting."

Spot, whose birth name is Glen Lockett, was one of the eccentric personalities circumnavigating Greg Ginn in the late 1970s. Born to an African-American father and Caucasian mother in 1951, Spot grew up in the same upper-middle-class Hollywood that Ray Charles called home for some time. In World War II, Spot's father was one of the Tuskegee Airmen, the famously efficient all-black combat unit and the first African-American pilots in the U.S. military.

Having done some production work for Black Flag, Spot became SST's in-house producer as the label gathered steam. By 1982, he had produced practically every SST record as well as bands outside of the camp like D.O.A. His preferred mode of transport was a pair of roller skates—and despite what various episodes of *CHiPs* may have suggested, it was not easy to get around L.A. on a pair of roller skates.

The three days allotted to record an album's worth of material allowed no laboring over song craft. All of the tracks recorded at Total Access had been tightened up during recent live shows. "All of *Everything Falls Apart* was already written," states Greg Norton. "None of it was written in the studio. This became a Hüsker trademark—touring the record that you were about to record, not the one that was just released."

"They were really primed to record [the songs]. That's what makes *Falls Apart* sound so immediate," Katzman continues. "They never really achieved that sound again; they got a different sound, but not that one. The reason it's good is that it sounds like them playing live. A lot of great records sound like people playing together in a room, and that's what that record sounds like. They were obviously playing close to one another; that's one thing that made that record so special."

Around the time that Hüsker Dü was recording *Everything Falls Apart*, the Replacements released the classic *Stink* EP on Twin/Tone, the follow-up to their debut album and, in a sense, their own final statement on hardcore.

The Replacements and Hüsker Dü were on separate trajectories by then. The much-touted "rivalry" was not what it was the previous year, nor was it what music journalists have since made it out to be. "They were doing two things that were parallel but also separate," remembers Twin/Tone co-founder and Replacements manager

Peter Jesperson. "Hüsker Dü was very of the times, and I think that the Replacements might have looked on that as a little bandwagonism or something, rightly or wrongly. Hüsker Dü might have looked at the Replacements and thought 'It sounds like they've been listening to the Rolling Stones.' To some degree, Hüsker Dü didn't get the Replacements' music and the Replacements didn't get Hüsker Dü's music."

Jesperson also concludes, however, that both bands respected one another and that Hüsker Dü was very helpful to the Replacements. "It's important to remember that Hüsker Dü were established when the Replacements came along," he explains. "There were times when Hüsker Dü took the Replacements under their wing, letting them open out-of-town shows."

I   I   I

What Hüsker Dü brought back to Minneapolis in late July 1982 was not *Land Speed Record, Part II: In The Studio* or an album-length translation of *In a Free Land*. There was only one conceivable direction in which to creatively move, and Hüsker Dü was a band that moved creatively. Hart describes pre–*Everything Falls Apart* Hüsker Dü as "a fly speck—all we had that we could brag about was velocity; that was the only thing we could really claim." Pop and melody are identifiable in tracks other than the hum-able title track, and overall the album plays out more tunefully than other examples of Midwestern hardcore contemporaries, even with the half-minute blasts "Punch Drunk" and "Bricklayer" that would not be out of place on a Negative Approach release from the same period. Even so, *Everything Falls Apart* lacks the suffocating nihilism of Bob's beloved *Damaged*. The influence of the Flag masterpiece is certainly noticeable on *Everything Falls Apart*, but so are the post-punk brilliance of Mission of Burma and the adroit hardcore/pop hybrid aced by the Descendents during this era.

Norton's "From the Gut" starts with a choppy riff not unlike Mission of Burma's "Outlaw." Listened to sequentially, the similarity is uncanny. Melody takes over when the song switches into a twice-repeated bridge of ascending riffs locked to the bass and drums. This serves as a tight, vocal-less hook between the artfully yelped (think

Pere Ubu) lyrics. "From the Gut" is miles removed from a love song, though the lyrics are personally emotive.

"Blah, Blah, Blah," Norton's other contribution to *Everything Falls Apart*, is a breakneck punker with clean vocals somewhere between screaming and singing. Norton's bass line steers the song and is uncharacteristically complicated for hardcore. Bob and Grant shout the "Blahblahblah!!!" chorus (if it can be called a "chorus") indecipherably fast. The song ends with a recording of random party/club/bar conversation that goes on for thirty seconds.

"I was tired of people dictating dogma to everyone," says Norton. "I didn't want to be told what was cool or who was cool. This is when we started straying from the pack—not like we were ever a part of it."

At twenty-nine and thirty-four seconds long, respectively, "Punch Drunk" and "Bricklayer" are faster than anything on *Land Speed Record*. They are structurally similar, exploding along for the first fifteen seconds until Mould steps up and closes the second half with the ultimate hardcore no-no: a guitar solo. And it's not just any guitar solo—Mould wails like Yngwie Malmsteen's demented, art-damaged, hardcore alter-ego.

"Afraid of Being Wrong" comes across like "Bricklayer" stretched to the minute-and-a-half breaking point. Like the latter, the pace is mind-numbingly fast, the guitar solo goes off out of nowhere, and the lyrics reflect Mould's increased focus on personal politics, calling out the hardcore herds with sentiments like "You think you're so self-righteous/But your mind is out of touch."

"The lyrics are more personal, no 'Reagan's fucked,' none of that; it's all personal stuff," Mould told *Flipside* in 1983 shortly after the album was released. "It's pretty much a self-analysis thing. People can look into the lyrics for what they want; it's a personal thing this time—how we're fucked or everybody's a little fucked at one time or another."

The trio's cover of Donovan's "Sunshine Superman" demonstrates a critical difference between Hüsker Dü and other hardcore bands. The Circle Jerks, for instance, covered '60s and '70s pop hits with tongues planted firmly in cheeks, trying to corrupt the originals' intentions with aggression, light-speed interpretation, or gratuitous curse words. Mould's arrangement of Donovan is appropriately punked-up and fast, wrapping up in under two minutes, but compared to the rest of *Everything Falls Apart* and one hundred percent of what Hüsker Dü had released before it, the cover sounds like a Christopher Cross hit. Calling it loyal might be a stretch, but calling it downright un-hardcore is not. Bob's guitar swarms all over the song, updating yet respecting the light psychedelia of the original, and Hart's vocals are shiny and inviting. In avoiding a backhanded retelling of a pop hit, Hüsker Dü stood out once again from what surrounded them. Here was a band with a wide frame of reference and a daunting knowledge of music, and a band that was unafraid of exposing a love for genres that most hardcore folks found terminally uncool.

"Sunshine Superman" has grown to be one of Hart's negative recollections of the *Everything Falls Apart* experience. "At the time I didn't give too much thought to it, but Bob suggesting 'Sunshine Superman' as the first cover song we ever recorded in a studio, then wanting me to be the singer?" asks Hart. "I often wonder if it was because my hair was growing a little longer, or if it betrayed a motive. I did wonder at the time, 'Why do I have to sing this song, and how come, out of this entire long album, there's not more of my songs?'" Hart saw Mould's asking him to sing the track as an act of placation, a bone thrown his way. He wasn't happy with how the cover turned out, either: "There's a lot of twelve counts that turn into eight counts . . . there's a lot more going on in the Donovan version than there is in the Hüsker version, which was kind of dumbed down."

Selected to open side two, "Signals from Above" greets the lis-tener with a paint-peeling squall of Mould's Ibanez before ripping into another hardcore detonation. The original version of "Signals" was scrapped from the *In a Free Land* sessions and added to the *Barefoot & Pregnant* cassette released by Reflex earlier that spring.

The album's title track makes good on the promise made by *In a Free Land*, showing that the band was indeed capable of following an even more melodic path. *In a Free Land* threatens to bury key ele-ments of Hüsker Dü's development in a hardcore maelstrom, yet with "Everything Falls Apart," the listener cannot deny Mould's signature vocal delivery and trademark high-end guitar sound, the unapolo-getic pop hooks at the forefront as opposed to the background, and the unique hybrid of bold melodies and hardcore-derived noise that both Mould *and* Hart would utilize (differently) to shape entire albums in the future. The band's live set had seen pop float in and out since its formation in 1979, namely with Hart's "Diane," a set list regular for two years by early 1983. "There were a lot of songs from '81 and '82 that were written in the tradition of 'Everything Falls Apart' and 'Gravity' that never got an airing," explains Katzman.

"They still had the pop thing going on even when they were releasing the hardcore stuff." Recording and releasing a song as catchy as "Everything Falls Apart" was a new step, however.

"I really don't have a clue as to what that song is supposed to be about," says Hart. "With it being the title track, I think [Mould] was posing it to be a single from the album, if we were to do that. Releasing singles from albums was still pretty alien to us. Bob was pleased with himself about the song, but then sabotaging it, regarding radio play, with the word 'fuck,' when it could have easily been replaced with something else . . . 'everything is so screwed up.' That doesn't sound like a compromise."

The song is also unusually verbose for an early Hüsker Dü composition. Mould's guitar solo is gone before it starts, his vocal hooks dominating the song from start to finish. The track could have been split into two equally memorable songs, as the hooks are not limited to just the chorus. Hart views the song as a possible respite from the brevity and volume of the rest of the album. "Compared to the other songs on the album, it doesn't belong. It could be deliberate, like how 'Data Control' stands out on *Land Speed*—it's a relief," says Hart, who, despite his feelings about other aspects of the album, agrees that "Everything Falls Apart" is a vital statement. "As far as Hüsker Dü material is concerned, that song is a milestone."

The energy of "Everything Falls Apart" did nothing to alienate the hardcore audience who might not have realized the song was bubble-gum pop obscured by breakneck speed and ample distortion. A set staple for months leading up to the *Everything Falls Apart* sessions, the song underwent an exhilarating transformation when played live. Hart's backing vocals gave the title track a new identity, as did the band's tendency to tear through it at such velocity that forty-five seconds were shaved from the studio version's runtime. "'Falls Apart' was a perfect combination of both worlds," says Katzman.

"Wheels" is the only Grant Hart composition on *Everything Fall Apart*. While it's unknown exactly what other songs Hart had ready to bring to the table, he believes one would have fit nicely on *Everything*, saying, "[T]his would have been a good time to bring out 'Diane.'"

"Wheels," a mid-tempo repetitive rocker, is neither instantly gripping nor forgettable. It's pleasantly inoffensive in sonic terms, but the lyrics touch on taboo iconography that had yet to attract a hipster cache. *On a date with Sharon Tate/I'm gonna pick her up in my new crate*, foreshadowed Hart's later success with murderous subject matter and Sonic Youth's later Manson obsession (*Bad Moon Rising*'s "Death Valley '69" in 1985). Like "Sunshine Superman," mention of "Wheels" exhumes a bad studio memory for Hart. While Mould was taking a break, Hart and Spot had recorded the song's ending: the sound of a hubcap rolling to a stop. "Spot and I had it done in five minutes. Take one of the drum mics and turn it around, take a hubcap off of the van and let it [makes the noise of a hubcap rolling to a stop]," recalls Hart.

A slightly different version of Mould's "Target" was previewed on Reflex's *Barefoot* compilation, and as with "Signals from Above," the song dates back to the *In a Free Land* sessions of February 1982. The album's token attack on hardcore single-mindedness uses what was by then the Mould hardcore formula, meaning it sounds like hardcore until that crazy guitar solo comes out of left field. And, with what might be an act of parody, the vocals are chanted by all three members.

Mould's "Obnoxious" is an explicit nod to Black Flag's *Damaged*, but the raucous spurt is nowhere near as interesting as what follows. "Gravity" is mostly removed from hardcore, punk, pop, or any combination thereof. Not that the track is completely devoid of discernable influence; a few seconds resemble a "hook," but "Gravity" is otherwise a lumbering beast that intimates an affinity for Flipper or the Black Flag songs that had just started to agitate hardcore fans. Fundamental to the song's weirdness is Norton's rubbery, post-punk bass line pouncing on Mould's noisy sheets of guitar, the latter a sign that Bob was finding the sound that would soon become his trademark. "I think a key transition into what they could really become, away from what they were, is the song 'Gravity,'" says Katzman. "That really propelled them into a new place, and in all sincerity I think that song is one of the greatest songs they ever wrote. The melodic displays were getting a little bit more complicated, they were stretching out . . . I think it was a big mistake when they dropped it from the live set later on."

I   I   I

In 1982, Hüsker Dü played more than thirty out-of-town gigs and a greater number of local shows. The underground touring network still had a lot of kinks to be worked out, and performing nationally, in any capacity, distinguished the trio from the majority of their Twin

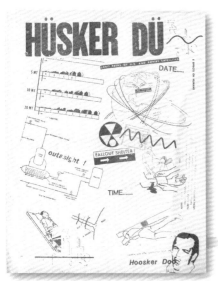

■ Hüsker Dü's first poster, designed by Grant Hart, 1979.
Courtesy Minnesota Historical Society, gift of Greg Norton

■ Gig flyer, 1980.
Steve Hengstler collection, special thanks to Annie Hengstler

■ The Longhorn, 1980.
© Kathy Chapman/kathychapman.com

■ 7th Street Entry, 1980. © *Greg Helgeson*

■ Hangin' downtown, 1980. © *Greg Helgeson*

■ Mould shreds the purple Mosrite, 7th Street Entry, 1980.
© Greg Helgeson

■ The first 7th Street Entry shows, 1980.
Steve Hengstler collection, special thanks to Annie Hengstler

HÜSKER DÜ
APPEARING WITH WILMA & THE WILBERS

MARCH 26 AND 27

2 FOR 1 DRINKS ALL NIGHT WEDNESDAY
2 FOR 1 DRINKS UNTIL NINE-THIRTY THURSDAY

7TH ST. ENTRY
UNDER UNCLE SAM'S

Gig flyer, 1981. *Courtesy Minnesota Historical Society, gift of Greg Norton*

■ The previously unpublished photographs on this spread are among dozens taken of the band in 1980 and 1981 by the late Minneapolis photographer Steve Hengstler. *Steve Hengstler photos, special thanks to Annie Hengstler*

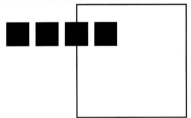

■ Gig flyer, 1981. *Steve Hengstler collection, special thanks to Annie Hengstler*

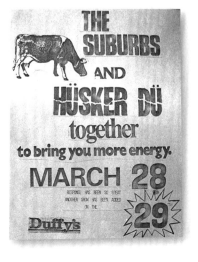

THE SUBURBS AND HÜSKER DÜ together to bring you more energy. MARCH 28 29TH

RESPONSE HAS BEEN SO GREAT ANOTHER SHOW HAS BEEN ADDED ON THE

Duffy's

■ From Seattle's *Desperate Times*, Vol. 1, No. 2. The ad announces dates on the Children's Crusade tour as well as the "Statues" single. In his review of the WREX show that accompanied this Skip Beattie photo, Wilum Pugmyr wrote, "Hopefully it won't be too long before we are treated with a live album. Wow!" *Courtesy Maire M. Masco*

■ Reflex Records stamp, circa 1981. *Courtesy Minnesota Historical Society, gift of Greg Norton*

■ Reflex C was a 1982 cassette compilation rereleased on CD in 1999. In addition to the Hüskers, it featured Minneapolis stalwarts like Rifle Sport, Man Sized Action, Todlachen, and Loud Fast Rules (as Proud Crass Fools), all recorded at Goofy's Upper Deck in October 1982.

■ The Hüskers' first real recorded "pop" moment.

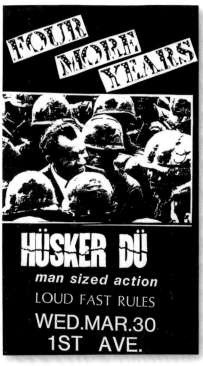

■ Handbill for 1983 First Avenue show featuring Man Sized Action, whose first LP was released on Reflex that year, and Loud Fast Rules (later Soul Asylum). *Courtesy Minnesota Historical Society, gift of Greg Norton*

■ Backstage at Maverick's during the band's first trip to Boston and the East Coast, April 1983. © *Kathy Chapman/kathychapman.com*

■ Answering questions from The Mystery Girls at M.I.T.'s student-run radio station, WMBR, April 1983. © *Kathy Chapman/kathychapman.com*

Cities peers. At the time, they were the only band in the Minneapolis underground to place any serious weight on transcending the city limits by way of live performance.

"With the touring, this is when we starting learning how to effectively spend our time," remembers Hart. "It no longer made sense for us to have a week off in Boulder, when that week in Minneapolis could be so productive. We weren't willing to waste so much time on the road. We'd discovered that three out of four directions—we were in the center—we could pie-cut the country. We were establishing patterns, but if you're on your way to do a string of two-hundred-dollar gigs, and three hundred miles north, you're offered the first five-hundred-dollar gig, you reestablish or break patterns."

A multi-date trip in 1982 began in Chicago, which was also the final stop before returning home. The city could be relied upon to deliver decent to great crowds. The Effigies, Naked Raygun, Articles of Faith, and, for a short time, Strike Under dominated the Chicago punk rock scene in their own unique ways, and these bands had become friends and colleagues of Hüsker Dü. When a Chicago band played Minneapolis, the gig was secured by Mould and company, who also provided a floor to crash on. The favor was always returned, and Hüsker Dü's tireless DIY ethic did not go unnoticed.

The second half of 1982 found Hüsker Dü workshopping new material in front of local audiences and planning the future of Reflex Records. "They were playing out a lot, but also trying to get ideas, thinking about what they were going to record next, writing songs," says Katzman. "It was kind of a weird time; it was just before the next inspiration, sort of caught in between."

When the band returned to Minneapolis with *Everything Falls Apart* in the can, they secured financial help from Twin/Tone's distro arm, Twin Cities Distribution, to release the album on Reflex. Hart contends that the band could have benefited from taking the LP to another label: "Releasing the album on Reflex, I think that might have been a step backwards. We had a standing offer with SST, we had released on New Alliance . . . maybe the decision had something to do with 'clouting up' [Reflex] with a record of our own so that other Reflex products would have sales." As for the "standing offer" from SST, it's Norton's recollection that Joe Carducci passed on *Everything*, hence the release through Reflex.

Whether releasing the album on Reflex was a free or forced decision, it wasn't out of the ordinary. "It happened in Chicago, in

Portland, in L.A., a lot of bands would start putting out records for their own benefit, then realize they had developed a sort of routine where they could get a record out and into the hands of distributors," says Steve Albini, who in 1982–1983 was writing for the influential Chicago 'zine *Matter* and elevating his bedroom recording project Big Black to a full-blown band. "That became a resource that their friends' bands could utilize to get records out. Ruthless Records in Chicago was like that, Trap Records in Portland, SST in L.A. . . ."

Reflex held a live multi-band benefit on October 8 and 9, 1982, booking a weekend at Goofy's Upper Deck that would provide the content for the *Kitten* cassette compilation, the third title in the Reflex catalog. The door money, along with the aforementioned Twin Cities Distribution deal, would also help fund the release of *Everything Falls Apart*. "*Barefoot & Pregnant* and *Kitten*, things that we did to promote the scene, were things that we saw in other cities around the country, something to say 'Hey, check out our scene,'" explains Norton. "We didn't really start thinking about putting other bands out on Reflex until after the *Barefoot* and *Kitten* compilations. That's when you see Terry Katzman get more involved."

Everything Falls Apart was released in late January 1983 and sold swiftly, necessitating a repress of another five thousand units by summer. Hüsker Dü took the album on the road with them in 1983. "That was when the touring really started to get going," says Katzman. "That was the catalyst for *Everything Falls Apart*—it was basically designed as a touring vehicle, designed to get them out of Minneapolis and to have a record to promote when they played, to play in towns where stores would have it."

Be it the advanced snippets of hardcore with head-spinning guitar solos that fall under a minute, the stretched-out noise and melody of "Gravity," Hart's bizarre and somewhat No Wave–influenced "Wheels," or the bubblegum-meets-hardcore of the title track, *Everything* reaches out and grabs the listener as a time capsule of amazing energy seldom heard in 1983. Terry Katzman attributes this to the short recording session: "All records that are done that way sound better than any record that's labored over, because the feeling is captured without a lot of bullshit surrounding it. That's true of all really great first efforts in a studio, [the Replacements'] *Sorry Ma* is another example; it's something that's not going to get captured ever again in a band's history. It's a one-time thing."

Everything Falls Apart may have pointed toward Hüsker Dü's future, but the album was mostly governed by short blasts of pulverizing and complex songs. Hart's "Wheels" may have been a dissonant, even difficult, twisted pop song, but it wasn't hardcore, and the drummer feels as though this had something to do with his low profile on the album. "Maybe it would have spoiled the thirty-second songs to have, well, fewer thirty-second songs, though I think the thirty-second songs set a good scene for 'Gravity' and contrast that song nicely," Hart says. "If I would have felt the need to do the thirty-second songs, I think I would have found more of my songs on there. I think it was reactionary, but not having written any of those songs, I'm merely speculating. For a fellow that must have, at that time, still felt like an isolated outsider, it was [Mould's] way of feeling like a part of something. It was his way of feeling a connection to all of the other thirty-second-song composers."

Peter Davis of *Your Flesh* maintains a lukewarm opinion of *Everything*: "I just didn't think it was all they were capable of, especially as a follow-up to the concise wallop the *In A Free Land* 7-inch was, and as what ostensibly stood as their first full-length studio offering." Parts of *Everything* do indeed sound tame compared to the preceding EP and absolutely commercial compared to *Land Speed Record*.

The cover of *Everything Falls Apart* showed the band's visual presentation to be advancing: blue and white with the Hüsker Dü logo stretching across the top over twelve Rorschach blotters, and the album title through the middle. The full-color cover was a first for Hüsker Dü, but, then again, the album represented many firsts for the band: first full-length studio effort, first album recorded outside of the Twin Cities, first album recorded with Spot producing, first album with a glaring pop element, and first album to fly off the shelves by previous standards. Just as important, it was the final major statement in the Hüsker Dü "hardcore" chapter and the only Hüsker Dü studio-recorded long player that's classifiable as a hardcore album when no other assessments will do.

Tom Hazelmyer sums it up: "The record was amazing. It had more depth and variety than a lot occurring at that moment. It showed that even within the confines of hardcore at that moment, every song didn't need to be formulaic, and that there was room to expand the confines that were starting to solidify at that time. The non-ironic cover of 'Sunshine Superman' was a nice eye-opening twist as well. It certainly was one of the first mixes of hardcore-style aggression, speed, and sonic terror, with hooks you found yourself humming." ǂ

ALL TENSED UP

6

Before they created their own genre, the Hüskers aligned with one. It's important to step away briefly from the chronological process and examine the elements that elevated Hüsker Dü above the standard, accelerated punk rock of the early '80s—what would later be widely referred to as "hardcore." The term itself wouldn't come into frequent use until the idiom was dumbed down and made formulaic in the mid-'80s. "In '80 or '81, you'd hear the term 'hardcore,' but it didn't specifically mean any style of music. It was a time when Naked Raygun, the "Misfits, the Effigies, Hüsker Dü, and Black Flag would all be described as 'hardcore,'" explains Steve Albini.

"Contrary to popular belief, today's punk bands don't all sound alike—there are a lot of experimental bands that are hardcore just because they are so experimental," Bob Mould told Minneapolis' *City Pages* in the fall of 1981.

It could be said that Hüsker Dü created a groundbreaking, short-lived, left-field version of hardcore and then quickly moved on, while the scene became congested with mediocrity. By the time *Metal Circus* hit stores in October 1983, Hüsker Dü was its own animal. The band was no longer sonically toiling in hardcore, nor did it care anything for the style's regimented terms.

In the strict but confused revisionist history of hardcore punk, Hüsker Dü is always reserved some biographical space. Bob Mould was a hustling networker in the Midwest hardcore scene, for his own band as well as for touring bands and the Minneapolis underlings he exposed through the Reflex label. In Stephen Blush's widely read *American Hardcore*, the band is awarded a short "chapter" in the book's regional section. For obvious reasons, Hüsker Dü is considered the Minneapolis/St. Paul area's most important contribution to the 1980–1986 heyday of hardcore (the band's name also pops up very briefly in the film version of the book). "Hüsker Dü first hit the road playing Chicago in late '80 and '81," he writes. "Greg Ginn and Chuck Dukowski of Black Flag caught one gig; totally blown away, they initiated SST Records' long relationship with the trio. A call to Mould could usually guarantee a traveling HC outfit a Twin Cities date, and one of the Hüskers'd always put up out-of-town vanloads for the night."

Blush then moves on to homophobia and, in a milder affront, plain old misinformation in his description of the band, describing them as "all gay men hung out with outcast teenage boys" [sic] and claiming their "sonic maturation was probably a good thing, because they were an unsuccessful HC group."

The Hüskers had no idea what hardcore punk rock was until they toured and witnessed other bands playing fast. They had had very little exposure to it, other than Mould's love of Minneapolis' by-then defunct Suicide Commandos and Grant Hart's and Greg Norton's various shifts at record stores. Unlike their brethren in Black Flag, who were based in L.A. and surrounded by a scene that they helped create, Hüsker Dü's unique stab at hardcore was mostly born of isolation. Once Hüsker Dü noticed Black Flag, the Subhumans, D.O.A., and the punk rock scene of Chicago, they absolutely had to outdo all of it. They had to play it faster and with far more abandon. A band as progressive as Hüsker Dü can only do this for a short time before maturing into something else altogether, as they promptly did with *Everything Falls Apart*.

Thus, only a small portion of Hüsker Dü's recorded output can be considered hardcore, and as suggested, aside from some minor missteps, it was far ahead of the pack. It was a style that Hüsker Dü had, to say the least, perfected on the Children's Crusade tour of '81 that resulted in the homecoming performance captured on *Land Speed Record*. The lightning-fast noise rock of this live album is discernable as hardcore but comes off as completely alien when compared to traditional hardcore bands like Minor Threat and Youth Brigade. "They never had a kinship with hardcore punk. This was only a perceived thing," explains Terry Katzman. "Instead of a rebellion against society or your elders, Hüsker Dü of this period was more of an exploration of restlessness."

"While I was at *Maximumrocknroll* in the early '80s, the perception was that the Hüsker records were great and energetic, and as long as they weren't racist, there wasn't going to be a problem at *MRR* with Hüsker Dü, whereas Hüsker Dü may have had a problem with this overarching philosophy of the magazine and the hardcore movement," explains Ray Farrell, a San Francisco native who would go on to join Joe Carducci as an employee of SST in the mid-'80s.

Similar to like-minded bands Mission of Burma, Black Flag, and the Minutemen, Hüsker Dü dressed conservatively and avoided the negative attention brought about by mohawks, dog collars, and dyed hair. Hart liked to joke that G.B.H. stood for "Great Big Hair Cut." Mould looked like a well-fed grain elevator operator until witnessed in a live setting, with his very un-hardcore Ibanez Flying V knockoff swinging in half-circles to the insane energy of his playing. Hüsker Dü was the consummate anti–fashion statement in hardcore punk rock, enough so that the band's anti-statement became a statement. "When they first started, they didn't look that different from any other bands, but when Grant started to grow his hair out really bad and started to walk around barefoot everywhere, people took note of that," says Albini. "There were things that distinguished them from other bands on the scene, but no one took it very seriously. Grant's behavior and bare feet were seen as a sort of affectation and no one was bothered by it."

Hüsker Dü saw negative attention as counterproductive. Getting banned from clubs, attracting the police, violence at shows—none of these elements of hardcore were at all attractive to them. "We learned how to not be noticed, how to avoid calling attention to ourselves, to put on a shroud of invisibility, to not invite any conflicts that would impose upon our progress," explains Hart. "Other hardcore punk bands were negative-attention freaks, and as it would turn out, so many of those so-called radical elements would have the biggest ace in the hole—where someone's father was an ACLU lawyer. It was often bands picking fights that they could always win."

Simpleminded hardcore action figures of the early '80s were unhygienic for the sake of rejecting hygiene and came into music not because they were musicians but because they loved negative attention. Their anarchy went no further than another band's beer cooler. "Maybe they eventually learned some politics by hanging around enough squats," says Hart.

Though SST was composed of Hüsker Dü's peers and future business partners, the crew's habit of causing serious problems in L.A. and on the road was nothing that Hüsker Dü wanted to truck in. "To a certain extent, SST people took comfort in negative attention," Hart recalls. "They loved being banned from different suburbs in L.A. because it meant that they were dangerous. That ten thousand kids smashed windows during a Black Flag gig must signify some sort of importance." Hart found this mindset to be as flawed as the "Punk Rock 101" ideals flaunted by bands less intelligent than Black Flag. The "We must be important if The Man is so worried" belief worked against Hüsker Dü's agenda of making the most mind-blowing hardcore possible and turning people onto it at the same time. Thus, Hüsker Dü rarely endured the "Hey, punk rock faggots!" moments that fill the Youth Brigade and Social Distortion documentary *Another State of Mind*.

Regardless, Hart recalls one harrowing episode on the road: "We did have one incident during an early Midwest tour. We stopped at a place called Mr. Quik, which is like a Whatta-burger. It was right over the Indiana border, one of those places where you filled out your own order form and handed it to the cashier. You had to use a tiny pencil stub, and it said 'Mr. Quik Hamburgers' on it. I wanted to keep it as a souvenir, take it back to a friend. It was half a pencil. Bob had an enormous amount of some sort of pick-me-up on his person. We're sitting down waiting for our food, and a highway patrolman comes in, walks over to our table, and says, 'Okay, which one of you guys has the pencil?' That blew my mind. That was a brow-wiping moment."

In the band's hardcore phase, Mould kept an ear acutely tuned to contemporary punk rock. "Bob and I used to drink beer and listen to the English band Discharge. I think that they were the only band playing as fast as the Hüskers," says Katzman. It should come as no surprise that two of Mould's favorite East Coast bands of the era were D.C. metal proto-crossover weirdoes Void and Philly's YDI, a violent band fronted by a giant black singer named "Jackal." Bad Brains is another hardcore band that might have reached the velocities established on *Land Speed*, and that was capable of playing several styles prior to inhabiting the hardcore movement.

Hart, meanwhile, needed to step back in order to have a clear head with which to compose. "I definitely considered Naked Raygun to be peers," he says. "I patiently accepted Articles of Faith as peers, though I thought that they were far too intelligent for their music. The Effigies were a little thuggish, we sort of avoided each other. The best thing about them was the name."

Hart has never regretted missing much of early-'80s hardcore. In fact, at the time, he and Norton were listening to a lot of free jazz and experimental post-punk. "When we opened for Mission of Burma, it was the first time I'd ever asked a band to autograph a record," he says. "And in '81 or '82, I was still catching up on bands that I'd missed the first time around, like Pere Ubu."

Over the course of the band's flirtations with hardcore, Mould remained very quiet about his sexuality, while Hart was more open about his. Although it wasn't a secret in the scene, sexuality was not a hindering factor. Several other hardcore bands, mostly from Texas (MDC, the Big Boys, the Dicks), advertised an alternative sexual preference and worked it into their aesthetic. "It was taken as 'Okay, they're gay' and an aspect of their personal lives that was no one's business, but everyone knew," says Albini. "Being gay wasn't shocking in the punk scene." One reason for this was that gay bars failing in Chicago and other large cities during the early '80s turned themselves over to the punk scene and flourished. Essentially, the punk scene survived on the dregs of the gay bar scene. For a time, any venue a punk band played in a decent-sized city seemed to be a gay bar.

Hart adds, "There was a bit of an ultra-mystique there, particularly up until *Metal Circus*. People first regarded us as a freak accident because we came from Minneapolis/St. Paul in the first place, and when the rumors circulated around—dealing with anything from hairstyle, clothing choices, bedroom partners, those types of things—it made some people think that we were the ultimate expression, because so many of the obvious punk rock rules were ignored."

I   I   I

Hüsker Dü had the best of both worlds in hardcore punk rock. They released an avant masterpiece, *Land Speed Record*, which sold well, relatively speaking, especially considering it was perhaps one of the more uncompromising recordings of 1982. The album's success was surprising given that hardcore audiences could be closed-minded and unreceptive to bands that broke the mold. The album's speed and intensity were unprecedented in hardcore. That, combined with the live reputation the Hüskers had built up prior to its release, made for a very popular hardcore band with an enigmatic album. "The style that they chose for *Land Speed* was kind of bulletproof," says Albini. "A set like that, when you are playing super thrashy, you become immune to criticism—anyone that doesn't like it can be accused of not getting it, and for the audiences that did like it, it was an easy victory."

The simplistic hardcore theme of "Guns at My School" did belie the band's stature as an exemplary punk rock band. Terry Katzman refers to the song as "a really stupid hardcore song that they should have thrown out," a sentiment that the lyrics, which could have been scrawled in the notebook of an eleventh-grade punk rocker, bear out: *Guns at my school/Think that's cool?/You like violence?/Think it makes sense?/(Fuck, no)*.

"Ultracore," a song that Hart claims was Mould's attempt at sarcasm toward the hardcore scene, features the lyrics *Fight for your country/Fight for your life/Days are numbered/Soon dismembered*. "If there's one thing we always were, even in those early days, it was a band of sarcastic motherfuckers," Hart muses.

In *Our Band Could Be Your Life*, Michael Azerrad compares *Land Speed Record* to free jazz or very fast folk music. Both comparisons are valid, but a subtler, less often noticed quality is the swirling urban psychedelic guitar in which Mould wraps the longer numbers, namely the opener, "All Tensed Up," and the pummeling drone of Hart's "Data Control." Mould flies away from the loose structure of the songs, wailing away on choppy solos before returning to the cacophony like a boomerang thrown from the explosion. "I would say that a lot of their fans, early on, didn't grasp the subtleties to what they were doing, and just sort of saw it as this loud, thrash music," says Albini.

"*Land Speed* wiped the whole slate clean," Mike Watt remembers. "When we first heard the tapes, D. Boon and I thought that it sounded like really fast Blue Öyster Cult. We had no idea what to make of it—like Blue Öyster Cult blown up on itself. When we later knew of Coltrane and free jazz and shit like that, we might have made that comparison, but not at the beginning."

Mould's love of industrial noiseniks Throbbing Gristle is apparent throughout the omnipresent scraping abrasion of *Land Speed Record*. Mould clearly wanted to make a very noisy, discordant album as an opening statement.

The choice to release a live LP as a debut was not financial. Rather, it was the only way to capture and bottle the Hüsker Dü that had just left jaws scraping floors across the upper Midwest and western Canada, and down the West Coast. "Bob knew they would only do one record like that, like *Land Speed*, and he knew they would only do one record like *In a Free Land*," says Katzman. "There were inklings of their hardcore on other records, but nothing like that *Metal Machine Music* meets punk rock of *Land Speed*, that extremely ferocious thing."

The *In a Free Land* EP—only the second studio recording by the Hüskers (after the "Statues" b/w "Amusement" debut 7-inch)—connected with hardcore audiences to an even greater degree. "Every fanzine that reviewed it, loved it," Watt notes. Hints of the melody that would emerge later, beginning with the *Everything Falls Apart* 12-inch, creep into the title track's assault, despite its being sterling hardcore all the way through. "It's my belief that they thought, 'Let's write and record the ultimate hardcore song' before they deserted the style, and they accomplished that with 'In a Free Land,'" says Katzman. "It was the end of their hardcore journey."

The sleeve's dirt-cheap cut-and-paste collage of the Statue of Liberty with a crumpled-up American flag probably helped the EP sell fairly well to politico punks ready for a Minor Threat–style message, all while band members were crashing through the emotional catastrophes of their next album, *Everything Falls Apart*, in a live setting, perplexing the masses of simpleton skinhead drones.

❚   ❚   ❚

Hüsker Dü considered the road a testing and development ground both for their super-noisy songs and for their more melodic material. This was a first in hardcore. The band chose sets in accordance with what type of people were in the audience, and these audiences were always blown away, not driven away. "With the set that became *Land Speed*, we thought that we were playing Circle Jerks tempos, but it ended up being something much faster," says Hart.

If Hüsker Dü was an unknown entity when they arrived in a town, they were on everyone's tongues when they left. Not to mention that playing the *Land Speed* set was physically exhausting. As Hart remembers, "It was like rolling down a hill aware of the bumps, but focusing on blowing people's minds and completely wearing out the audience."

The Hüskers were also renowned for playing the entirety of their next album live, so a lot of the typical call-and-response with the audience was not there. Even early on, Mould never stopped his guitar, so there were no breaks in between songs. The end of the set marked the audience's first chance to process what had happened.

When Hüsker Dü left for the Children's Crusade tour, the hardcore touring network was young and unstable, having only been recently built by Black Flag. Hüsker Dü helped stabilize this blueprint, which exists to this day, playing wherever they could. "One thing that definitely made Hüsker Dü a hardcore band was the fact that they toured at all," says Watt. "You have to understand that bands just didn't tour back then, not before Black Flag, and Hüsker Dü, they played wherever they could—VFW halls, teen centers, anywhere."

Touring was indeed alien to the first wave of punk rock bands, unless they played huge cities on a major label tab, like the Sire bands (the Ramones, Dead Boys, Television, Blondie, etc.). It was unheard of at that time for a band like Hüsker Dü, on the low end of the totem pole, to pile into a van and travel five hundred miles or more to gigs in small to moderately sized cities, only to remain on the low end of the totem pole. People were constantly asking the band why they didn't have a bus, as if touring automatically equaled fame or major-label funding.

Still, the relative hardships of DIY van tours undertaken by the second wave of punk and indie bands were not without their rewards. "I've heard a lot of those first-wave punkers lament, 'Why didn't we get in the fuckin' van?'" Watt notes.

Hüsker Dü's relationship with the SST crew had a massive impact on the band's attitude toward the scene, as did playing the birthplace of hardcore. By this point, Los Angeles was overrun with every conceivable stripe of hardcore, most of it thuggishly fighting its way out of the South Bay suburbs of Hermosa Beach and Orange County. "When Hüsker first played L.A., I think they felt on edge," Carducci recalls. "Black Flag had a unique standing back then, and L.A. is a strange landscape to get used to. I think they loosened up as they saw how little the Minutemen, Descendents, Black Flag, and others cared for the supposed big issues of hardcore that carried such weight elsewhere around the country. Hüsker Dü always played great in L.A. when I saw them, though the audience didn't seem as tuned in to them compared to the bands from town, and when they played in front of the non-SST hardcore crowd at the Olympic Auditorium, they were adequate to that audience's needs though they didn't have a skinhead singer in boots and chains to get over visually."

The Hüskers assumed incorrectly that L.A. would be a punk rock convention, that they would exchange hardcore punk war stories with the bands outside of the SST faction. What they found was a blown-up version of experiences in other parts of the country.

"L.A. was the deflation of a myth. We had imagined this place where all of these bands were going to be, [but] it was like the other live situations," says Hart. "With the exception of a few people in Vancouver, these other hardcore people were yuppies, and in the place of a mall it was a punk rock ghetto. They were just exchanging one uniform for another."

In California, the band got along best with those who had gravitated toward leadership—like Greg Ginn, D. Boon, Mike Watt, and, to a lesser extent, Jello Biafra—and with the bands that didn't write lyrics by watching the local news or reading the newspaper.

Mould expressed more discontent with the punk scene during an interview with Peter Davis for *Your Flesh*: "There was a real pressure to say good things about other bands, a real pressure towards general conformity. Everyone was a non-conforming conformist. We just said, 'Fuck, we're just three people.'"

▌   ▌   ▌

Hüsker Dü's hardcore phase had an expiration date from the very beginning. The perfect pop of *Everything Falls Apart*'s title track is evidence of this. "They were in a perpetual state of change even in the beginning," says Katzman. "When they got to *Land Speed*, that was actually the end of their first phase. They kind of became stars—they didn't just belong to Minneapolis anymore."

Hart concludes, "I just didn't have that much to scream about. My brain cannot avoid melody. I was never able to satisfy a search for a voice in that medium. Later, there was a point where Bob, he could scream like a motherfucker, but he could only do the hardcore thing for so long."

Most hardcore bands, even the ones that later incorporated more melody or put out an extraordinary album or two before breaking up or shifting to thrash metal, had not shuffled through disparate styles before deciding on hardcore. And no hardcore band offered the acute wallop of something like *Land Speed Record* or *In a Free Land*. Hüsker Dü's unprecedented approach to hardcore foreshadowed the inventive inspiration that they would show in spades two or three years down the road.

As Mould told *Flipside* in February 1983 when asked about *Everything Falls Apart*, "The lyrics are more personal, no 'Reagan's fucked,' none of that; it's all personal stuff. People can look into the lyrics for what they want; it's a personal thing this time. Politics will come and go, but we're still people. That will never change, and that's what we're gonna sing about. That is just what I've got in my head. We're not worried if Reagan gets re-elected that much anymore. I'll be here, you'll still be here."

IT'S NOT FUNNY ANYMORE

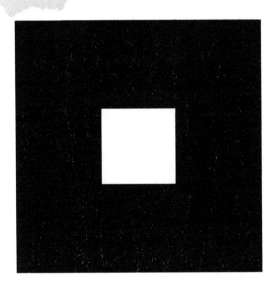

7

SET ONE
Old Milwaukee
Russian Safari
First of the Last Calls
It's Not Funny Anymore
Real World
Standing by the Sea
Deadly Skies
Out on a Limb (Don't Fall)
What Do I Want/M.I.C./Data
Control

SET TWO
In a Free Land
Target
From the Gut
Blah, Blah, Blah
Wheels
Drug Party
Everything Falls Apart
Sunshine Superman
Tired of Doing Things
Strange Week
Big Sky
Statues
Can't See You Anymore (??)
Sex Dolls
Do the Bee
M.I.C.

n Terry Katzman's vast collection of Hüsker Dü live material, there is a tape labeled "Hüskers Goodbye, pre-tour, December 14th, 1982." This selection says volumes about this stage of Hüsker Dü, as well as the band's affection for the hometown audience (see sidebar). The first two songs date back to the pre–*Land Speed* days, a time prior to the "hardcore" makeover, when the band was as green as it gets, trying out several styles. "That was probably the last time they ever played those, which were on their way out," says Katzman. "'Old Milwaukee' is sort of a straight rocker, and 'Russian Safari' is almost like a surf rock tune."

The set includes a snippet of each step in the Hüsker ladder. Examples of forward motion without compare, the key live staples from *Everything Falls Apart*, an album that wasn't even out yet, are nestled in with almost every song that Hüsker Dü would record with Spot at Total Access Studios just a few weeks later for an as-yet-untitled album that wouldn't see the light of day for almost a year. Understandably, it behooved the band to nail down those particular tracks, since waffling around in the studio was not something for which Hüsker Dü was known.

The December 14 show wrapped up three months of regular playing around the Twin Cities, cut with the practicing schedule of a well-oiled machine. "We were never one of those practice-once-a-week bands. We practiced at least four times a week at my place in St. Paul," recalls Grant Hart. "By this time, we were writing, we weren't playing at writing or learning how to write, and we had a pretty rough idea of what was going to be recorded for *Metal Circus* when we went on the road to record it."

Down in California, a contrary assumption had reared its head. "The Hüskers would provoke a lot of discussion within the SST camp," remembers Mike Watt. "It would become a healthy rivalry. People would say, 'You know the Hüskers don't practice' and the Black Flag thing was heavy into practice—seven, eight hours a day—and it was rumored that the Hüskers would just get together right before a tour."

Local reception of Hüsker Dü live shows had turned a page during the second half of 1982. "We were no longer the youngest kids in show biz in the Twin Cities. There was no longer a 'for as young as you are' sentiment," remembers Hart. "Having brought attention to Minneapolis by that point, people started respecting us, people that had never endorsed us before, and now you might hear people say, 'Oh, I get it now' or 'Now they're into something interesting,' and in a way, we took this to mean that we could take it further artistically."

Tom Hazelmyer, future founder of the bruising power trio Halo of Flies and the celebrated Amphetamine Reptile label, was a young fan in 1982 and a part of the tight-knit Reflex Records/Hüsker Dü community as an early member of Otto's Chemical Lounge. "I will *never* forget them coming back from a long tour in '82," he says. "They fucking ripped everyone's heads off, and this was one of the only rock show experiences I recall where I literally saw open jaws en masse."

Everything Falls Apart, soon to be released in January 1983, right around the time that the band was scheduled to record more new material at Total Access, would be the last Hüsker Dü title on Reflex. Before leaving on their winter 1982 tour, the band announced that *Everything*'s follow-up would carry the SST imprint. "The original plan was for [*Metal Circus*] to come out on Reflex, but I knew that wasn't going to happen," explains Katzman. Hüsker Dü needed the distribution power of SST or a similarly sized label; everything pointed in that direction, including the fact that they had spent the previous year and a half building a relationship with the Southern California crew. "I don't think that Bob or Grant really ever had the full-blown intention of it coming out on Reflex," Katzman continues. "They wanted to step it up a level, they were starting to sell some records. And as much as they trusted me, I think they wanted something a little bit more tied down and tied in than Terry Katzman to distribute their product."

The SST "deal" had more or less been on the table since the days of *Land Speed Record*, when Ginn and Co. had to pass on that album's release due to a lack of finances. *Everything Falls Apart* came out on Reflex because, as Hart claims, "We were distracted by the idea of running our own record label" (a claim that runs contradictory to Norton's recollection that *Everything*, like *Land Speed*, was also offered to SST). There was no written contract with SST until later, when "exit paperwork" (as Hart puts it) was needed to facilitate the band's move to Warners. Despite the seamless, unsurprising nature of the band's move to SST, Joe Carducci, who had been the primary liaison between the label and band, remembers that it could have gone differently: "I was surprised to learn that *Metal Circus* wasn't going to come out on New Alliance. SST had far more to do than we could afford to pull off, but Greg [Ginn] and Chuck [Dukowski] didn't often recognize economic reality and that just got more done than I considered possible. I got a cassette [of *Metal Circus*] from Spot, but I didn't consider it a demo submitted to SST or anything."

SST was strapped for cash in 1982 and dealing with a very messy production and distribution predicament with Unicorn Records, which temporarily banned the label from releasing any new material by its breadwinner, Black Flag. SST dealt with the situation by releasing a ton of non–Black Flag product in 1982 and 1983, but this strategy stretched the label's finances almost to the breaking point. Releases by the Stains, Meat Puppets, Saint Vitus, and Overkill (not the New York City thrash-metal band) required a lot of monetary attention in their various stages of completion, and the need to keep Black Flag's backlist in print was an additional challenge. Carducci had to dig into his own pockets to help pay for the Minutemen's *The Punch Line* and Saccharine Trust's *Paganicons*. By the time that the Dicks' *Kill from the Heart* EP was done, SST had to release it through a separate production and distribution deal with Enigma Records.

The Hüsker Dü/SST marriage was a two-way street. Carducci explains, "It was Greg and Chuck who came to me with the need to add a band that would tour and thus more easily sell their records. The Minutemen did not tour yet due to jobs they had. The Descendents didn't for the same reasons. SST was about to have Mugger quitting the Black Flag tour crew and joining me full time, and Hüsker could see that we would be able to push harder than [Reflex] could."

The trio inaugurated the winter 1982 tour with a Chicago show on December 19, then played St. Louis, Tulsa, Dallas, San Antonio, and Tucson. At the Backstage in Tucson, Hüsker Dü shared the bill with a young and now sadly overlooked hardcore band, Conflict (not to be confused with the better-known British hardcore band of the same name). Guitarist Bill Cuevas, nineteen at the time, remembers being confounded by Hüsker Dü's refusal to play by the hardcore rules. "I was skeptical at first," he says. "They didn't 'fit the bill.' The bassist had a mustache and played a Gibson Thunderbird or the like, very rare. The other members were sorta pasty, overweight, and the guitarist used a chorus pedal, something that only U2 cover bands did at the time." Cuevas' apprehension was quickly placed on the backburner as the sound leveled the crowd of thirty. "From the first few bars, the intensity and sincerity swept me away," Cuevas continues. "My memory is of Bob, all his mass balanced on his forefoot at the mic stand, strumming for his life. Then, look! The drummer is hammering and singing just as hard! And the friggin' weird-looking bass player with the handlebar mustache, he's right on target. It was the perfect storm. By the end of the set everyone was screaming bloody murder."

The band arrived in Fullerton, California, to find that a New Year's Eve gig was cancelled. They tore back to Minneapolis for a New Year's Eve show at the 7th Street Entry, then were back in Southern California for a Santa Barbara gig and the time allotted at Total Access.

It would be a few months before the Hüskers truly conquered the East Coast, but this tour substantiated the trio's live domination of the Midwest and West Coast. The new material significantly widened the gap between Hüsker Dü and hardcore. Steve Albini remembers, "They were gradually becoming quite well-known. I was impressed by their energy, and I thought that they had come onto a different sort of music. I appreciated their early hardcore thing, but when they started to slow down and get a little bit more rich texturally, I thought that it was a good development."

The Replacements' third album, *Hootenanny*, would be released that April. What was seen as a rivalry between the two bands a year earlier had died down. The 'Mats and the Hüskers were the two biggest indie bands in the Twin Cities. They shared mutual appreciation and criticism for each other, but each band was maturing and focusing on its respective route. As live acts (they would occasionally meet up on the road but rarely played together locally by 1983), there was no similarity. "Folks go on about the hit-or-miss Replacements shows, but nobody came close to the attack unleashed by the Hüskers of that era," says Hazelmyer.

Mould lacked any hint of self-deprecation and instead hemorrhaged self-assurance. "There was a cockiness about them that kind of put me off a little bit on a personal level," Albini continues, "but that was fine. They were an awesome band. You can't really fault someone for thinking he's the shit when he is, you know?"

Though Hüsker Dü and the Minutemen would eventually release sprawling double albums in July 1984, begetting comparisons for eternity, Mike Watt, D. Boon, and George Hurley aired a humility that their friends and colleagues in Hüsker Dü had discarded by the 1982–1983 period. "When I would talk to them about the next record, the always amazing thing about Hüsker Dü was the unfathomable confidence, you know, not really conceited, but they would say, 'This next one is going to be the greatest,'" recalls Watt. "We were always saying 'Oh, I hope our next one is okay,' but they never had doubts."

The brand-new songs were honed and ready for tape when Hüsker Dü arrived at Total Access during the second week of January to record what would become *Metal Circus*. In *Our Band Could Be Your Life*, Michael Azerrad writes that the band intended to record an entire album in one day but that this became "impossible" when the studio's electricity was cut, allowing the completion of only seven songs. Azerrad quotes Mould: "We were trying to jump power from other parts of the building. . . . Stuff like that really freaks people out."

Hart has a different recollection: "We had permission to use someone else's power. It was a neighborly gesture within that little industrial complex. Bob had a tendency, especially at that time, to reach for a conspiratorial angle."

Another cassette from Katzman's archives, which he recalls "were final mixes that came straight from Bob's hand" when they returned in early 1983 from touring and recording, is labeled "Hüsker Dü: Metal Circus Mixes, Winter '83" and contains thirteen songs: "Heavy Handed," "Real World," "Obnoxious," "Deadly Skies," "Today's the Day," "First of the Last Calls," "Lifeline," "Won't Change," "You Think I'm Scared," "Out on a Limb (Don't Fall)," "Standing by the Sea," "Diane," and "It's Not Funny Anymore." Hart's "Standing by the Sea" turned up in far superior form on *Zen Arcade*, while "Won't Change," "Today's the Day," "You Think I'm Scared," and "Heavy

Handed" either surfaced later as compilation contributions or circulate as bootlegs. So many tracks would seem to discount any intention of completing the recording in one day.

"The duration of the power outage would not have been so great as to cause a serious dent in what we were doing," concludes Hart. "We would have had to have been recording and mixing a song every fifteen minutes. It sounds like as good an explanation as 'my dog ate the homework.'"

Hüsker Dü left Southern California in mid-January. The tour ended like it started: in Chicago. On January 30, the band appeared at the Cubby Bear on yet another bill that epitomized Hüsker Dü's removal from the punk rock norm of the day.

"They opened for Rights of the Accused and the Antibodies," says Joe Carducci, who happened to be at the gig. "ROTA were sloppy and English-sounding; Antibodies were better. By then there was a small Chicago hardcore scene, but . . . it was kind of retarded."

Planning for an October release of *Metal Circus*, the Hüskers hunkered down in mid-1983, occupying their time with the EP's visual aspects, the running of Reflex Records, plenty of local shows, writing the material that would become *Zen Arcade*, and shorter jaunts out of town. "It was a combination of getting their profile up, watching over the bands on Reflex, making T-shirts," recalls Katzman. "They were really starting to get into the merchandising of their name. They were always conscious of it, but once they were sure they were signed to someone else, they started to push a little harder and stay busier. This was a period of fine-tuning."

With brand-new LPs by Rifle Sport (*Voice of Reason*) and Man Sized Action (*Claustrophobia*), the summer of '83 was a productive time for Reflex Records. With Hüsker Dü as a headliner, the label held a party on June 4 to celebrate a distribution deal with Dutch East. "That was the one time that it felt like a real label, we were doing what records labels do . . . like having parties," remembers Hart.

Hart's approach to *Metal Circus*' cover art indicates that he was fully aware of the band's growing status and that the EP would be a turning point. It is a treasure-trove of hidden trivia for the hardcore Hüsker fan or Twin Cities pop-cultural historian. Due to the band's strenuous touring schedule, Hart had since moved out of the Milton Building and was living at home in South St. Paul. Still close with many of the people who lived and worked there, he secured the interior of a ground-floor office for the photo shoot. Occupying the office at the time was the father of Dez Dickerson, Prince's most famous guitarist. Sticking with the Twin Cities phenomenon since the beginning in 1977 and known for his rising-sun headband, Dickerson departed the Revolution the same year the photo was taken.

Hart started at break of dawn, painting the logo on the glass, using a paper template taped to the outside to keep the letters level. Inside the office, he arranged a series of props to represent the Hüsker Dü discography to date. A model airplane sits on the desk in the lower right-hand corner. On the plane's wing Hart painted the tiny alpha-numeric sequence "NAR007"—New Alliance Records 007, the catalog number for *Land Speed Record*. The calendar on the wall is open to a picture of the Statue of Liberty, representing the cover of *In a Free Land*. On the desk is a framed picture of Chairman Mao to suggest the cover art for the "Statues" single. Finally, if one looks very, very closely at the newspaper, also on the desk, the back cover logo of *Everything Falls Apart* can be seen.

The promotional poster for *Metal Circus* was shot from the outside in, with the letters reading correctly, the glass reflecting the building across the street. "The whole thing was the most satisfying graphics project that I ever connected with Hüsker Dü," says Hart. "By the time it was all set up, I had to race the sun and deal with drunken street revelers getting in the way of the shot. The shoot was on St. Patrick's Day, and there were a lot of throwaways where you can see the tips of those party horns entering the frame."

When *Metal Circus* was released in October, Hüsker Dü was on a short West Coast tour that would lead to their first headlining trip to the East Coast. Armed with a set that included several numbers that would later appear on *Zen Arcade*, the band was again ready to move on, but *Metal Circus* did new and deserved wonders for the trio, both in sound and the acquisition of a wider audience.

For a band interested in severing its ties with the hardcore scene, there's no better way to open an album than with "Real World." It annihilates the competition with Mould's scream-sung vocals and first genuine use of the guitar-wash that trademarks his playing to this day. Hart's backing vocals are ultra-melodic and reminiscent of the Descendents' landmark album from the year before, *Milo Goes to College*. Mould's lyrics attack the hardcore archetype with caustic aplomb and are encased in what is, well, one of the more intense hardcore songs of 1983.

"Deadly Skies" is also an ear-shredder, but it lacks melodic sense and tones down Mould's signature guitar work (though it does have two wild solos that last several seconds apiece). The lyrics shift between sincere concern over nuclear warfare and the futility of protesting the problem. The point is wrapped up neatly within a minute and a half. Mould explained the song during an interview with the *Suburban Punk* 'zine in early 1984: "Yeah, it also deals a lot with people who see protesters walking around carrying signs that someone else painted for them to try to get attention for a cause they know nothing about. As far as the whole thing with nuclear war is concerned, I don't think that anybody's even come up with a half-baked idea of how to cut down on the chances for nuclear war. It's like, 'Oh, let's cut back the weapons.' Well, what's the difference between the 40,000, which there is now, and 500? It's like the war was over and everybody lost the second they made the first one. We all lost right then. There's nothing we can do about it—it's fucked."

"Deadly Skies" is followed by the one-two punch of "It's Not Funny Anymore" and "First of the Last Calls"—Hart's strongest moment to date backed by the same from Mould. The two songs together anchor the EP and accurately predict the band's next five years: hair-raising energy with beautiful hooks.

"It's Not Funny Anymore" is Hüsker Dü running into the loving arms of hook-filled noise-pop, and they wouldn't be as unapologetic about the form until two and a half years later with *Flip Your Wig*'s "Makes No Sense at All." The song is a thinly veiled proclamation: "Like it or not, we are going to do this pop thing." The backup hook is in Norton's bass line, which carries the song but, if removed, could almost be the basis for an entirely different composition. This brings to light one of *Metal Circus*'s minor mysteries: Why was Greg's bass so low in the mix? "Greg Ginn noticed how Greg's bass was turned down, because it was so important to the Hüskers' sound," recalls Mike Watt. "For me to say something like that would be totally biased, but for Ginn to notice it, a lead guitarist, I thought that was kind of insightful."

With its tunefully barked lyrics, "First of the Last Calls" is Mould tackling alcoholism and marks the only time in the Hüsker discography that he would do this in such an obvious manner. "I didn't realize that Bob thought his drinking was a problem until he announced he was quitting, later on," says Katzman.

As in the closing minute of "Real World," Grant's backing vocals add a pleasant flourish to the final, incredibly fierce chorus. The spine-tingling, pure rock 'n' roll release felt in this track would only be surpassed by the band's infamous, as-yet-released cover of "Eight Miles High."

If anything on *Metal Circus* resembles filler, it's track five. Mould's "Lifeline" is the last time Hüsker Dü earnestly released something close to generic hardcore. Perhaps the song was a preemptive strike against what followed.

The next-to-last track on *Metal Circus* catapulted Hüsker Dü into the underground limelight. Hart's "Diane" gave Hüsker Dü a not-so-gentle nudge into the realm of headlining tours and college-radio favor. A spiked ballad, it was certainly slow by Hüsker standards. Hart's chorus was nothing more than the word "Diane" repeated over and over, salvaging the building blocks of '60s bubblegum pop. But the real punch came from the lyrics: The story told in Hart's murderous tale is a real one.

In 1980, Joe Ture, a drifter and occasional employee of the Ford Motor Company, abducted, raped, and murdered a nineteen-year-old Minneapolis waitress named Diane Edwards. Convicted of the crime and sentenced to life in 1981, Ture was also behind a string of attacks in Minnesota in the 1970s and was convicted of other murders as recently as 2007.

Many listeners were unaware of the song's intention, much less what it referenced. In April 1983, during the band's first East Coast tour, the band met Josiah McElheny and Lou Giordano in Boston. Both ran the sound at local shows and would serve the band in different capacities until 1988. McElheny remembers the April show: "The club [Mavericks] was very strange. I worked there on a number of gigs and for a single week as the house soundman. During the day, it was a businessman's lunch place with strippers, at night a punk rock club. . . . At that gig there was a lot of discussion of 'Diane,' as at the time there was a good deal of controversy about the lyrics. People did not understand its irony or voice in terms of it being a protest. Also, there was a lot of talk of how loud the band was. There was a baby there on the shoulders of a dad, wearing red earphone hearing protectors."

A live staple written before the release of *Land Speed Record*, it goes without saying that "Diane" was not pro-rape/murder. "There was talk of this treacherous, really crazy song that Grant had come up with," says Katzman. "I was kind of scared the first time I heard it. Up to that point, he really didn't have anything quite like that."

Hart found himself answering for the song's content during numerous 'zine and college radio interviews. "Grant probably got pretty fucking tired of having to explain that song all the time," adds Watt. "It's just like Greg Ginn having to explain 'White Minority' all the time, and when we shaved our heads people would ask the Minutemen if we were skinheads."

Metal Circus is prescient in its method of closure as well, but in a manner different than "It's Not Funny Anymore" and "First of the Last Calls." The discordant madness of Mould's "Out on a Limb" presents a bizarre ending of cathartic primal scream therapy on top of a Flipper-influenced dirge. Mould's atonal, Eddie Van Halen–with-all-thumbs guitar solos are enough to make first-time listeners jump out of their seats. "They would go on to do this, when you look at the records that came after *Metal Circus*, a 'let's end with something really freaking nuts,'" notes Katzman. "They did it with 'Plans I Make' on *New Day Rising*."

Spot's early-'80s production techniques drew perpetual criticism, especially in hindsight, but albums like *Metal Circus* are not to be enjoyed for sound quality—they are to be cherished for documenting rapidly changing bands in an era of great importance. "The early Spot records sounded kind of crappy, I don't think that's debatable," says Albini, "but I also think that they existed is way more important than what they sounded like. That he was cooperative and friendly and competent enough to keep getting work . . . that says an awful lot more than just listening to those records and passing judgment on the sound quality. It's like peeking through a window at a very active sex scene—just because you're not standing at the foot of the bed doesn't mean you don't know what's going on."

Despite its urgency, compact delivery, and relative accessibility, *Metal Circus* took a week or two to sink in with the buying public but soon became Hüsker Dü's biggest seller to that point. "It was a pretty strong seller, but I don't remember it going out with the velocity of *Everything Falls Apart*," remembers Katzman. "It took a little longer, and then people started snapping it up. It was a little quiet at first."

The success of *Metal Circus* was vital to the stability of SST, helping set the label's course for the next two years. "I felt that the label got to be self-capitalizing from the releases of *Metal Circus* and the Minutemen's *Buzz or Howl* [*Under the Influence of Heat*] in '83," says Carducci. "Gradually, we could keep everything in print, distributors were more interested and paid up front so as to get the next release, et cetera." There would be problems for a particular future Hüsker album, but for the time being, SST could get *Metal Circus* into eager hands all over the country, including the college radio network that, thanks in large part to R.E.M., was now beginning to accept new and challenging sounds.

Metal Circus was the first Hüsker Dü release to clearly segregate Hart's and Mould's compositions. With Norton out of the picture as a songwriter, the Bob and Grant Show had officially commenced. "This was the first time that you had 'Are you a Bob Mould fan, or a Grant Hart fan?' appearing in the appreciation of our records," says Hart, "and I remember that record being referred to later, by Bob, as the Grant-heavy album, because of the attention that 'Diane' got, but that's when he started being aware of those judgments and criticisms of other people."

"It was the first Hüsker Dü record that I thought sounded awesome," says Albini. "The previous records gave you an impression of what the band was like, but that one was a good distillation of that stage of development in the band. That record didn't seem like it was heading in the direction of the mundane, whereas at the time an awful lot of bands, the more records they put out, the more simple their approach got— they were defining what they did to the point that it became a gag."

The stylistic gap between *Everything Falls Apart* and *Metal Circus* is the biggest in the entire sequence of Hüsker Dü albums. When the band entered the studio back in January 1983, committing those songs to tape, they would create a microcosm of an entire career. A great deal of what would go on to solidify the trio as a groundbreaking, enigmatic force in music was laid out with *Metal Circus*. That five songs were scrapped, leaving an eighteen-and-a-half-minute EP, is even that much more astonishing considering the end result. The Hüsker Dü "sound"—the reason the band changed lives and inspired countless bands to form—was established with *Metal Circus*.

"People are always saying, 'Then there was *Zen Arcade*,' and I say, 'No, you need to take a look at what came right before that,'" concludes Hart. ǂ

COFFEE-TABLE HARDCORE

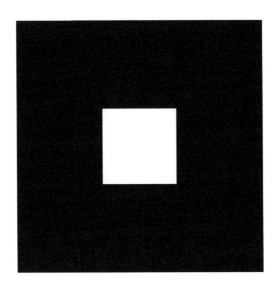

8

n what was becoming a signature of Hüsker Dü's unequaled progress, Bob Mould, Grant Hart, and Greg Norton entered Total Access in October 1983 to record their next album as *Metal Circus* was hitting stores. When it came to making records, the band had shown an astonishing degree of development, not just within the context of hardcore, but in the context of rock 'n' roll in general. It was a rare case of decision-making and efficient execution resulting in unique, inspired results without one minute of music coming off as forced, contrived, or insincere.

The band's discography up to this point had shown an astonishing degree of variety. There was the debut single ("Statues" b/w "Amusement"); a live album as a debut (*Land Speed Record*); the three-song "In a Free Land" 7-inch (essentially an EP); a proper full-length LP (*Everything Falls Apart*); and a meaty EP more accurately described as a mini album (*Metal Circus*). The LP documenting Hüsker Dü's October 1983 sessions would require a format previously absent from the band's discography and absent from hardcore in general. The tapes that the band brought back to Minnesota that fall indicated *Metal Circus'* follow-up would not only be longer than seven songs, it would be a double album. Whether or not the band was prepared to finish a double album's worth of material when they entered Total Access is debatable, as is the idea that they conceived the album's much-touted concept before arriving at the studio. Regardless, the result was *Zen Arcade*, the album that most critics and fans consider the most important statement of their career.

In *Our Band Could Be Your Life*, Michael Azerrad writes, "the band recorded twenty-five tracks—at least twenty-one of them first takes—with Spot in California at Total Access in a remarkable forty-five hours, then mixed it all in one marathon forty-hour session, bringing the whole thing in for $3,200."

In reality, Hüsker Dü spent more time hanging out than they did in the studio. In all, the band spent two-and-a-half to three weeks in the L.A. area, barring short jaunts to play other cities. "I really don't recall on that album there being a time pressure like there was with *Everything Falls Apart*," says Hart. "We just worked very expeditiously because of having the experiences of *Metal Circus* and *Everything Falls Apart*."

"They often smoked and drank beer at SST, ate at Rod's Char-Broiled on Artesia," says Joe Carducci. "[SST staff] didn't eat there. We ate Mexican if we had cash. There are Naomi Peterson photos of them around the neighborhood and in Total Access horsing around." The downtime is indicative of a band that had reached a stage where they could play the process of recording and not have it play them.

Interestingly, the Minutemen had finished their next full-length and were hanging around the SST offices a lot as well. Hüsker Dü took to the Minutemen more than any other SST entity. Before returning to Minneapolis, Mould had become outwardly enthusiastic about the new material and revealed to Mike Watt that it would be a double album. The revelation planted the seed for the Minutemen's own two-record masterpiece, *Double Nickels on the Dime*.

"Minutemen and Hüskers bonded on the power-trio trip," remembers Dave Markey, a 'zine publisher, filmmaker, and leader of SST's Painted Willie. "They were peers of each other. Watt first put out Hüskers on New Alliance before Ginn would take notice and later snatch them up. Clearly, *Double Nickels* was an answer to *Zen*. No other SST band was going to follow suit with a double LP. If anyone could match it—and probably upstage it—it would be the Minutemen. That said, both are fantastic in their own way."

The Hüskers may have been bonding with their fellow trio from San Pedro, but October 1983 in L.A. may have been one of the last times the three band members felt at ease around one another—not that they made it a habit of airing their dirty laundry to outsiders no matter how bad things were. During the year, Mould had gradually assumed the position of band mouthpiece for 'zine and radio interviews (a subtle change that foretold of a more fractured dynamic). "Bob seemed to be the spokesman for the band at the time. Either that or it's just how it worked out with the interviews I did with them," says Markey. "Bob knew the band was going off in a different direction, yet he wasn't quite sure what it was yet. He was excited about the music and was interested in seeing what the reaction would be from the punkers. Everyone did their share of talking, actually, and they seemed relaxed and also excited to be in L.A."

In the September 1983 issue of *Matter*, Mould had hinted at an epic statement during an interview with Steve Albini: "Right now we're at a stage where we have to think things through in a big way. We're going to try to do something bigger than anything like rock and roll and the whole puny band touring idea. I don't know what it's going to be, we have to work that out, but it's going to go beyond the whole idea of 'punk rock' or whatever."

Later, while talking with *Ink Disease* for the January 1984 issue, Mould gave a concise but dead-on preview of the by then recorded but unreleased *Zen Arcade*: "The hardcore is more hardcore than we've ever done, the melodic pop stuff is more melodic, the experimental stuff is more experimental. There's a few straight-ahead rockers, a few psychedelic, a few country songs. There's like 25 songs."

Mould also was interviewed by *Suburban Punk* publisher Al Quint around the same time and had a humorous but no doubt honest answer to his favorite album question:

> **Al:** Which of your records do you feel most proud of?
> **Bob:** The one that hasn't come out yet. We have a double album coming out in April.
> **Al:** You did quite a few songs I haven't heard before. Are those going to be on the album?
> **Bob:** Yeah. Most of those are the big ones off the album. There's about 25 on the new one. "Masochism World" is the new one with the weird stops in it.

Following Hüsker Dü's return to Minneapolis after recording *Zen Arcade*, the band members got their collective bearings, worked on Reflex business, dealt with the stir of activity following the release of *Metal Circus*, and played only three dates (one local and two in Wisconsin, at Madison and Oshkosh) during the entire month of November 1983. In mid-December, they popped over to the East Coast for a handful of dates, including their second-ever Boston show. In just eight blurry months, Hüsker Dü had amassed a respectable East Coast following.

When discussing the Hüskers' live act, people often note that the band habitually performed material from their next as-yet-unreleased album (or sometimes the album after the next one). However, their live sets always acknowledged the full breadth of their discography. This time out, though, because *Metal Circus* was a seven-song EP and the forthcoming release would be a double LP, the illusion was given that the band had already eschewed the new release for a set-anchoring cluster of songs that would appear on the follow-up.

Back in April 1983 on their first trip to Boston, the band had told Lou Giordano that when they next came to town, he was invited to join them on tour and mix a few dates, after which they would fly him home. Giordano remembers:

> Let's face it, to be in a rock band, you have to have some kind of ego. And admittedly, I didn't know what to expect, so I went in with an open mind. A few years of studio work gave me the skills to communicate well with musicians in search of a sound, and I found the Hüskers to be about the most anti-rock stars you could possibly imagine. I ended up mixing a few East Coast dates in December '83 and on the main tour, which began in March '84. It didn't really matter that I was a rookie soundman, it was more important that I understood the music. From the earliest days of four guys in the van, I made it up as we went along, advancing PAs, making up a sound rider, threatening house sound guys to beef up their wimpy PAs. Hüsker Dü were great folks to work for, always made me feel like a fourth band member. They knew we would get substandard PAs at some gigs and never complained about it. As long as I could get the vocals above the roar, everyone was happy.

Earlier in the year, the band had blown away the New York audience at Gildersleeves when they unleashed their cover of "Eight Miles High." One of the few outtakes from the *Zen Arcade* sessions, it was released as a stopgap single in April 1984 before *Zen Arcade*'s proposed release date in the summer. By that point, the song had gained a little notoriety as an encore favorite, a spot it would hold for some time in the band's constantly changing set.

"For me it was a major moment when they started to play it live," McElheny remembers. "It was and is my favorite Hüsker Dü performance. There was definitely a sense that it was a change in the set list, being the first cover. It was usually, if not always, played as an encore, and the reaction was insane, not least because Bob would go insane himself with the Ibanez Flying V and the vocals. It definitely replaced 'Diane' as 'the song' . . . . In fact, my memory is that they mostly stopped playing 'Diane' around that time."

"Eight Miles High" satisfied Mould's love of '60s pop, just like the cover of "Sunshine Superman" on *Everything Falls Apart*. "Mould always loved the Byrds, and the other contender was going to be a Hollies song, which never came to be—maybe 'Carrie Anne' or one of those," remembers Katzman. "Mould's a big Hollies fan, too. The Hollies' *Greatest Hits* was on the turntable a lot when we were getting together in the early days. It would have fit on [*Zen Arcade*]—it wouldn't have been out of place—but I don't think Mould wanted a cover on the album."

While the band's cover of "Sunshine Superman" was a fairly straightforward affair, the ferocity with which the band, and especially Mould, attacked "Eight Miles High" set the song apart. The sonic assault also served another purpose. Back in Los Angeles, primarily, an altogether different subset of post-punk was flourishing with a group of bands eventually termed "the Paisley Underground." The exceptional and superior Dream Syndicate led the way for the slightly lesser sounds of the Three O'Clock (formerly known as the amazing psych garage punk band the Salvation Army) and the Bangles (also formerly known in much better form as the Bangs). Sharing those bands' '60s influences but leaning more toward punk rock were the Leaving Trains (then a new SST acquisition) and Redd Kross. Like-minded but adopting a much more blues-influenced take on post-punk were the Gun Club and Green on Red. "Eight Miles High" was Hüsker Dü's answer to the way these bands approached their '60s influences. "Those bands . . . didn't add anything to the sound," says Hart. "If they had covered 'Eight Miles High,' it wouldn't have sounded that much different from the original. We created an entirely new song out of it."

Identifiable as the Byrds classic by Mould's super-trebly, distorted appropriation of the song's main riff, as well as his vocals over the first half of the song, the cover quickly explodes into a cathartic and moving piece of rock 'n' roll, sending more and more chills up the spine as its four minutes play out.

B-sided with a live version of "Masochism World" (the studio version would appear on *Zen Arcade*), the single was thrown together and released in March 1984 so that the band would have something to tour on before the summer release of *Zen Arcade*. "It was a rush job. They got that thing together in next to no time," Katzman remembers, adding, "It was a weak B-side . . . they were getting those live tracks mailed in by people on the road."

Giordano describes "Eight Miles High" as "always a barn-burner. Their arrangement was one of the best things they did. It was hard to come down after this one, so it ended up being an encore, if I remember correctly."

Giordano also traveled as Hüsker Dü's soundman on the longer *Metal Circus* tour that began in March 1984 and led up to and followed the release of "Eight Miles High." It was his first extended tour with the band; together, he and McElheny would cover every subsequent Hüsker Dü live performance until the band's demise. An important aspect of the Hüskers' live set—one that is usually overshadowed by the band's velocity and energy—was volume. Hüsker Dü was one of the first bands of the American '80s underground to harness volume in a way that made the air in a club move. Giordano recalls: "Volume was always maxed out, drums and bass in the low end, guitars and vocals in the middle, and everything washing out the top end. It was difficult to get the vocals above the roar, and after experimenting with different mics, we ended up using Sennheiser MD431s. These kept the leakage to a minimum and let me mix the vocals loud, which everyone loved. The harmony singing really set Hüsker Dü apart from the rest, as well as the wall of sound. It really was as simple as 'make everything loud.' There weren't any decisions to be made other than getting a powerful enough PA, and sometimes harassing promoters to beef up their existing house systems to meet our spec."

While on tour, at least through the release of *Zen Arcade* (the band played more than fifty out-of-town gigs and no shortage of local ones between the recording of *Zen Arcade* in October 1983 and its release in June 1984), Mould, Hart, and Norton seemed to share a common ability to click with new people whom they deemed worthy of their inner tier. Mike LaVella played in a number of Pittsburgh hardcore bands, most notably Half Life, and befriended the band around this time in mid-1983. Whenever the Hüskers played Pittsburgh's Electric Banana, they always stayed with LaVella, who would often pull what Hart termed "the roadie scam," riding with the band to the next city or two and getting into shows free by helping with the load-in. LaVella remembers one particular incident from the period:

I lived at this punk house called "the Hell House." There was a shower in the basement and a bathtub on the third floor. So Bob decides to take a bath one night after a show . . . He grabs one of those back scrubbers, and starts telling me about giving guitar lessons to one of the Minnesota North Stars [hockey] players. He was thrilled about this. Then he says, "You know, when you're on tour, you have to stop and try to get some of the grime off—just scrub off the grime—but you never really get clean."

The period spanning mid-1983 through the end of 1984 was important for relations within the band as well. As they gathered momentum, drawing people to shows and selling records (all the results of their incredibly diligent DIY work ethic), the members' respective moods were elevated, if not constantly, at least on occasion. The band was much more confident, not just on stage, but walking across the bar and showing up at afterparties. In a January 1984 *Ink Disease* interview, for example, the following exchange took place with Mould and Hart:

ID: How many songs do you think you've written?

B: A couple hundred.

ID: Do your songs still run together like on your live album?

B: Yeah.

ID: Did you tour on the way out?

B: Yeah, but this was essentially a mission—to get this album done while we were at a peak. We were starting to write songs so fast over the last few months that we knew we were going to have to record immediately, and it was gonna have to be more than a single album. Moneywise we're doing okay. We can get from place to place and eat with the money we got playing shows.

ID: Next to MDC and Sammy Hagar you tour more than anyone I know. Why is that?

G: Bringing the music to the people, meeting people, folks like you.

ID: Do you think you've been successful?

B: We've enlightened a few people. That's not to sound religious; I think we've got something to say that a lot of people can understand. We're not trying to talk about communism or anarchy or any of that stuff. We're just trying to talk about shit that everybody knows, but if they hear somebody else say [it] they feel a little better inside. They go, "Yeah, I was thinking that, but I didn't know quite how to say it." Trying to get people to realize things that they know. We're not so grand and intelligent; we just know what we know. I think I know what a lot of other people are thinking about. If you can help them get it out of their systems, it might be good.

Zen Arcade is the first Hüsker Dü release to feature a wide variety of songcraft. While each Hüsker Dü album boasts at least one innovation—a "first" that would be honed as the band tore along at its precocious pace—*Zen Arcade* is packed with more of these creative instances than any album in the trio's career, before or after. Some succeed; some do not.

The world's introduction to *Zen Arcade*, via Hart's drums and five seconds of Norton's bass, would become one of the more recognizable sound bites in the entire Hüsker Dü catalog. "Something I Learned Today" is signature Hüsker Dü post-hardcore noise-pop, but it's also top-shelf, straight-up punk rock that bears more than a passing likeness to hardcore. Mould's barnburner, "Broken Home, Broken Heart," follows, applying some of the preceding song's stylistic innovations but coming off as less catchy.

The song does serve as a quasi-introduction to the album's loose narrative, though it was one of the future *Zen* songs debuted during the summer of 1983, several months before the probable invention of the narrative. As the double album is examined, it becomes obvious that its oft-claimed conceptual nature could easily have been concocted as the track order was sequenced. The familiar plot line revisits more than it follows a disenchanted teen escaping a tumultuous home life, experiencing the harsh realities of the world, then awakening to find that the whole affair was nothing but a dream. It seems entirely conceivable that Hart, Norton, and Mould were too busy creating music to notice that they'd composed a storyline that had a lot in common with an after-school special.

"My opinion is that it wasn't envisioned as a concept in the 'pre' stage, but the 'post' stage," says Katzman. "The other version is more romantic, but that's what I think. Then there is the [fact] of it being a double album, but that's just a long album. I doubt the Beatles even envisioned the White Album to be a double album; it just turned out that way. I think this is a similar metamorphosis for Hüsker Dü."

Especially notable among *Zen Arcade*'s twenty-three tracks is Hart's "Never Talking to You Again," which appears three songs into the A-side and is the band's first recorded use of an acoustic track. The style would never dominate Hüsker Dü's subsequent albums, but it's not the song's acoustic nature that qualifies it as prescient; it's the headlong dive into flagrantly melodic waters. The song's lyrics supposedly detail a sentiment felt by the protagonist, one aimed squarely at his parents if one buys into the storyline. Bob's moderately fast and forceful strumming takes the place of percussion, while Hart's traditional construction and memorable vocal hook have made it one of the more popular songs on the album and even in the band's entire predominately electric songbook. The song also did wonders to establish Hart as a melodic force. (For all practical purposes, "Diane" was Hart's last time on record in the minds of most fans, who probably didn't give the live version of "Masochism World" a second listen.

Grant's soaring melodies are bolstered by another Hüsker Dü first: a guest musician. Backing vocals are courtesy of former Black Flag guitarist/vocalist Dez Cadena, then a fixture and occasional employee of SST. Departing the ranks of Black Flag earlier in the year, Cadena had tutored his vocal replacement, Henry Rollins, in 1981 before switching to guitar and adding an essential element to the Flag's most powerful lineup. Cadena had recently formed the trio DC3 with drummer Jeff Dahl and keyboardist/bassist Paul Roessler (brother of Kira, future Black Flag bassist).

As the final acoustic downstroke of "Never Talking . . ." is muted after reverberating for a split second, Mould's Ibanez opens "Chartered Trips" with the type of melodic chord fans would come to know and love. The song is the noise-pop of *Metal Circus*' "First of the Last Calls" perfected: quintessential Mould-driven Hüsker Dü that helped to cement the band's reputation. As a "type" of Hüsker Dü track, it would be heard later on *Zen Arcade*, on almost every *New Day Rising* track that Mould composed, and in future standouts like *Flip Your Wig*'s "Private Plane" and "Divide and Conquer." Lyrically, the song's wanderlust supposedly answers the separation anxiety of "Never Talking to You Again," though it does nothing to quell the suspicion that most of *Zen Arcade*'s songs originated in a mental space removed from the album's narrative.

The midsection of side one ("Never Talking to You Again," "Chartered Trips," and "Dreams Reoccurring" [*sic*]) shows the band making as great a gain in three songs as they did when they followed *Everything Falls Apart* with *Metal Circus*—and none of the songs are within the realm of hardcore. At two minutes and seven seconds, "Indecision Time," the song that follows "Dreams Reoccurring," is hardcore claustrophobia worthy of *Everything Falls Apart*. Mould incorporates pick slides and other string-torturing tricks into his flailing chaos, the lyrics screamed over this cacophony.

Side two of *Zen Arcade* is commonly considered the final resting place for whatever hardcore tendencies remained in the minds of Mould and, to a lesser extent, Hart. Calling this side "hardcore" has always been an easy out for critics and fans who save their superlatives for sides one and three. However, Mould's four tracks are quite prescient, in retrospect.

Mould's four-song block of musical catharsis that kicks off side two is arresting, to say the least. If layers of terrifying release, aural violence, impenetrable density, and guitar pyrotechnics were shaved from "Beyond the Threshold," "Pride," "I'll Never Forget You," and "The Biggest Lie," these four tracks would still annihilate any of the hardcore that dominated *Everything Falls Apart*, peppered *Metal Circus*, or defined *Land Speed Record*. In 1984, there was simply nothing on hardcore's radar with a comparable wallop. More so than on the aforementioned releases, this is where the influence of Discharge on Mould truly shines through—if Discharge were more enamored with psychedelic noise than with metal, that is.

Lyrically, these songs yet again raise the question that may never be answered: how premeditated was the narrative concept allegedly driving *Zen Arcade*? Did the band really set out with a narrative in mind, or did they construct it after seeing the body of songs they'd assembled? If one were to swing a bat in a gymnasium filled with early- to mid-'80s hardcore bands, one would never fail to strike the author of several songs concerning teen alienation, frustration, and self-inflicted separation from a constricting family life.

"Pride" offers undiluted angst to a degree the guitarist had never before displayed, and never would again. Mould goes from angrily screaming a wounded, despondent plea in "Pride" to something else entirely in the song's follow-up, "I'll Never Forget You." Lyrically and vocally unremarkable until after the one-minute mark, the latter song is then thrust into a netherworld of anguish by the repetition of the title, in which Mould assumes a genuinely threatening wail. As a pure communication of pain atop a bludgeoning dirge of down-stroked riffing and circulating noise, the song would have far more in common with the future of the American underground than with anything associated with the year 1984. The real inheritor of the song's aggro-noise histrionics was Dinosaur Jr, a band that closed its 1988 album, *Bug*, with the similarly cathartic kiss-off "Don't," in which bassist Lou

Barlow repeatedly wails/roars the question "Why don't you like me?!" over a plodding rhythm track and J Mascis' psychedelia-drenched riffing and noodling. (Appropriately, *Bug* turned out to be Mascis' kiss-offs to both Barlow and SST.)

Mould's "The Biggest Lie" brings side two back around to more familiar territory. The song would never make it to the band's live set, but "Pride" and "I'll Never Forget You" were both debuted in the summer of 1983. Like "Broken Home. . ." and "Indecision Time," however, neither lasted very long as live staples after being recorded in October.

The second half of side two ("What's Going On," "Masochism World," and "Standing by the Sea") best debunks the sometimes stated notion that this section of *Zen Arcade* was the band's final stab at hardcore. Hart's "What's Going On" is a raging rocker, yes, but it's not hardcore. The drummer's more aggressive numbers tend to be longer, and this one is no exception at almost four and a half minutes. Following Mould's four-song block of terror, "What's Going On" still fits into side two's relentless agenda. Cadena returns to provide vocals, a duty that Norton would fulfill in a live situation. "On 'What's Going On' I let [Greg] take over singing duties live, so he'd have something to sing off of *Zen Arcade*, and also because I thought that he and Dez had similar vocals," explains Hart.

Closing out side two, "Standing by the Sea" is a thick monster of ascending riffs and Hart's from-the-edge-of-the-earth vocals, which strike a nice balance between melodic yelling and traditional singing. Used to propel the later claims that the album has a narrative, "Standing by the Sea" tells of the sensory overload suffered by the protagonist. As one of four outtakes from the *Metal Circus* sessions and a live staple from the same time period, it's most likely the oldest track on *Zen*, further supporting the theory that Hart most likely did not originally envision a double album based on a runaway's coming-of-age story.

On side three, "Somewhere," "Newest Industry," and "Whatever" feature Mould in peak form, continuing the sublime, hair-raising power of "Chartered Trips." Again, along with that track, these songs are the first true examples of Mould songcraft that helped make Hüsker Dü such an influential band.

The drug death described in the lyrics of "Pink Turns to Blue" supposedly happens to a girlfriend the protagonist meets during his travels, the title referring to the hue of one's lips when they suffer such demise. Situated amid Mould's "Somewhere"–"Newest Industry"–"Whatever" trifecta, the song shows Hart matching Mould's level of songcraft and laying the groundwork for his own future influence.

Interestingly, beginning with *Zen Arcade*, Mould made the declaration that every Hüsker album would have individual songwriting credits. Allegedly, the decision was based on Hart's layout of a Man Size Action album, which excluded individual songwriting credits. It's worth considering, however, that Mould's decision followed the recording and release of *Metal Circus*, nearly half of which was written by Hart, and a strong half at that. "It never occurred to me or the guys in Man Sized Action to include individual songwriting credits," Hart remembers. "It was never mentioned . . . it was never an issue with that band."

Individual song credits aside, *Zen Arcade* Hüsker Dü operating as a peerless force, rarely looking over their shoulders at the mindset(s) behind *Land Speed Record*, *In a Free Land*, and *Everything Falls Apart*. The band's music was reliably turned a notch to the left, cranked through the roof, and played with an intensity that surpassed most of what was happening in the rapidly stagnating hardcore scene. It seems appropriate that the "hardcore" songs on *Zen Arcade* either never made it into the live set or were scrapped very shortly after the release of the album. Most of them, penned by Mould and featured, were the kinds of expression that Mould would get down on record once and rarely acknowledge again. The progression away from hardcore becomes more obvious when looking at *Metal Circus* as being roughly half hardcore, then realizing that *Zen's* follow-up, *New Day Rising*, was the first Hüsker Dü album to eschew the genre altogether.

In Steve Waksman's fantastic revisionist history of post-1970 rock, *This Ain't the Summer of Love: Conflict and Crossover in Metal and Punk*, the author writes:

> Many performers who assumed a more open or eclectic approach to their music were compelled to announce a break with hardcore as their sound began to diversify. Hüsker Dü generated tension with their move to a more pop-oriented approach to melody in their songwriting and the increased prominence of the band's neopsychedelic trappings, which also involved Bob Mould playing more extended solo breaks. Alongside the Minutemen's *Double Nickels on the Dime*, Hüsker Dü's *Zen Arcade*—both released at the same time by SST—marked the moment at which

the most musically-exploratory elements of hardcore broke away from the form and were reconstituted into the more open-ended style that came to be labeled indie-rock.

Compare this to Michael Azerrad writing in *Our Band Could Be Your Life*: "*Zen Arcade* was Hüsker Dü's most strenuous refutation of hardcore orthodoxy," and it had "stretched the hardcore format to its most extreme limits; it was the final word on the genre, a scorching of musical earth." To hear a "scorching of musical earth" in 1984, however, one would do better to seek out the then current Septic Death, Siege, Corrosion of Conformity, or Deep Wound, rather than the album that has "Never Talking to You Again" and "Pink Turns to Blue" as standouts. Azerrad closes his sentiment with "any hardcore after *Zen Arcade* would be derivative, retrograde . . . formulaic."

But *Zen Arcade* did not destroy the relevance of future hardcore or preclude it from evolving in other directions, nor did it create indie rock. The truth is, hardcore was simply arriving at a point that many genres reach once saturated with mediocrity or unintentional self-parody. In fact, it could be argued that hardcore enjoyed its first developmental heyday from 1980 until 1984, then had a creative heyday beginning in the late '80s and lasting through the entire '90s. The latter time period found one of several national home bases in Minneapolis with the Profane Existence and Havoc labels. Instead of negating hardcore—a nervy assessment, indeed—*Zen Arcade* influenced the next quarter-century of hardcore as well as indie rock.

❙   ❙   ❙

It's tempting to imagine an alternate history in which *Zen Arcade* was issued as a single album stuffed with nothing but its strongest moments, an exercise often undertaken with *Exile on Main St.* and the White Album. To this day, voicing a negative comment about *Zen Arcade* is the rock-critic equivalent of racism in certain circles. This critical behavior should always raise red flags. While *Zen Arcade* remains perhaps the most important album of the band's career, much of that importance lies in the fact that particular strides—the melodic nature of "Pink Turns to Blue," the acoustic arrangement of "Never Talking to You Again," Mould finding his trademark fury-and-hooks formula, the post-hardcore/proto-aggro that starts side two—were made for the first time, rather than in the quality of those particular strides. Is *Zen Arcade* four entire sides of innovation? Not quite. Enter the main gripe (when one does dare to issue such a thing about *Zen Arcade*): too much filler.

The brief "Dreams Reoccurring" (fifth track, side one) is an ethereal, backward-looped, structure-free (excepting rhythm), and harmless experiment credited to all three members of the band. Not only is it the first such work on *Zen Arcade*, "Dreams Reocurring" has no comparable tracks on any previous Hüsker Dü release. A minor offender at a minute and a half, it nonetheless hints at things to come.

Not even Hüsker Dü can resist the temptations of the novelty song. Like "Dreams Reoccurring," "Hare Krsna" is credited as a group effort, too, perhaps in an attempt to conceal the culprit behind this ridiculous shot at both humor and experimentation (rarely successful bedfellows in music). Unlike "Dreams Reocurring," "Hare Krsna" is less interlude and more proper song, placed at the end of side one and clocking in at 3:33. Driven by a Bo Diddley riff, the song resembles something the Butthole Surfers might have rejected as too silly. (Incidentally, the sun-damaged Texans' self-titled debut 12-inch was released the summer before the *Zen* sessions, and drummer King Coffey was a huge Hüsker Dü fan who allegedly sent the trio their first fan letter.)

While side two escapes the scourge of filler, the fate of side three is debatable. Hart's two solo piano interludes, "One Step at a Time" and "Monday Will Never Be the Same," are melodic and unobtrusive at 0:45 and 1:10 respectively. The former bleeds into "Pink Turns to Blue" and can be heard faintly tinkling away underneath that song's first thirty seconds. Sequencing "Newest Industry" and "Whatever" back-to-back would have been an overload of high-quality Mould, therefore the plaintive "Monday . . ." provides a wonderful intermission and excuse to keep Bob's two strongest tracks (barring "Chartered Trips") from coming and going with a one-two punch. Neither of Hart's simple but effectively melancholic pieces takes up significant room, but some critics deemed them self-indulgent detours that should have died on the cutting-room floor. What did get cut was Hart's best solo piano effort. Entitled, appropriately enough, "Grant's Untitled Piano Track," this gorgeous outtake surfaces on bootleg compilations and on the Internet. It most likely was rejected because of its upbeat, ragtime feel. For his part, Hart admits, "As much as [*Zen Arcade*] got hailed as an innovation, I don't know that the little piano segues were the finest of fine art. They functioned as the middle ground between point B and point E."

Also mentioned in the filler stakes, and closing out side three, is Mould's "The Tooth Fairy and the Princess," a disposable 2:43 that meanders like a subtle reprise of "Dreams Reoccurring." The track is all instrumental, save Mould mumbling repeated phrases like "Don't give up."

An argument could be made that "Dreams Reoccurring" has been written and blogged about more often than it has been played all the way through. When the term "filler" enters a discussion about *Zen Arcade*, it's more often than not in reference to this track. Eating up the final fourteen minutes of *Zen Arcade* and preceded by "Turn on the News," this unbridled, improvisational jam is not without its merits, but conspiratorial minds wonder if its length wasn't calculated to nab a full side of content. If edited down to the seven minutes that appropriate the riff from Led Zeppelin's "Communication Breakdown," the track provides an interesting look at a different side of the band. Hart and Norton were nurturing a nascent love for free jazz during the early '80s, while Mould had more than a casual interest in the harsh soundscapes of U.K. noiseniks Throbbing Gristle and Whitehouse. Few fans and critics were aware of these facts in 1984, however, so the avant-garde workout became a focal point of *Zen Arcade*'s "wow factor." In the end, however, it comes as no surprise that side four universally comes in mint condition on used copies of *Zen Arcade*.

Hart's "Turn on the News," while sounding laughably dated today, can take partial credit for bringing *Zen Arcade* to the attention of the mainstream music press. Filler, hardcore, or innovative works, a respectable majority of *Zen Arcade* has aged nicely. Sadly, "Turn on the News" is in the minority. Hart's Frampton-gone-political vocals and Mould's use of not one but two sections of Lynyrd Skynyrd's "Freebird" drown the track in heavy-handed and unintentional silliness. Hart's peace-punk lyrics are hard to stomach, especially in the context of a band that had moved away from such sentiments. Hart's lyrics also distance *Zen Arcade* from its much-touted narrative. As the last *Zen Arcade* track with vocals, "Turn on the News" is an extreme letdown next to the rest of the album.

Just as it's tempting to imagine a single-LP *Zen Arcade* without the filler, it's tempting to conclude that a large amount of the praise for *Zen* originates in the work's size and scope. There's no denying

139

that it took balls for a band this fresh out of hardcore to issue a double album, much less one sporting a concept, as has been alleged. Though pandering is not a practice that any of the three members of Hüsker Dü will ever confess to, neatly containing their last vestiges of hardcore on one side of the double-LP perhaps served a practical purpose (aside from constructing a narrative): it offered an easy exclusion option for Hüsker Dü's newfound college-rock fans.

The term "college rock" was used to describe whatever wasn't punk rock, hardcore, or straight-up weirdness or noise. Hüsker Dü, of course, wasn't dominated by any of those directions when "Eight Miles High" and *Zen Arcade* were released and processed by critics and listeners, thus they came to be considered a major mover in college rock. This reveals another aspect of that fledging genre that can only be seen in hindsight.

College rock included the American post-punk bands that directly predicted what would be called "indie rock" a few years later. While amassing a steadily growing number of college-rock fans, Hüsker Dü made music that precisely informed a particular aural attitude of the future: one that combined volume, speed, and noise with overt melody and hooks. For concrete examples, one need only look to Dinosaur Jr, My Bloody Valentine, the Jesus and Mary Chain, and the second, third, and fourth albums by Hüsker Dü's hometown colleagues, Soul Asylum. Some bands lumped into this genre released their seminal works parallel with or shortly after *Zen Arcade*; others made their mark a few years later.

Already having gravitated to "Diane," "It's Not Funny Anymore," and especially the more recent "Eight Miles High," by 1984, college radio was as ready as it was going to be for *Zen Arcade*. But when the album arrived at stations a week or two before the release date, *Zen Arcade* looked a bit different from what everyone was expecting. Nicking a major-label promo method, Joe Carducci had pressed up a very low number of single-sided LPs that featured what he considered to be the strongest tracks on *Zen Arcade* (a strategy he also used for *Double Nickels on the Dime*).

"I just thought that our promo list was big enough that it might make more sense factoring in mailing costs to cut a one-sided disc with no cover and mail that," Carducci explains. "We found the average Minutemen album had less impact with radio than did the 12-inch EP *Buzz or Howl*, where the non-hip could get a better handle on a smaller number of songs."

Highly sought-after by collectors, the *Zen Arcade* sampler often turns up with one-of-a-kind doodles or drawings, courtesy of the band. The track sequencing belies Carducci's claim that these samplers were engineered to attract the college-radio programmer with more traditional tastes. Scare the living crap out of them seems a little more likely with a track list that begins with "I'll Never Forget You" and "The Biggest Lie," the former hands-down the most intense song on *Zen Arcade*. This cobweb-clearing duo is followed by the friendlier "Newest Industry," "Whatever," and "Somewhere." Then Hart's "Pink Turns to Blue" arrives to confound and amaze with a hook bigger and better than any of Grant's previous journeys into the pop arena. "Turn on the News" is followed by the three-month-old "Eight Miles High," which closes the sampler.

It's hard to get too much "Eight Miles High," but why put a previously released single that's not even on the album on a sampler when recipients already may be familiar with the track? In fact, this track listing says volumes about Carducci, Greg Ginn, and the SST mindset: their collective intuition was not its strongest when dealing with the positive impact a hook has on a listener's brain. Ginn wrote Black Flag's music specifically to sound anti-melodic as the band morphed into an avant-garde metal enigma. Henry Rollins' vocals often move through notes in a manner exactly the opposite of pop melodies. More than once, Ginn was quoted as saying that he felt like Black Flag had achieved something if show attendees were "bummed out" when they left. But the biggest piece of evidence supporting SST's anti-hook agenda is *Rock and the Pop Narcotic*, the massive tome authored by Carducci following his departure from the label. In it, Carducci spends little time trumpeting the importance of melody.

Unsurprisingly, some of the most engaging writing on Hüsker Dü appeared in response to *Zen Arcade*. In September 1984, an essay ran in the British weekly *New Musical Express* containing this passage: "That these quickfire missives scattershot across four sides don't become unrelentingly bleak, then, is down to Hüsker Dü's distillation of grey, wasted lives into concentrated instants of minimal duration but greater quality. They hone in on emotional flashpoints—be it personal disappointments or a newsflash—and edit them into songs of cartoon bubble efficiency and invigorating directness."

Legendary music writer Robert Palmer took a liking to *Zen Arcade* and wrote this review for the *New York Times* (incidentally crediting Mould for three of Hart's songs):

Hüsker Dü is often compared to the Minutemen; both bands are trios of guitar, bass and drums, both play at death-defying tempos, and both record for the SST label. Now both bands have made new double albums. The Hüsker Dü double *Zen Arcade*, is the most impressive album of the batch under discussion, and arguably the best to have emerged from the hardcore scene.

The band's guitarist, Bob Mould, is turning into an exceptionally gifted songwriter; the three most immediately impressive songs on *Zen Arcade* ("Turn on the News," "Standing by the Sea," and "Pink Turns to Blue") would be superb material on any band's album. There are several lyrical, dreamlike instrumental tunes, and the album's concluding track is a 14-minute jam that piles dissonance on top of dissonance. . . . It is not as successful as the improvisation on the recent Hüsker Dü single, a revival of the Byrds' "Eight Miles High," but it certainly shows that Hüsker Dü has found a number of avenues to explore, a number of ways out of the trap of more-faster-louder that many more conventional hardcore bands fall into.

Robert Christgau raved about *Zen Arcade* generally, and "Turn on the News" specifically, in the *Village Voice*'s 1984 "Pazz & Jop" poll, while noting that New York City musician and journalist Tim Sommer had dubbed *Zen* and *Double Nickels* "coffee-table hardcore."

Many of the band's Twin Cities contemporaries still agree with the critical accolades. "That was the beginning of a great, positive, creative moment for the band, and it was also a loss of the more collaborative efforts between the three," Katzman says. "Many people would see *Zen Arcade* as the complete opposite of that. They were firing together, but it's also true that something got left behind, because then, they made a record that no one could ignore, you could ignore the other records if you wanted, but that record you couldn't ignore."

"It was a massive breakthrough," says Tom Hazelmyer. "They had been rushing headlong through releases at that point—all amazing—but *Zen Arcade* jumped more than a few rungs in the ladder. There was a depth that no band with hardcore roots had achieved, especially while a majority of that initial wave of hardcore bands was creatively imploding. 'Gobsmacked' is about the best word for when I first dropped the needle on it."

As for one of the album's creators? "With the exception of Greg— and that's just because I haven't read anything he's said about *Zen*

Arcade—I think Bob and I are both a little bit tired of the dispropor-
tionate attention that album has gotten," says Hart. "There's nothing
that will spark my interest more than a person coming up and saying
'*Metal Circus*, that's the album that changed my mind about music,'
or 'N*ew Day Rising*, man!' But usually if they say *Zen Arcade*, they're
wearing it on their sleeve." ‡

THE PRODUCERS

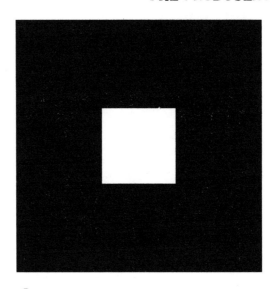

9

True to *Zen Arcade*'s liner notes, Joe Carducci indeed did want another Hüsker Dü album. People *bought* Hüsker Dü records. People also bought Black Flag records, and they would have not one but an astonishing *four* new Flag titles to choose from by the time 1984 came to a close. Not surprisingly, Black Flag and Hüsker Dü accounted for much of SST's revenue in summer 1984, though they would soon be joined by the Minutemen and the Meat Puppets. On the same day in July, SST released *Zen Arcade*, the Minutemen's *Double Nickels on the Dime*, and the Meat Puppets' third full-length, *Up on the Sun*, none of which would sit around taking up space in record stores (especially *Zen Arcade*).

Since the conception of *Zen Arcade* some nine months before in fall 1983, the trio had held at least the passing interest of a major label or two. But the idea of the Hüskers on a major held no allure for the band, even as their profile, popularity, and workload increased dramatically after *Zen*'s release. Ironically, it was this heightened profile and popularity that led SST to make the one mistake of which a major would never be found guilty.

"On the tour to record *Zen Arcade*, there were the first rumblings of major label interest," Greg Norton remembers. "This was when Grant got a letter or a fax, I think it was from someone at MCA, and it just said 'I love your band' over and over and over. But right after *Zen* was released, we started getting actively solicited. Guys would show up at gigs, or they would call, but it didn't make sense because SST had been doing a good job. Now, this was also the time that we were two weeks into the first tour after *Zen Arcade*'s release, and when we'd show up in town, people would tell us that they couldn't get the record because it was already out of print."

In an interview with a New Jersey–based fanzine called *No Place to Hide*, Mould was uncharacteristically candid about what was happening with the band in the fall of 1984:

> **How long are you guys out here for?**
>> Three weeks. Anything longer than that we just get burned out real quick. We get sick and we don't feel like playing. And if you don't feel like playing you might as well not play. You're just ripping people off. We had a bad night last night. We played Maxwell's in Hoboken and it's a two o'clock club. We got out of there at a quarter to seven in the morning. We stayed up all night with the owner and got plowed. We did shots for about four hours. I quit drinking last night. One of those nights. No hair of the dog. I had the whole dog last night; there was nothing left, no hair, no nothing. Hair of the dragon maybe.
>
> **How do you guys feel about your new-found [*sic*] success?**
>> *Zen Arcade* sold out of its first pressing. There's a lot of heavy shit going down.
>
> **I listened to *Land Speed* the other day. It was just filed away in the dust of my records. I didn't like it when I first got it but it's really pretty good. I like bad recordings.**
>> They have a certain charm. It was more of a document than a project. But anyway it sounds like our record's out of print. They only did 6,000. Can you believe that? They do twenty or thirty thousand of Black Flag. We're the biggest seller on the label right now. It seems to me like we're the most in demand. They suggest that we do tours, but what good is it to do a tour if you come to a city and your records aren't available in the stores? They're supposed to be repressing it right now, but those will go out the door in a week and a half and everybody will be complaining. I think we can sell 15, 20, 30 thousand copies.

Norton adds that, despite SST's gaffe, the band members were their own managers, press agents, and tour-bookers—all while having to deal with just one guy, Carducci—so they "didn't see a major label as being a large step forward in success because there wasn't anything a major label could offer us at that point that we or SST couldn't provide."

The same month *Zen Arcade* was released, the band already had a new album's worth of material. Rather than waiting for the trio to schedule a tour around recording sessions as it had done in the past (not that the process would have taken long for Hüsker Dü), SST flew Spot to Minneapolis in July 1984. Flying a producer to a band's hometown was not, nor has it become, common practice for independent labels, but Hüsker Dü was not Saccharine Trust.

In *Our Band Could Be Your Life*, Michael Azerrad writes that SST flew Spot to Minneapolis to supervise the recording process so that it would not become too expensive for the label to handle. It's highly unlikely that SST was concerned that the trio would pull a Clash and follow their *London Calling* with a *Sandinista!*, or submit anything longer than a proper album, for that matter. Even though they've never received the recognition they've deserved alongside Minor Threat and Black Flag as consummate DIY trailblazers, it's difficult to imagine Hüsker Dü engaging in money-wasting behavior when it came time to record an album.

"Spot had told me after a bunch of work in '83 that Hüsker was who he enjoyed working with the most," says Carducci. "So I passed that along to Bob with an offer to fly Spot to Minneapolis for *New Day Rising* if they wanted, and he said sure."

"We could sleep in our own beds . . . we can add an instrument that's in our living room whereas before it was something sitting around the studio or something we'd have to rent . . . and we never rented anything," says Hart. "Because of this you have an expansion of sounds that took place on that album."

The sessions that resulted in what would soon carry the title *New Day Rising* took place at Nicollet Studios in the building shared by Twin/Tone and Hüsker Dü/Reflex Records. In fact, *New Day Rising* was recorded in Minnesota's longest-running commercial recording studio.

America's initial indie-label boom actually occurred in the 1950s, albeit this was one of different motives and ethics than those that accompanied the indie-label boom that nurtured the hardcore movement three decades later. Even so, affordable and small studios were in big demand, and no structure catered to this need better than an unused neighborhood movie theater, which were in abundance due to the nation's newfound romance with television. Garrick Theatre was located at 2541 Nicollet Avenue until 1955, when it was converted into a studio by the engineer Bruce Swedien, who later worked with B. B. King, Nat King Cole, Michael Jackson, and Quincy Jones, among others. After Vernon C. Bank purchased the studio in 1957 (renaming it Kay Bank Studios for his wife, Kay), the Heilicher brothers (Daniel and Amos, formerly Bank's partners in the deal) took it into the '60s in a big way with smash hits like

"Surfin' Bird" by the Trashmen and "Six Days on the Road" by Dave Dudley. Forming Soma Records (Amos spelled backwards), the brothers were the driving force behind the creation of Minneapolis' fervent '60s garage rock scene and the "Kay Bank sound" (three tracks and lots of echo). For $495, they offered local bands three hours in the studio, a thousand 45s, and fifty promo packages delivered to radio stations across the Midwest. The studio changed names and hands several times throughout the '70s until Twin/Tone moved into the building in 1983, rechristening the included three-room recording facility "Nicollet Studios." Soon after, as Reflex Records and Hüsker activity steadily increased, operations were moved into an available office. Once rolling in the latter part of the 1980s, Tom Hazelmyer's Amphetamine Reptile Records took offices at 2541 Nicollet, the unassuming and very cube-like brick building with perhaps the richest musical history of any structure in Minnesota.

Hart sums up the *New Day* studio atmosphere as a power struggle, plain and not so simple: "Say you walk up to two guys fixing a car and they ask you for help, and you say, 'Okay, I need a left-handed, metric spindle-nut driver.' By virtue of that, they're going to think you're quite a bit more of an expert than you actually are. I seem to remember a lot of this. How is a band supposed to respond to that, other than as some sort of flaunting of importance or authority?"

Terry Katzman remembers his brief time in the studio during the *New Day* sessions: "It was [the song] 'Terms of Psychic Warfare' and they were mixing. . . . I was only there for about an hour. I remember coming out in the lounge area of Nicollet and Bob was pacing around like a caged animal. I could see that things weren't working out with Spot. There was some sort of doubt registered there. Those sessions were very cloaked, very secretive. I'm surprised Grant invited me over that night."

"Spot's a good guy, and you have to understand that . . . well, our first time recording with him, for *Everything Falls Apart*, I remember Bob watching Spot's every move and asking a lot of questions like 'Okay, so what are you going to do next?' and 'What did you just do?'" says Norton.

The *New Day Rising* sessions were a clear case of too many cooks in the kitchen, resulting in a record that suffered on the production end. In audiophile parlance, *New Day Rising* is one of the unintentionally "hottest" recordings since the dawn of punk rock. Every format—cassette, vinyl, and especially the poorly made CDs of the late

'80s—pegs VU meters no matter what type of stereo equipment is used to play it. From a song's start until its finish, the needle stays affixed to the right side of the meter, with very little shivering or variance.

"It's dangerous to go into a new studio because no one knows the monitors, the biases, et cetera. You can't be sure the record will sound like it does in that studio," says Carducci. "The musicians knew a lot about what they were doing, but I often thought that they could never really know what they sounded like from the audience, and had a hard time riding their own self-consciousness to hear their own recordings clearly."

For his part, in *Our Band Could Be Your Life*, Spot is quoted as saying, "They wanted to produce it themselves and then I was there. I had to do what the record company wanted. And it was one of those situations where I knew my territory and I did my job, whether it was popular or not."

"So Spot was disappointed both personally and professionally as well, as they were making technical mistakes with noise gates and other things they were using to try to advance," continues Carducci. "Because they were also less a playing band at this point and more a writing/producing band, they were getting caught between rock and pop, and the studio was going to reveal this. Spot went through a lot more with Black Flag, of course, so I wouldn't stress that it was a new experience for him, just that Hüsker was no longer an enjoyable relief from Black Flag."

"With some exceptions I was able to actually have a second take on the vocals. The horrible 'The Girl Who Lives on Heaven Hill' . . . the sound of my vocals is fucking terrible," Hart says, "I remember the vocal room at the studio was full of, uh, not really a storage room, but there was a lot of lumber, it was a little compromised, but it was the type of compromise we were used to working around. At Total Access, the big recording room would have a shitload of stuff in there that wasn't supposed to affect the sound."

"It's clear that they were coming up with some really great songs and then having to produce them themselves. I think that they thought they were ready, but they might not have been," says Katzman. "It did have something to do with the first inkling that there was going to be some other labels. They were losing their patience with [Spot], he was out of his element . . . this wasn't Total Access. He had argued that the record suffers from a poor mix, which is true, but there was more going on."

"I'm not happy with how that record sounds, no, not at all," says Hart. "Now, it's very possible that we wanted to get the fuck out of the studio by the time we were mixing. I remember a distinct 'When is this guy going to get out of here?' attitude towards Spot."

Soundman Josiah McElheny was not around for the recording sessions but remembers that the studio situation merited discussion when he traveled with the band for the *New Day Rising* tour more than half a year later.

"I was not there but heard a good deal about it from the band while on that tour, especially from Bob," he says. "My memory is that he was really frustrated in general with Spot, in part because he had such specific ideas about how things should be mixed. But at the time I remember being confused because *Zen Arcade* seemed to me to echo so well the band's live sound, especially Bob's guitar setup with the Fender on top of the Marshall. I think that it was less an issue of philosophic disagreement between Spot and the band and more of a transition period where the band wanted more control in general as well as a change in the kind of songs that both Grant and Bob wanted to write. This became really clear later—that they wanted to have a much clearer kind of sound for the songs, as opposed to the 'wall of sound.'"

If Bob and Grant shared some solidarity against what was perceived as a common issue (Spot), it certainly wasn't apparent to Hart. During the *New Day Rising* sessions and the simultaneous release hoopla surrounding *Zen Arcade*, the existing cracks in their relationship became chasms. While only the closest inner-circle colleagues like Katzman could occasionally pick up on this, it's a safe assumption that Bob and Grant had reached the point of no return during (or even in the months leading up to) the *New Day* sessions. As Katzman puts it, this was "the beginning of the real creative, artistic struggle between the two of them."

Hart claims that during the *New Day* sessions he was treated with an unprecedented degree of disdain by Bob and whomever Bob could rally in his corner, even Spot. Allegedly, Mould tilted the competitive edge in his favor by taking extra time to get his parts just right, leaving Hart in a position that differed very little from a time-sensitive session thousands of miles away at Total Access.

"Had there not been a piano to rehearse, there's no way, for example, on 'Books about UFOs,' Bob would have tolerated me rehearsing the part on studio time," Hart says. "I would have had to have done it when he was doing something else, or on my own time. On 'The Girl Who Lives on Heaven Hill' we have the notorious slide guitar. Bob and Spot erased the take after the rough mix had been made, which I cannot locate. It was one of the first and few times I can remember a 'We need to have a band meeting' kind of vibe. Bob said, 'You take your pick: you want the piano part on 'Books About UFOs' or do you want the slide guitar on 'The Girl Who Lives on Heaven Hill?' That really was the point where it became reinforced with me that there are boundaries here that exist for no other reason than people's egos. Bob made sure, before the meeting, that Greg knew what side of the argument to be on. It was a shocking moment for me."

Songs on *New Day Rising* without writing credits are Mould compositions. Hart does not have a standout track like "Pink Turns to Blue" or "Diane" on *New Day Rising*. "Heaven Hill" and "Books about UFOs" are inoffensive pop songs with rollicking '60s *Nuggets*-style melodies and sound nothing like Mould's strongest efforts on the LP, "Celebrated Summer," "I Apologize," and "59 Times the Pain," wherein Mould nailed the formula that would make his Hüsker Dü creations famous. The album closer, "Plans I Make," comprises four minutes of Mould-style, antagonistic noise-core, just like the tracks that end *Zen* and *Metal Circus*.

There was but one outtake from the *New Day* sessions, Mould's fantastic "Erase Today." At 1:30, it may have been "too hardcore" for a writer who often seemed to overthink stylistic barriers. When SST released the second *Blasting Concept* compilation LP in 1986, the track made the cut.

Hart illustrates a few important factors that made this a period of major productivity for the band: "With Hüsker, as with a band like the Byrds, you have the writer advantage. A band with one writer could put out a record every two years; a band with two writers . . . it doesn't jump additively, it jumps exponentially, where two writers are actually doing three writers' work. It's really ego-driven. . . . It's like 'This guy is going to bury me with songs if I don't crank some of these ideas into finished product,' and I think the significance of that period of time, that's where its origins may lie. Here's two very competitive guys, and with *Metal Circus* and *Zen Arcade* we could kind of live in both worlds, the hardcore and the non-hardcore world, and still pass the music off."

In the six months between the releases of *Zen* and *New Day*, Hüsker Dü spent much of their time playing out. Bulking up the touring schedule even more than before, they spent July and August at home (with several local gigs) because of the recording and mixing, but more than half of October was devoted to touring, with ten or more days in September and December used for the same purpose. November passed without a local gig or a tour.

Locally, the band had graduated to playing the main room at First Avenue. Only rarely did the band play the tiny 7th Street Entry next door anymore. Though the band had played a handful of shows in the larger space, the release of *Zen Arcade* not only exploded its fan base nationally, but in the Twin Cities as well. "The move was suggested by the club management. Instead of overselling a small room, let's undersell a big room, and we didn't undersell it for long. Right here is where we're seeing the latest influx into the tent in terms of fans," says Hart.

The change locally was a snapshot of the change nationally. *Zen Arcade*, with its glowing review in *Rolling Stone* and the general elevation of the band out of the 'zine world, attracted the college-aged curious out of the woodwork. Who is this band with the weird, usually mispronounced moniker that keeps popping up everywhere? Mould reflected on the band's growing audience and its prospects, again in *No Place to Hide*:

Do you think you'll ever break into Top Forties?
   I don't know. Not on SST we won't.
Why do you think you have gotten so popular?
   We've got a higher profile. When you start getting that much straight press in *Creem*, *Musician Magazine*, *Rolling Stone*, that's all different markets. . . .
Why all of a sudden were they interested in you?
   Because we're probably the only thing that's worth talking about this year. I don't know. I'm not trying to be sarcastic but we're probably the only thing that's going this year. We're not putting on airs about it. We don't dress up . . .
But lots of bands don't dress up. That's not what makes you appeal to people.
   I don't know what it is. I just like to think that we're better than all the other bands.

Hüsker Dü showed a new audience that not every band stood in one place during performances. Along with Black Flag, Hüsker Dü was one of the more visually entertaining live bands being absorbed by non-hardcore fans in 1984. Footage from the era presents a band of peerless intensity. As always, there were no breaks in between the songs, and the encores became the stuff of legend. On December 31, 1984, the band played the first of their now legendary New Year's Eve gigs at Maxwell's in Hoboken, New Jersey. The highlight of these evenings became the band's encore treatment of "Eight Miles High." As one of the band's two traveling soundmen, Josiah McElheny remembers it well: "This was a time when most of the small shows would end up pretty much sold out. There was always a lot of talk about Hüsker Dü vs. Minutemen, but I think that people watching the band were so blown away because they could sense that the band was not just a touring punk band from the Midwest playing for kids but a major new sound. The crowds definitely started to seem less like the kids who would come to any punk all-ages shows, but 'fans.' This is the period as well when there started to be 'stalking' behavior and the transition to 'rock star' status, i.e., people writing poetry books to give to the band, people forming their self-declared identity around the band. At the same time this is the time when other really good bands started to really take notice, and there would always be a lot of musicians in the audience."

With barely six months to digest *Zen Arcade*, fans were blindsided by *New Day Rising*, a condensed, precise, and proper full-length exclusively dedicated to showcasing a direction that accounted for only part of *Zen Arcade*. There was no hopping around from nihilistic noise-core to hardcore, from melodic hardcore to an acoustic track and then to the noise-pop that the band, for all intents and purposes, invented with tracks like "Chartered Trips," "Pink Turns to Blue," and, earlier, "First of the Last Calls" and "It's Not Funny Anymore." *New Day Rising* was the near-perfection of this noise-pop, which, at that time, was unique to Hüsker Dü. Writing in the *Village Voice*, Robert Christgau raved about the album:

> With its dawn-over-the-lake cover, guitar chimes, and discernible melodies—on as many as ten of the fifteen songs!—this is the Hüskers' pastoral. I suppose a few hardcore urbanists will think it's wimpy or something, but by any vaguely normal standard it's clearly their finest record even if they have turned off the news in pursuit of a maturity I trust they'll outgrow. Not that they haven't matured. Bob Mould's ambivalence gets him two places instead of none, and I love Grant Hart's love objects—one

with a big messy room and "a worn out smile that she'll wear some more," another who's heavily into UFOs. Play loud—this is one band that deserves it. Grade: A

Noting that the band was riding a wave of popularity gained after *Zen* and following the double LP with another *Village Voice* "Pazz & Jop" poll-topping effort, Hart adds that *New Day Rising* was "not sides five and six of *Zen* but definitely a part of the same creative rush."

One spin through *New Day Rising* lays to rest any question of the band concerning itself with retaining its original hardcore audience. "I wouldn't use the term 'emancipated,' but the fact that we had the balls to abandon what was possibly the mainstay of our original fan base. . . . We took the big risk of losing all of the international followers of the *Land Speed Record*–style of Hüsker Dü," Hart adds.

College radio was poised for a Hüsker track it could wear out, and it got what it was looking for in "Celebrated Summer." Certainly a mainstay in the canon of gold-standard Hüsker songs, the song is a burning pop showpiece not quite as simple as something like "Everything Falls Apart," not as abrasive as "Chartered Trips" or "Eight Miles High," but claiming a middle ground where the best of Mould's compositions would be found from now on. The song's two acoustic/vocal breakdowns helped endear the longish track to new listeners looking for something more adventurous than R.E.M. "It was around this time that you started to see college radio stations doing Hüsker marathons," says Grant about the new step in the band's development.

"I think that 'Celebrated Summer'—and I'm not saying that Grant's songs didn't draw attention too—but it was 'Celebrated Summer' that got a lot of people's attention who thought Hüsker Dü was a little too noisy for them," says Katzman. "It was a palatable thing that they could like from a hardcore band. That's pretty much what *New Day* was—it was the push for college radio, the college push record. I mean, that's the way I view it and that's the way they viewed it back then, too, that it was very accessible. There's a few weird [songs], but enough poppy ones and accessible ones that everyone would find something they would like. That was the concept behind that one, basically."

SST would also get what they were looking for with *New Day*. Pressing an appropriate number this time, the label moved 30,000 units in a mere four months after the release. The cover, widely believed to be

Grant's photo of a sunrise over one of Minneapolis' dozen lakes, is in reality a sunset. With two dogs strolling into the frame through the shallow water, the presentation was subtle and more or less unique within the music scene that surrounded the band.

"We were the money horse in the stable at SST," says Hart, explaining that as long as Hüsker Dü delivered their albums on time, SST could finance other bands' albums. "*New Day Rising* is the first record for SST in which there wasn't a lengthy waiting period between final mix and mastering. All things considered, it was a time when the realization of the records was at its peak."

Once again, a progressive release that was wholly unlike its predecessor grew Hüsker Dü's profile to thrilling new proportions. The album's title track is one of the more uncompromising songs on the album—easily as intense as much of side two of *Zen Arcade*—and it really cleanses the palate for what's to follow. It seems rather odd that this song attracted the attention of Robert Palmer. No, the immensely respected music writer didn't return to write up a glowing essay about *New Day Rising* for the *New York Times*, but the massively popular mainstream radio-rocker of the period who shared the music critic's name *did* include an earnest cover of "New Day Rising" in his encore for some time. This rumor, long circulated among Hüsker Dü fans, is confirmed by Westwood One radio network's *Superstar Concert Series* No. 87-10, a 1987 triple-album release that features a Palmer gig in which "New Day Rising" appears as the second number in a nine-minute, four-song encore.

Back on planet earth, the Hüskers hit the road behind *New Day Rising* in February 1985, predictably rocking a set that included a sizeable chunk of brand-new material that would appear on *New Day*'s follow-up in September of the same year. For a two-night gig headlining Seattle's Omni Ballroom on the weekend of February 22, 1985, the Hüskers were supported by two unknown bands calling themselves the Melvins and Soundgarden. A few days later, Hüsker Dü co-headlined SST's "The Tour" with the Meat Puppets and Minutemen (Saccharine Trust and SWA opened each date). Not so much a tour as it was a jaunt, The Tour was booked for San Francisco, San Diego, Los Angeles, and Palo Alto. Finishing up with an unrelated two-nighter in Boulder, Colorado, the band returned home and played a March 30 party at the 7th Street Entry before taking three months off to record the album that would break everything wide open: *Flip Your Wig.* ∓

TICKET TO RIDE

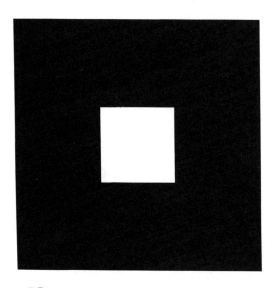

10

Hüsker Dü's career was one of perpetual transitions, but no year was as transitional and chaotic as 1985. In a single twelve-month period, the band released one album, recorded and released another album, recorded *that* album's follow-up, and released a single. They also toured Europe for the first time, shot their first video, sped to the top of the college charts, and made their historic move to a major label.

When Hüsker Dü toured in support of *New Day Rising* during the first four months of 1985, audiences were treated to a band at the height of its powers. As archival footage shows, "Eight Miles High" was at its apex as a chilling display of everything that made Hüsker Dü the best live act in the country that year. It often began with a minute or so of noisy free-jazz-like improv before Mould sliced off the opening chords. Once Mould was lost in one of the song's several vocal screams, he looked like he might fall over from a heart attack. And it's not a silly analogy to suggest that, as the song built into an impossible storm of tension in its final minute and a half, he most closely resembled Bill Bixby's transformation into Lou Ferrigno's Incredible Hulk.

Hüsker Dü left enough of a live impression during a March gig that the band made the cover of the spring '85 *Puncture* (issue number nine), the professionally done 'zine (later a proper magazine) that would become a mainstay of the underground music press into the 1990s. Inside, the band earned hyperbolic praise from writer Jean Debbs:

> For their encore, the Hüskers opened with the outstanding "Pink Turns to Blue," followed by their astonishing and still improving reconstruction job on "Eight Miles High." The title line has by now turned into a full-scale

roar from the depths of Bob Mould's throat, but in contrast he delivers the rest of the verse almost tenderly, singing slow, clear, and low in a minor key—like a harmony vocal line without the lead. An equally great "Ticket to Ride" finally sealed my conviction that Bob and Grant are up there with Phil and Don (Everly, of course!) in the vocal harmony stakes, and to follow it with the *Mary Tyler Moore Show* theme ("You're Gonna Make It After All") . . . clearly, *this* band *is* God.

On March 30, Hüsker Dü reentered the 7th Street Entry for the first time since a double set the previous September. The Entry was celebrating its fifth anniversary, and the choice of band for the occasion was a fitting one—no other local outfit had steered the room to its status as a standalone Twin Cities institution like the Hüskers. Gig flyers were photocopied jobs depicting the *New Day Rising* cover with one of the dogs uttering, "Happy Anniversary, You Bitch." The small room undoubtedly reached capacity in no time, especially given that this would be the band's farewell to the Entry after demonstrating its ability to pack the much larger and adjoining First Avenue "main room" during *New Day*'s record-release celebration back in January. "There may have been some transitional gigs in the main room, but it wasn't long before we were selling out First Ave.," says Hart.

The band took April off from touring to begin work on *New Day Rising*'s follow-up. With each new Hüsker album a breakthrough in its own right, this next effort, *Flip Your Wig*, would be the breakthrough of breakthroughs, ushering in changes that were merely speculative at the time of an interview for the May 1985 *Alternative Focus*. Happily taking a backseat to Grant and Bob when the need arose for a spokesperson, here Norton gave a rare solo interview (if not his only solo interview during the band's lifespan). Refreshingly humble, intensely likeable, and as genuine as they come, Norton is in typical form as a neutralizing force between the band's two pillars of personality:

AF: So, what is the band's current relationship with SST records? I have been hearing a couple of different stories.

GREG: Our relationship with SST records is that we make records, and they put them out for us. And we do our tours, and they help us out in terms of promotional things: They do the promos of the albums for us in terms of radio and stuff like that. It's a good, healthy working relationship.

AF: Have you had any major record companies looking at the band, without mentioning any names?

GREG: Yes, there are some.

AF: Have you been considering any of them, or are you happy with SST?

GREG: We are not looking around for anything. We are not shopping around for labels. We have never solicited a major label to come and listen to us or anything like that. Anything that has happened, they have done on their own. We have not gone to anybody; they have come to us. We have not called anyone and said, "Oh, come and hear our band." It has just happened by itself.

AF: If you were signed to a major label, your music would have a much greater possibility of breaking mainstream listening venues and becoming what most people would consider commercial. How would you respond to that?

GREG: Like I said before, we are not out there trying to make that happen. If we had a hit song, fine. But we are not going out of our way to make that happen. I don't think a bigger label would necessarily indicate we would be breaking into Top 40 or anything like that anyway.

AF: How is your reception in Europe?

GREG: We have never played there, so we can't really say what our audiences are like there. We still get a lot of mail from Europe, and our records are available over there. We should be going over there in September. Records in Europe are difficult to keep track of, so it is hard to say how they are doing over there. It is a lot harder to call up someone in Europe and see how a record is doing than to call SST in California. We will only be there for like three weeks and will try to get to as many places as possible. We seem to have a good following in Italy and will try to get down there if possible, as well as Denmark, the UK, and possibly France, etc., depending on time.

As it turned out, after the band booked some summer dates stateside, they were invited last minute by Trilion Pictures to play a one-off gig at London's Camden Palace on May 14, 1985. The gig—the band's first-ever overseas—fell on an off day between two U.S. shows, without so much as twenty-four hours of wiggle room in either direction. Exclusively shot for the *Live from London* TV show, the performance was later released as a home video by Trilion Pictures, something the band had expressly forbidden in its contract. This led to the Hüskers' first, but not last, venture into the legal realm via a cease-and-desist that was slapped on Trilion. Major geographical and technological distances being what they were in 1985, this failed to stop the VHS release from seeing the light of day as the nineteen-track *Makes No Sense . . . .*

On the positive side, the concert footage is today a hi-fi beacon in an online glut of poor-quality offerings, and like other Hüsker shows captured from this era, it features a blood-boiling "Eight Miles High," not to mention the fine-tuned rush of "Everything Falls Apart" (perhaps one of the oldest set staples at this point) and the band's newly added cover of "Ticket to Ride." Despite the legal action, the video was also released in a Japanese version (four minutes shorter) and later appended with interview footage and edited to fit into the video compilation (or "video magazine") *Punk Overload*, in which the Hüskers keep company with the decidedly un-punk Lords of the New Church and Flesh for Lulu. (To their credit, the producers did include UK Subs for a little punk flavor.) At least two of these versions are still (illegally) available for the cost of a legit concert DVD.

The earliest live coverage of the Camden Palace show came courtesy of the May 25 issue of *New Musical Express*. Unsurprisingly, writer Richard Cook was in the full backhanded-hyperbole mode that has come to signify the UK's journalistic handling of American bands. In his piece titled "New Rock Rising," although the Neanderthal references flow like warm ale, they carry golden compliment after golden compliment:

> If they played like they looked, Hüsker Dü's music would be a slobbering mastodon rock without grace or curves or beauty. But from these angry grubs come gorgeous lepidoptera that arch and sting sweetly in the ears. They are playing this earth's most magnificent rock.
>
> It's not, as I had glancingly feared, heavy metal for sophisticates. True, they have discovered an amazing blend of the primitive and the progressive—they are like bludgeoning, deranged cavemen in calm command of technical resource. Yet the exhaustive ferocity of the music comes in a language that's poetry, an expression that runs in colors. "Celebrated Summer" is so crushingly beautiful on record that a foaming live performance of the song must surely tear and ruin it—instead it's, well, almost transcendent.
>
> In the endless thunderstorm of "Recurring Dream" [*sic*], Hüsker Dü indulge their frightmares—this obliterating, all-consuming feedback is chilling. But their short takes, spliced together in a terrific blur, hold their true selves. I could be cute and call them a Buzzcocks grown huge and

desperate, but they are far more. As Swans are the sound of rock finally breaking, Hüsker Dü are the noise of it crashing together again.

This piece, however, is absolutely nothing compared to Andy Gill's June 8 assessment of the band, also published in *NME* and incorporating coverage of the live gig with an interview. Gill begins with band IDs so unflattering the respective Hüskers couldn't be blamed if they shielded family members' from reading them:

> Bob Mould—guitarist, singer and songwriter—is soft-spoken, short-haired, paunchy, and wears an anorak over a sweatshirt bearing the legend "American Wrestling Association." He looks like he might indulge himself—serious wrestling in America is a noble sport; but no, he likes to watch it on TV (Bob watches a lot of TV) and the real showbiz kind, at that. Bob says it's the modern-day equivalent of Shakespeare, the only place the common man can get a full-blown morality play, with a bit of gymnastics thrown in for good measure. It's one of the few subjects on which Bob gets mildly animated. His greatest desire, while in Britain, is not to see St. Paul's, the Tower or Big Ben, but to see Big Daddy, a monument among men.
>
> Grant Hart—drummer, singer and songwriter—is swarthy, paunchy, with shoulder-length hair that covers his face like a Hawkwind helmet when he's drumming, and he wears white Hüsker boots with half-size laces, no socks, a garage T-shirt and a rumpled paisley jacket. He's rather more rowdy than Bob, given to one-line interjections, sometimes accompanied by a cynical snort. Strangely enough, Grant's songs have a buoyancy, a wistful pop lyricism that provides many of the group's most memorable—hummable—moments.
>
> Greg Norton—bassist—writes no songs, sings no songs, says few words, but is the snappiest dresser of the three. He also has a magnificent handlebar moustache, a veritable Salvador Dali of an upper lip. Apart from this, he seems quite sensible. Onstage, he leaps higher than anyone since Pete Townshend in his heyday, which is just as well, since Bob's Couch Potato style and low-slung guitar (at the Camden Palace, there was some difficulty in finding a guitar strap long enough for Bob) militate against excessive gymnastic displays. Together, they look like the rock 'n' roll equivalent of the Pontypool front row.

Mould, after weathering the usual "Do you consider yourself hardcore?" and "What do hardcore audiences think of you?" line of questioning that he'd grown tired of in the States, gives Gill a choice answer or two and offers at least one backhanded dig at Hart (specifically the latter's non-rock contributions to *Zen Arcade*):

But don't you find the guitar/bass/drums line-up limiting?

"Not for this band," says Bob. "The function of this band is to be guitar, bass, drums and vocals. Anything beyond that, in theory, is not really the band. We don't have synthesisers off to the side, or roll on the grand piano and stuff, which was what 'Zen Arcade' was leaning towards. Fortunately, we got a hold of ourselves and brought it back to reality, started realising the context in which we performed.

"If a song calls for something, then we'll get it. The record we're working on now, there isn't even an acoustic guitar. The songs are strong enough that we didn't need to fuck around with the shit this time. It's sort of in the same vein as 'New Day Rising'—whichever direction—and it's more vocal-oriented, as opposed to a wall of sound. It's a cleaner production: we produced it ourselves, as opposed to having Spot from SST come in and do it, so it does sound a lot better."

Individual elements of their sound are recognisable, but there's no single neat little compartment you could shoe-horn them into, like 'Country Rock' or 'Psychedelia.' Not for them the structures of a Paisley Underground. . . .

"It's all a bunchahooey!" claims Grant, with customary frankness. "There's a lot of people that think they can slap on a paisley shirt and a pair of Roger McGuinn sunglasses and smoke pot and take acid and be psychedelic."

"There's a lot of that kind of stuff," agrees Bob. "A lot of talking in real abstract terms and being real surreal all the time . . . playing in a band and being fulla shit. . . ."

By the same token, the resurgence of interest in older musics receives short shrift, too.

"People lacking the imagination to draw from the future, draw from the past," says Grant, a trifle harshly perhaps.

Bob is somewhat more reasonable.

"What we're doing and what most of the bands are doing is not that new. Especially what we're doing—there's nothing incredibly new about it. We're not, like, The New Age. We're just doing what we do the best we can. There's some elements of change in the way we approach the topics, or weave in and out of topics—but again, I don't think that's anything new. It's just a change from what's going on, to some degree."

Is what you do Art, with a capital A, or something less precious than that?

"It's Music, with a capital M. With all capital letters."

In August 1985, three years to the month after their debut full-length album was released, the band issued a single that would be one of the three or four songs—depending whom you ask—forever identified as sterling Hüsker Dü.

Truthfully, "Makes No Sense at All" most resembles the Buzzcocks-like powerpop that the band was flirting with prior to adopting the charging onslaught heard on *Land Speed Record*. This unreleased material, circulated among the peer-to-peer community and the tape-trading underground that preceded it, is often tagged with the title "Savage Young Dü," though it is anything but savage.

The cover photo and layout for the "Makes No Sense at All" 7-inch is a spoof not lost on Beatles' fans, as the band began to toy with parallels being drawn in the music press, which went so far as to call Grant and Bob the "Lennon and McCartney of post-hardcore" (and variations thereof). Recorded in January 1985, the band's live cover of "Ticket to Ride" was submitted at the request of *NME*, which put it on a compilation 7-inch (that also included Tom Waits, the Jesus and Mary Chain, and Trouble Funk) to be included with the February 1986 issue. It stands as the trio's only gold record by virtue of the high number of *NME* issues distributed.

"We started to play into the whole Beatles thing with the 'Makes No Sense' sleeve layout and photo, and with the title of the record," explains Hart. "Some people got that one, some didn't, but *Flip Your Wig* was the name of the Beatles' board game, and here we are a band named after a board game."

Starting off with Hart machine-gunning his kit, the next two minutes and forty-odd seconds of the Mould-penned "Makes No Sense at All" did a "Smells Like Teen Spirit" on the college rock world of 1985—on a smaller scale of course, since there was no radio format that compared to the commercial "X-station" alternative-rock rat race of the early '90s (and apparently no daytime or primetime programmers at MTV willing to take a chance on the video). Still, the song and subsequent album, *Flip Your Wig* (released a month later in September), would stay at the top of the *CMJ* (*College Music Journal*) charts for months.

Shortly after the release of *Flip Your Wig*, *Boston Rock*, a supplement to the nationally distributed *U.S. Rock*, reported, "*Flip Your*

Wig and its popular single 'Makes No Sense at All' have broken commercial barriers, getting the Hüskers airplay on a number of AOR stations that one would never imagine to play such a vitally original band." Mould, quick to make sure the band wasn't confused with the Fixx or another DIY-allergic band, and answering an accusation that wasn't made, stated in the interview, "I really think it has a lot to do with the amount of records we put out and the amount of touring that we do. A lot of people will resent us for that, but I think that we deserve everything that we're getting. We've worked hard for it and I don't think we've copped out at all."

The lyrics to "Makes No Sense at All" are standard Mould fare of the "relationship complaint" strain, but it is the vocal melodies that forever stamp the song in the brains of all who hear it. Ask any fan of the trio, casual or obsessed, and they will often cite it as their introduction to Hüsker Dü.

In addition to being the band's first "hit," so to speak, "Makes No Sense at All" marked another notable first in Hüsker Dü's career: a vehicle to explore the waters of music videos. Though MTV's *120 Minutes* wouldn't occupy its famous Sunday-night slot until March 1986—where it would serve for seventeen years as the main pre-Internet impetus for indic bands to make videos—avenues existed for underground and indie bands to secure airplay for videos. In fact, MTV was desperate for late-night/early-morning material, and it wasn't uncommon to see an R.E.M. or Cure video during these hours. Someone at the network had the foresight to snap up the IRS Records–produced video program *The Cutting Edge*, which was previously offered to certain markets and as a video magazine on VHS. In 1983, MTV began airing the program on the last Sunday of each month until *120 Minutes* took over the same slot each week. Predictably, the show was heavy with IRS artists like R.E.M., of course, but sometimes aired more challenging artists like Lydia Lunch and Einstürzende Neubauten. "Makes No Sense at All" was definitely aired on *The Cutting Edge* during its October 1985 broadcast. The band appeared as guests on the same episode, indulging the host in a brief interview before showing the video for "Makes No Sense at All" plus the single's B-side, a cover of the *Mary Tyler Moore* theme (the entire video was shot to both songs). The appearance was released in 1987 as part of the *Best of The Cutting Edge, Vol. 2* compilation.

In addition to MTV, the USA Network aired the legendary *Night Flight* throughout the '80s. *Night Flight* was a mind-shattering amalgam of under- and above-ground culture, artist interviews, and music videos. The programming mirrored the underground video magazines that by then had capitalized on the exploding VHS market and were usually associated with a parent entity in the print medium. *Flipside* magazine, for example, one of the most famous punk rock fanzines of all time, had begun a series of VHS compilations in the early '80s. Live footage dominated the content, but scripted videos did make the cut. Their earliest release in the long-running series was *Flipside Video #1*. Twelve of the tape's one hundred and twenty minutes are given over to live footage of "Target," "Everything Falls Apart," "Out on a Limb," and "It's Not Funny Anymore," accompanied by a short interview with the band. Social Distortion, D.I., and Circle Jerks received similar treatment.

∎   ∎   ∎

Like *New Day Rising* before it, *Flip Your Wig* begins with a title track, but unlike its predecessor, "Flip Your Wig" is not a single-chord rave-up but rather one hundred percent Mould gold. It joins "Private Plane" and "Games" among the guitarist's best outings on the album, aside from the undeniable allure of "Makes No Sense at All," which no doubt propelled the album to its status as SST's highest seller yet. *Flip Your Wig* clocked fifty thousand units before 1985 came to a close.

Elsewhere on *Flip Your Wig*, "Divide and Conquer," "Hate Paper Doll," and "Green Eyes" were the oldest tracks, turning up in live sets as early as September 1984. "Divide and Conquer" is again classic Mould—hooks plus major power—à la "Chartered Trips" or "I Apologize." A slightly lesser version of the formula shows up with "Hate Paper Doll," a song that goes for an off-kilter rhythm instead of driving force. "Green Eyes" would be Hart's new high-water mark. The songwriting journey that started with "Diane" and includes "It's Not Funny Anymore" and "Pink Turns to Blue" reached a new level with this track.

Around this time, Andy Nystrom was a Redondo Beach resident and friend of the band, as well as a part-time employee of SST. "I was actually a quote-unquote 'accountant' for a couple of months," he recalls. "Chuck Dukowski would give me a stack of receipts and I went down to the market and bought a little notepad, wrote the stuff in, like 'Descendents – Gas - $20' . . . it was pretty exciting. They'd give me a hundred dollars a week to do that part-time, and I'd started college by then, this was in 1985, but I also did it for fun, just to be around. When you're in high school and you hear that SST Records is located around the corner from your house, you go and try to hang out."

Nystrom recalls the frenzy and attention that *Flip Your Wig* garnered, both at SST and on the airwaves: "There was definitely more press-release type stuff. They were the top priority around SST at that time. There was a lot more talk about them around the office, certainly. There was a big *L.A. Times* article on Hüsker Dü, and you knew they were getting bigger, that something was happening. They didn't play the typical five-band SST gigs anymore . . . they were headlining their own shows and playing bigger places like The Lingerie. It was still SST-flavored, if you will. They did play with SWA and DC3 in '85, but the Hüskers were standing out from the pack. It wasn't 'Hey, here's five SST bands'—it was 'Here's Hüsker Dü and four others.'"

Nystrom continues: "I thought they should have been huge. After I first heard 'Makes No Sense at All' and *Flip Your Wig*, I remember thinking, 'Oh no, people are going to know about them now, they're not going to be the underground band anymore.' I loved their hardcore stuff, I grew up in the hardcore scene, but even as early as *Everything Falls Apart* and *Metal Circus*, there's the melody creeping in. I remember thinking I loved the melody and the aggressiveness, then 'Chartered Trips' off of *Zen*, and 'Celebrated Summer' was the song I played on the car stereo and my mom was blown away. She asked, 'Who's this?' and I said, 'This is Hüsker Dü . . . you know, Bob and the guys you met.' She said, 'I like this one,' because she'd heard the loud screaming stuff.'"

The band's competitive songwriting climate reached a new high on *Flip Your Wig*. Hart wrote only five of the fourteen slots—not since the pre–*Metal Circus* days had the balance been so brazenly off. Nonetheless, his contributions to *Flip* mirror the previous few releases: one or two core numbers of a transcendent nature, as well as strong tracks that are overshadowed by the album's more sublime moments. "Green Eyes" and "Keep Hanging On" make up the former category, and "Every Everything" and "Flexible Flyer" can be counted in the latter. Hart also wrote "The Baby Song," a heartfelt, albeit forty-six-second, tribute to the recent birth of, as Hart puts it, "his love child with a wonderful woman."

"We did spend more time on *Flip Your Wig* than previous records, but less time than we would spend on *Candy Apple Grey*, because the *Flip* material was more focused," says Norton. "I will say that having the studio in your hometown, and having Bob and Grant living in Minneapolis, this is why all of the sudden you see something like 'The Baby Song' ending up on the record. I think there were a few times when someone thought, 'Gee, we're recording here in town, maybe I'll spend all day in the studio.'"

Then there's "The Wit and the Wisdom," which could be Mould's hardcore novelty, a metallized crescendo that collapses into formless noise and takes up a precious 3:41 in the process.

Among fans and critics, *Flip Your Wig* has cemented itself as either the consensus best offering in the band's discography or a close second after *Zen Arcade*. When the hairs are split, the sprawling double LP's unfocused inclusion of hardcore, experimentation, and genuine filler makes *Flip Your Wig* the obvious choice, despite the groundbreaking aspects of *Zen Arcade*.

As the antidote to *Zen Arcade*'s shortcomings, *New Day Rising* dispensed with the filler and became the succinct blueprint for *Flip Your Wig*. Sadly, *New Day Rising* featured brutally high-end production and less impressive overall songcraft in terms of "hits."

Flip Your Wig suffers from neither of these issues. Hart and Mould covered production duties themselves and apparently learned a thing or two after the *New Day Rising* debacle. "I hung out with Bob more than the other guys," Nystrom remembers. "We used to play basketball when they'd have time off in town. There was a park right by SST, and once when he came over to the house, my mom asked, 'Which one are you, Hüsker or Dü?' . . . just one of those friendly, mom things. . . .

"'Makes No Sense at All' really blew me away because it had everything you'd want in a hardcore pop song. I guess it wasn't hardcore in any way, but it still had the abrasive guitars. I remember telling Bob it was a great song, and maybe in kind of cocky way, he said, 'Yeah, that's the one.' They knew they'd hit a high point. Around the time of *Flip Your Wig*, you could tell they were growing beyond and that they were going places . . . they weren't unfriendly at all, but there was a new demeanor there."

"With *Flip*, it was like you took a handkerchief off of *New Day Rising*," says Terry Katzman. "*Flip* was when everything came together; it was their White Album. I think that getting away from

Spot was a plus. I came over for a couple of the *Flip* sessions, but they were so busy then, it was weird because I could just look across the street and know they were in there. I thought, 'Oh, I know they're really making something special this time. I know this is going to be the one.' I knew I needed to stay away until they got a bunch of stuff recorded, then I'd hear it."

More so than any other '80s underground album—even Sonic Youth's *Daydream Nation*—*Flip Your Wig* predicted the sound of the late-'80s/early-'90s indie-rock explosion. Sonic Youth may have encouraged indie rock's embrace of off-kilter tunings and artiness, but *Flip Your Wig* presented a simpler, more subtle formula for greater staying power, especially when later bands like Superchunk and Nirvana are considered. When a band (e.g., the Pixies) claims to be influenced by Hüsker Dü, or a music reviewer claims this influence for a band, *Flip Your Wig* is the sound referenced. Of course, the terms "indie rock" and "post-hardcore" did not exist in 1985, so *Flip Your Wig* was consumed as one of the then rare examples of a middle ground between hardcore and the sonic flimsiness of college rock. The album's brilliant pop and air-moving power can be traced back to 1982's "Everything Falls Apart"—the first time that Hüsker Dü married massive volume to massive hooks. The style peaked with *Flip Your Wig*.

"They spent more time on overdubs, more focusing, trying to get it right," says Katzman. "They weren't in the studio from March until June. They tracked it just as fast as they did the other records, and they were touring a lot between those months. I remember Bob telling me, 'This one's going to have a lot of vocals on it,' not like the other ones didn't have a lot of vocals, but that they were really going to concentrate on getting a much cleaner sound, because I think the muddiness of *New Day* was still sort of in their throat, the negative recording aspects. *Flip* is much more fully realized vocally, and in other ways, too."

In October 1985, Oar Folkjokeopus, in many ways ground zero of the Minneapolis music scene, was destroyed by fire. "I remember carrying melted copies of *Flip* to the dumpster," says Katzman, who was also an employee of the store. Afterward, Katzman co-founded Garage D'or Records a few blocks east and across Nicollet Avenue from the building that housed Twin/Tone and Nicollet Studios. He also found himself with nothing to do on the Reflex side of things, since that summer's release, the Minutemen's *Tour Spiel* 7-inch, proved to be the label's last. The situation with the Arizona DJ who raised a stink about not being properly credited on the back sleeve of *Tour Spiel* and then threatened to sue and bootlegged the release (see Chapter 4), combined with the tense Hüsker Dü schedule, served as reasons to quietly shut down the label. "I remember Bob coming up to me as all of that was going on and saying, 'You know, Terry, this is going to be the last Reflex release,' and I said, 'Okay,' and that was it," says Katzman, "This was the point in time that my role was starting to diminish. Not only were they getting bigger . . . but I had a store to run, I was getting married in the near future. We'd still hang out all the time, but things were starting to change a bit. I moved into being more of an observer and not a participant."

As with *Zen Arcade*, Mould decided to close *Flip Your Wig* with a noisy exercise, "Don't Know Yet." And again, Greg Norton did not appear on the album as a songwriter or singer. "There was one time that I remember there being tension," Nystrom says. "It was the Halloween '85 show at Fender's Ballroom in Long Beach, and by that time they were staying in a hotel up the street from the venue. They were far beyond crashing on the floor at SST. So I walked up to the hotel with all three of them, and me being naïve and inquisitive asked, 'So, why doesn't Greg sing any songs anymore?' That was met with dead silence. . . . Greg kind of looked at me and shrugged and Bob got up and walked out of the room."

Band tensions had started to show several releases prior but had remained manageable up until the recording of *New Day Rising*. Now those tensions began to show a ruinous side as *Flip Your Wig* was released and as recording began immediately on the next album, in true Hüsker fashion. For the most part, band members played their cards close to the chest in professional situations, and that included not letting on that bad blood was beginning to flow at an unprecedented rate. "They would roll into town," Nystrom recalls, "Bob might play around on the guitar, just hanging out . . . it was very friendly and very inclusive, cracking jokes, nothing to outsiders that would indicate that they weren't getting along." ‡

BEDDING THE BUNNY

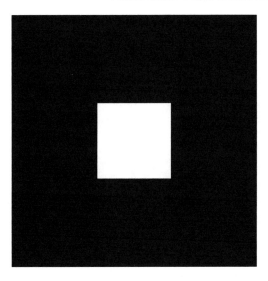

The year 1985 marked serious change in the national underground, and nowhere was it more apparent than at SST. The label's roster was growing at an amazing rate, due in no small part to album sales of the Meat Puppets, Black Flag, the Minutemen, and especially Hüsker Dü. A new Hüsker LP could bankroll releases by the other aforementioned acts, which in turn meant more titles for Greg Ginn's vanity interests—the very thing that would eventually bring the label's downfall.

The second half of 1984, along with the entirety of 1985, marked the beginning of a fateful change in the SST discography that Mike Watt succinctly explains as "The music that Greg liked." If it's conceivable that a label head could have his heart in the right place while exercising extreme selfishness, then Greg Ginn was that label head. Throughout 1985, he forged ahead with his campaign to flood the market with personal favorites, clogging college radio mail slots and record store bins with product that still collects dust.

"Presumably most stations had one or two hip DJs whose shows would've really begun to identify what was happening musically, and so maybe they were playing Slovenly, Toiling Midgets, and some buzz-less others," recalls Joe Carducci. "You'd have to look through back issues of *CMJ* or old playlists to recall the sheer amount of garbage that stole air from living musicians. Crimes yet unsolved and prosecuted."

Up until the summer of '84, SST had been regarded as "Black Flag's label" or " Hüsker Dü's label" or perhaps "the label with Black Flag, Minutemen, Hüsker Dü, Meat Puppets, Descendents, and Saccharine Trust, but I haven't listened to any records by the latter." By the end of 1985, SST was flush with proceeds from *New Day Rising* and *Flip Your Wig*, as well as the Meat Puppets' successful third LP, *Up on the Sun*; the Minutemen's *Double Nickels on the Dime* follow-up, *Project: Mersh*; and no shortage of Black Flag albums. Even so, the label would become regarded not as a veritable "Who's Who" but rather a veritable "Who's That?"

In restrospect, Ginn's vision seems almost supernatural in its prescience, but in 1985, peddling '70s butt rock, sludgy proto–doom metal, spazzy Zappa and Beefheart rip-offs, and improvisational jazz-rock hybrids were all absurdly unfashionable notions despite the growing open-mindedness of underground music fans. Their minds weren't opening *that* fast.

SST held college radio stations and record stores hostage by threatening to hold back prime product unless those stations and stores played and ordered titles by the unsellable (and in some cases, unlistenable) Saint Vitus, D.C.3, SWA, Wurm, Angst, October Faction, Saccharine Trust, and Overkill (*not* the New York City thrash band, but a punk-metal marriage of an altogether different and awful stripe that was posthumously named Overkill L.A. to avoid confusion—not that there could be any). "Because we could work fast, it did give SST the advantage as far as collecting bills was concerned," says Grant Hart. "If you want the new Hüsker, you're going to pay for the old Saccharine Trust."

Wurm, SWA, D.C.3, and October Faction either featured Ginn or past and present members of Black Flag. The powerpop-informed cow punk of San Francisco's Angst could have appealed to a wider audience but didn't. Saint Vitus, along with Chicago's Trouble, was arguably one of the first bands to create a style that would cause an underground sensation in years to come, namely "doom metal." In the mid-'80s, however, no one would confuse the music of Saint Vitus with the word "sensation."

Observers and fans couldn't be blamed for sensing that SST's boy's club mentality prevailed in everything from SST's releases to their office politics, with Kira Roessler representing the only female voice in the house. More females could and would be drawn to the new underground, as Sonic Youth and the lesser-known (though excellent) Salem 66 proved. Still, SST wouldn't boast the acquisition of Sonic Youth until 1986, so while Hüsker Dü and the Meat Puppets didn't have a female in their ranks, they nonetheless reigned as the only SST bands with music that didn't spew testosterone in all directions.

I   I   I

A sizeable piece in the July 18–August 1, 1985, issue of *Rolling Stone* featured Hüsker Dü prominently alongside contemporaries Minutemen, Meat Puppets, and Black Flag (the latter cited as "the most infamous punk band since the Sex Pistols"). Titled "Punk Lives" and beset with the angle-exposing subhead of "They don't sound like the Ramones and they don't look like the Sex Pistols, but bands like Black Flag, Hüsker Dü, the Minutemen and the Meat Puppets are keeping the spirit of '77 alive," the lengthy article made a decent enough stab at the impossible: telling the '79 to '85 history of the American underground within the feature boundaries of a mainstream music magazine.

Writer Michael Goldberg highlighted SST's non-hardcore hippie element, the bands' hardscrabble existence, the inner workings of indie labels (mainly Subterranean, Twin/Tone, and SST), and album sales before reaching closure with the subject of major labels and their reticence toward the bands profiled. "I think being outside the mainstream music business is good," Mould tells Goldberg. "When you tie yourself down to a major label, you give up all your individual control over things. You become part of a machine. It wouldn't seem right for Hüsker Dü to come out on Polymer Records."

Interestingly, it's a safe wager that the Hüskers were already in talks with their future label home, Warner Bros., when the *Rolling Stone* interview (the Hüskers' so-far highest degree of print publicity) hit the streets in mid-July 1985. Magazine lead-time gives Mould the benefit of the doubt, but the same can't be said for a *Boston Rocker* feature that ran that October:

> Understandably, rumors of Hüsker Dü leaving California's SST Records in favor of a major label abound. "A lot of majors have been calling," says Mould, "and they're all really interested in the band, but I don't really know if we're all that interested in them. We're pretty much happy with what we've got now. With SST, the records have been getting out in a relatively sufficient number and we've been able to do things the way we've wanted to do them. I think the question regarding major labels at the moment concerns us being what we want to be versus the majors and what they want us to be."

"When we were working on *Zen Arcade*, we started to get major label attention," says Greg Norton. "Then after the album was released, we actually started to get solicited. Guys would show up at gigs or people would call. [Signing to a major label] didn't make sense at the time, as SST was doing a fine job. We didn't see that a major label could do anything for us. But it's not like they were sending us bouquets of flowers or prostitutes. Keep in mind that in '84 and '85, there were very few A&R people that were into what we were doing. They were still looking for the next Dokken and didn't think that Joe Strummer could play his way out of a paper sack."

"The first thing I can recall is when it got back to us that there was a rumor that we were talking to the majors. These originated from people at the bars, because so-and-so with this label or that label was coming in, asking about us," says Grant Hart. "We didn't know who they were by sight, but the local club people [in] Chicago, New York would let us know after the show. 'Oh, so-and-so was here.' And this was awhile before they started dropping business cards."

One of the most widely accepted myths about Hüsker Dü's Warner Bros. deal is that it occurred before any other American indie or hardcore band signed to a major. Quite simply, the ink dried on the Hüsker contract with Warners almost a full year *after* the Replacements signed to Sire. Almost a decade before, in the same city, the Suicide Commandos, the only Minneapolis punk rock band of any note at the time, became the first punk rock band from Minneapolis to tour a nonexistent network of not-quite-venues, and in 1977 they became the first Minneapolis punk band to sign to a major (Mercury's "punk rock" Blank imprint).

Elsewhere in the world, Black Flag tried to release their legendary *Damaged* album on MCA-affiliated Unicorn, though the situation turned into a serious mess for all involved. After the first wave of "Seymour Stein Punk" (as Mike Watt calls it, after Stein's signing of the Ramones, Talking Heads, Television, Dead Boys, Blondie, etc.), the Gang of Four released the groundbreaking *Entertainment!* on Warner Bros. after one measly 45 on an indie. L.A. co-ed punk/country-punk combo institution X defected to Elektra in 1982 for their third LP, after the legendary *Los Angeles* and *Wild Gift* were released on Slash (when it was still a quasi-independent label).

Hüsker Dü was underground royalty by 1985. *Flip Your Wig*, released as the summer came to a close, marked the third time in a year and a half that the trio delivered a groundbreaking and mag-netic full-length album. "Makes No Sense at All" even dropped in on commercial classic rock radio when DJs and programmers felt adventurous. The song's video was licensed to several "video magazines" and soon popped up on MTV's attempts at tapping the college-radio crowd, the most successful of which was the long-running *120 Minutes*. The band was lavished with attention in Europe, and especially the UK, which was saturated with heavy-handed goth-pop drenched in keyboards and drum machines (along with a strange bedfellow in the sonically abrasive squatter-punk scene). The UK underground managed to float the Jesus and Mary Chain and the Wedding Present to the top, both of which built on developments made across the pond, most notably by the Hüskers.

Indeed, Hüsker Dü was also leaving a permanent mark on the American indie scene. Squirrel Bait, a Louisville, Kentucky, quartet of high school seniors and college freshmen (who would eventually form such timeless indie and post-hardcore outfits as Slint, Bastro, Gastr del Sol, and Bitch Magnet), released a stunning self-titled seventeen-minute debut on Homestead Records in 1985, thanks to the dual efforts of Steve Albini and Gerard Cosloy (two keener sets of ears didn't exist in 1985). Inevitable Hüsker comparisons followed as something of a mutual-admiration society developed. Hart himself noted, "This is definitely the best $400 I've ever heard" (a reference to the reported cost of recording the EP), while Mould told *SPIN* that the release was "on par with anything we've done."

Though Squirrel Bait's Hüsker influence does slap listeners across the face, their debut was also thick with the high school urgency of hardcore (namely in the emerging style of Washington, D.C.'s Dischord Records) and the manner in which Seattle bands of the day were utilizing metal (something that would lead, of course, to the grunge explosion a few years later). Squirrel Bait's second album, *Skag Heaven* (1987), built on the greatness of the band's debut and was colored with an even heavier debt to the Dü.

The two bands had become acquainted in early 1985 when Squirrel Bait opened for Hüsker Dü. "Squirrel Bait played exactly once with Hüsker Dü, at the Jockey Club in Newport, Kentucky, not long after *New Day Rising* came out," recalls Squirrel Bait guitarist David Grubbs. "Several months after that, Hüsker Dü said some very flattering things about Squirrel Bait in a *SPIN* magazine article, and it really helped to spread the word about our first record. They were a prime inspiration for Squirrel Bait, and the show that we saw them play in Newport when *Zen Arcade* came out—Brian McMahan's mother drove us up there and waited in the car, if I remember correctly—was one of the most awesome rock shows I've ever had the pleasure to experience."

Terry Katzman recalls first sensing a jump to the majors was imminent. "It was around the concert and big article in *SPIN* magazine," he says, referring to the same three-page December 1985 piece in which Mould name-checked Squirrel Bait. "A major label was the next logical step to make at this point. There's nowhere else you can go after making an album like *Flip*."

The concert in question was an August 28, 1985, *SPIN*-sponsored event at First Avenue held as part of the magazine's concert series. It has become the most bootlegged performance of the band's career. (*SPIN* had a promo double LP pressed of the concert for distribution to radio stations around the country.) The set (see sidebar) contains almost a third of the band's future major label debut, *Candy Apple Grey*. A few days after this concert, *Flip Your Wig* was released on SST under the guise of "owing the label another record," and it was soon revealed that the band had signed to Warner Bros. through the pursuance of the late A&R legend Karen Berg.

Berg was a behind-the-scenes force for Warner Bros. beginning in the mid-'70s. Always concerned with the development side of A&R, Berg's signings included Dire Straits, Television, the Church, Gang of Four, and Laurie Anderson, and she nurtured an unwavering affinity for Hüsker Dü. Julie Panebianco, one of the three or four Warners employees under Berg who were in charge of organizational, hands-on needs (also known as "handlers"), had met the Hüskers the previous year.

"They were on tour with R.E.M., around the *New Day Rising* time," she says. "We were part of the Alternative Marketing Department that Warners pioneered. No other major label was doing this at the time. Part of my job was to do something I was going to be doing anyway, which was going out to see bands in clubs. We were told to keep an eye out for great bands to sign."

Warners had long held a reputation for being the most artist-friendly,

SPIN MAGAZINE CONCERT
First Avenue, Minneapolis
August 28, 1985

Flip Your Wig
Every Everything
Makes No Sense at All
The Girl Who Lives on Heaven Hill
I Apologize
If I Told You
Folklore
Don't Want to Know If You Are Lonely
I Don't Know for Sure
Terms of Psychic Warfare
Powerline
Books about UFOs
Hardly Getting Over It
Sorry Somehow
(You're So Square) Baby I Don't Care
The Wit and the Wisdom
Celebrated Summer
All Work and No Play
Green Eyes
Divide and Conquer

open-minded of any major label. "We were playing bigger venues and things were really starting to take off for the band, and this is when Karen Berg appears on the scene," remembers Norton. "Karen was the first A&R person that seemed to genuinely get what we were doing, and she seemed to love it as a fan."

Hüsker Dü was never the subject of a bidding war, which were more common in the post-Nirvana feeding frenzies of the early to mid-'90s. "There were phone calls, people sending faxes, and even then, we never actually had a situation where someone said anything like, 'Well, we'll give you a hundred grand more than that label,'" Hart remembers. "It was us saying, 'This is what we'll accept' and it was Warner Bros. that separated themselves from the pack very early on when Karen Berg announced, 'We don't want to have any involvement in the band aside from releasing your records and we'll give you money to make them.' It was really the only circumstances that we were going to entertain . . . we were doing fine on SST."

When Hüsker Dü decided to go with Warner Bros., one the band's closest sonic contemporaries were the Replacements, who released their own major-label debut, *Tim*, six months before *Candy Apple Grey* hit the shelves in March 1986. The albums couldn't have any more different. The Replacements had been signed to Sire since the winter of 1984. But with their more palatable sound, not to mention their professed aspirations of success, few cries of sell-out were heard in reference to their major-label debut.

"With the Replacements, there were several labels involved in that situation," Panebianco remembers. "There were lots of people around them. Karen wasn't one of those A&R people that went after everybody. Karen was old-school about things—it wasn't 'How many records are they going to sell?' or 'How much money are they going to make?' With our [department], it was 'How good are they?'"

According to Hart, Hüsker Dü should've beaten their Minneapolis colleagues to the major-label punch. "Warners was supposed to get *Flip Your Wig*, and in a perfect world, they would have," he reveals. "Karen Berg was convinced she could make a college-rock hit, or some sort of hit, out of 'Green Eyes.' . . . They could have gotten [*Flip Your Wig*]. I mean, they were there in time, and it wouldn't have been a big yanking of the carpet out from under the feet of SST. There was enough time for everyone to have been accommodated in that situation."

"There was an option that we could have given *Flip* to Warners, as we signed the contract before the record was released," says Norton.

"I'm also of the opinion that Warners should have gotten the record. Bob felt that we owed SST one final record, and it was probably through loyalty to Carducci more than anything else."

"When Karen first came to town," Hart continues, "*Flip Your Wig* had been mixed. I was shooting the cover for it, and she offered to pay for the photo shoot, and I said, 'I don't want to do anything that will get me in trouble with the other guys.' And she respected that."

"Green Eyes" is college-rock hit material, no question about it, and all of the band's college-chart performers happened while they were still on SST, including "Makes No Sense at All," "Diane," and "Celebrated Summer." "Green Eyes" had similar, if not bigger, potential. Because it would be the band's last release on the label, everyone knew that SST was only going to pull one single from *Flip Your Wig*, and that position had already been filled by "Makes No Sense at All." But a major could have released more than one single and perhaps pushed "Green Eyes" beyond the confines of MTV's *120 Minutes*. Mould's insistence that the band release *Flip Your Wig* on SST would seem to make sense in this light.

"Ultimately, it's something that Bob thought would be better for the band, and in hindsight, that's proven to not have been the case," Hart concludes. "It made a big difference in how much [Warners] offered us and for how long. They had offered us seven albums. We could have waited on *Flip Your Wig*. . . . You know, we already proved we could put out good record after good record."

❚   ❚   ❚

There's no doubt that Warners was one of the more forward-thinking major labels. In the mid-'80s—before the Internet or even the widespread availability of cable television—the vast majority of music purchased was released by major labels. An obsessive Bruce Springsteen fan could collect every known recorded title and piece of Boss memorabilia and still have absolutely no idea that underneath this thick layer of major label/MTV artists there existed an extensive network of independently owned labels, retail outlets, publications, and bands. If the terms "underground" or "indie" were heard emanating from a major-label conference room or power-lunch, it usually was just another way of saying "it sucks." The masses made the money for the labels, and the customer was always correct. If the mainstream music fan had never heard of a band, how could they possibly be any good?

When majors other than Warners took risks on the underground, it was with a relatively safe gamble such as thrash or speed metal. The same month that Hüsker Dü released *Candy Apple Grey*, for example, Metallica wowed the industry (and their label, Elektra) with *Master of Puppets*. One of the heaviest records to have a major's backing up to that time, it soon revealed a tape-trading army of fans that could fill a stadium to see a band that had never charted or had a video in rotation on MTV.

Earlier, when the Hüskers were shaking hands with Warners in mid-1985, they unknowingly dropped their own little surprise on their new label: they had never enlisted the services of a manager.

"One thing that usually comes up is that Warners required all of its bands to have a manager," says Panebianco. "Hüsker Dü was putting out records and touring without a manager. It wasn't really an issue at all. Warners just wanted someone to be there. Someone that wasn't in the band." The band knew any warm body would suffice, so David Savoy, a coworker of Mould's boyfriend at the time, was hired to fill the role. This quick and seemingly harmless act would prove a major factor in the band's eventual undoing.

The passive-aggressive nature of Hüsker Dü's internal strife—which was perhaps in its most complicated stage in the months surrounding the recording and release of *Candy Apple Grey*—was only apparent to outsiders who looked really hard. "For my first meeting with the band, I thought it was a little strange that Bob and Grant traveled separately to New York," Panebianco remembers. "But Grant was the more social of the two. He was friends with all of the other bands—you'd see him out—and Bob was just a more private person. Bob was going down his own path. It still wasn't overt, but when Grant was riding in the car with us during tours, I eventually realized that it was because he didn't want to ride with Bob."

The Hüsker Dü story, as it is well-known, contains aspects that, as standalone subtexts, are complicated, to say the least. While drug use, Mould's and Hart's sexuality, and personal and professional rifts within the band are important to the story, their coverage over the years has drawn attention away from the band's accomplishments. Still, it would be idealistic to expect that a biographical work on Hüsker Dü could ignore these subjects altogether.

"I think it's important to note that Bob and Grant were smoking opium while they recorded [*Candy Apple Grey*]," says Greg Norton, who, as for his own drug use, readily admits, "I smoked a little pot, drank a little, did the occasional line of cocaine."

While most discussion of such issues has focused on Hart and Mould, Norton was by no means immune to extra-musical issues. But the bassist's partial absence from the *Candy Apple Grey* sessions, for example, was not a show of irresponsibility or apathy. After all, Norton was in a place—i.e., between Mould and Hart— as uncomfortable as any position the other two band members might find themselves in. Add to this a blatant gesture or two that excluded or alienated him, and maybe a camping trip seemed in order.

"Yeah, I took off to go camping for a couple of weeks and when I got back, I had to go in and do my parts," Norton begins. "I was listening to the rough mixes of what they had done so far, and just asked, 'What the hell did you do while I was gone?' That's how I came to find out about the opium smoking. I tried it—interesting stuff, nothing I'd do twice. I do think it had an impact on how that album sounds, and on the overall mood."

"So we signed with Warners and we get the big bad recording advance, and one of the first things that Bob, Grant, and Steve [Fjelstad] do is they go out and buy a lot of equipment for the studio, but they started their own little leasing company and they leased the equipment to the studio," the bassist recalls. "They bought tube compressors, all sorts of things. Even though there was still tension between Bob and Grant, they were still cooperative enough to align with Steve . . . I think they called the company 'Massive Leasing.'"

(The band members have always kept the exact amount of Hüsker Dü's Warners recording advance out of the media. The facts that Hart put $50,000 down on a house and had an additional $20,000 coming his way from the delivery advance (the portion of the advance that's paid upon completion of the album), strongly suggests the whole advance for *Candy Apple Grey* was in the neighborhood of $200,000 to $250,000—a very modest sum by mid-1990s post-*Nevermind* standards. This was most likely Mould's savvy business acumen at work: An advance, by its very name, is not a band's money, but rather a loan—a fact that gets many less-experienced bands in trouble after they're dropped from a major).

Norton continues: "And when the band broke up, this posed a bit of a problem, because all of the sudden, there was no money for the members of the band, but the people of Massive Leasing got paid for their investments—paid out of the band money, which I still don't really know how that went down, but I was not a part of Massive Leasing, so I didn't see any money. I think that it may have been written up so that Hüsker Dü the band had to lease the equipment, so when the band broke up, the individual members of Massive Leasing got paid by Hüsker Dü for the equipment that was used. That's where all the money went, and there was no money left over for anyone else, and that anyone else would be me."

I   I   I

For as long as there's been an underground beneath rock 'n' roll's mainstream, there has been a white elephant in the room: the "sellout" stigma. This aspect of Hüsker Dü's career has been greatly exaggerated over the years. While the band's major-label debut, *Candy Apple Grey*, proved far from the final coffin nail that some long-time fans and others predicted, the switch from SST to Warners did bring about substantial changes—negative, positive, and neutral—in Hüsker Dü's recorded and live products, in band members' lives, in their feelings toward one another, and in how they perceived the future of the band. *Candy Apple Grey* was not a sell-out, yet it has grown into a polarizing album since its March 1986 release. Still, in the years since its release, all three band members have been quick to point out that it was exactly the record they would have made for SST had they stayed with the label.

"There were a lot of people that I talked to that whined about us 'selling out,'" says Norton. "But let's put it this way: There will always be people that view a major label signing as money-motivated and an artistic compromise. I remember playing a gig down in Houston and the singer for Really Red was very bummed out that we'd signed to Warners, and I had to convince him that we didn't sell out, that we still had control over our music."

"Early on, there were not a lot of people coming to the shows, and later on, it was people playing catch-up," explains Hart. "Once we were signed, there would be these people coming up to us at shows and introducing themselves like 'Yeah, I'm going to be doing East Coast screwdriver maintenance for Warners.' In L.A. and New York, places where there were offices for Warners."

As far as the press was concerned, dissent surfaced exactly where it was expected: within the pages of *Maximumrocknroll.*

Joining *Forced Exposure*, *Your Flesh*, *Flipside*, and *Suburban Punk/Voice* as a survivor of the '81–'82 American hardcore 'zine explosion, *MRR* was pretty much the only one of these publications in 1985 to remain fixated on hardcore punk, including the lifestyle. What Hüsker Dü spent several albums moving away from was still there and still growing. *MRR* steadfastly refused to review any album on or affiliated with a major label, or run advertisements for such. In criticism of the Warners move, the February 1986 issue featured a very unflattering drawing of Hart modeling "Hüsker Dü Underoos."

MRR's "What th' Fuck!?!" was a short-lived feature in which one question was asked of a notable personality, who was then allowed to turn his or her answer into a column. The second ever "What th' Fuck!?!" featured Mould defending his band's major label move.

> **MRR:** There are a lot of rumors going around that you have signed to a major label. What impact do you think it will have on the independent/underground music scene (and do you feel any commitment to the underground scene)?
>
> **Bob:** First off, we'd like to say thanks for asking us about it. Hopefully, this will be one of the only times we'll be asked about it; we really don't want to spend the rest of our time on earth talking about signing with a major label. Yes, we've signed a deal with Warner Brothers Records; obviously we can't tell everyone everything that the contract contains. Generally speaking, their contract calls for at least two albums in the next two years, the first Warners LP to be released on March 17, 1986. The major part of the contract, at least to us, allows us complete artistic freedom on the project. Grant and I are preparing to mix the first LP this week, we're doing all the artwork in house, same as always. The songs we wrote for this LP were around long before the Warners deal was a reality, so I don't think there should be any radical changes in style. We were writing these songs for ourselves and we've always written songs that make us happy first. When we were an unknown quantity to the hardcore and punk crowd, we tried to express what we had on our minds as clearly as possible, in both what we do as human beings or musicians. On that thought, I don't think the Warners deal will change our attitude one bit.

A lot of people, especially on our European tour of September, confronted us about not being political enough. I agree completely with them. Earlier on in our days as a band, we attempted to deal with general global concerns (nuclear war, racism, and fascism) in very general and basic terms. We soon realized that we were not as well equipped as other bands around us to expound on certain political theories, but these things were, and still are, on our minds. To us, it seems more important to deal with why people are people and make certain people see things in such a negative way. That may sound like a cop out, especially now that we are in a better position to spread a certain "gospel" to the "masses" (whoever they may be).

Basically, we're not going to use music as a political tool when we don't have enough concrete knowledge about delicate political issues. It's better not to inform people than to misinform people about a subject of this magnitude. Of course we don't want to see any more wars, bigotry, or bulldozing of innocent people or countries. We're human beings with feelings and we have deep opinions on these subjects. I think the thing we're trying to make people realize is that most of the hatred and bigotry in the world starts right between your own ears, ours included. This society has stereotyped subcultures of all varieties through mass communications (be it TV, advertising, or the printed word), and it is repeatedly ingrained, day after day, through the entertainment and business worlds. . . . be it the Coors Light ad which portrays middle-American workers as beer drinking bar hounds, up to the ladies' cosmetic ads on any number of television shows portraying families living in projects or mansions— they're all guilty of displaying America as a completely factionalized society. People have to take a look at the society around them and decide where they stand and what attitudes that position might shape. That's what a song like "Real World" meant: who are you, why are you looking for some sort of religion to follow, punk or otherwise? We weren't knocking people who live within the Anarchist society, we were simply stating that anarchy was not the answer for us and may not be the way of life for a lot of people. We're just asking people to take a look at themselves and if they don't like what they see, do something about yourself before you take it out on someone else. No two people are alike; everyone is unique in one way or another and people should be proud of being different. It's a little unsettling when people are different like everyone else though. I'm sorry if we ruffled some people's feathers along the way, but maybe we're more interested in arguing with people than constantly agreeing just to seem in good graces with someone. If we presented a challenge to someone's personal philosophy—great, we've done our job. If we've insulted anyone personally, we apologize and ask you to take a second look. We don't have any answers that are right for everyone, but I'm sure, as I sit here putting this piece together, that we've got some damn good questions.

As far as our involvement in the underground scene goes, well, our little joke is that we're now the establishment—hardly likely considering how adamant we are about the way Hüsker Dü operates from day-to-day. I had talked to [*MRR* publisher Tim Yohannon] briefly on the phone about the sellout concept, and I think it goes a lot deeper than the "evil" major labels. In my mind, the real evils may lie within the management companies and booking agencies. Some of these companies are very good with bands like Hüsker Dü, some are not so good. We're still self-managed and we've hired one person for full time assistance with booking. We're still conscious of our audience, we're trying to play all-ages shows, we're trying to keep the ticket price down, and we are trying to keep people off the stage because we're tired of losing half our guarantee because of destroyed PA systems and half our teeth. It has nothing to do with elitism; we're concerned about ourselves staying in one piece, and not endangering unsuspecting people in the audience. Everyone has a right to see Hüsker Dü, not just the slammers in the pit. We haven't gone through a new image change 'cause we've never had one. Believe me, Hüsker Dü would be much more saleable if we had a look of any sort.

I don't think Hüsker Dü signing to a major label will have an effect on the underground scene at all. Just because we've signed to Warner Brothers doesn't mean that there won't be ten new bands next week. If anything, it might be a sign that something is happening, that some people are finally listening to the underground, and they might even respect what's going on. Nobody at Warners has asked us to tone down; they haven't asked us to sound like U2, they're completely happy with the high-end distortion and tons of ride cymbals and people yelling and singing pretty and writing any kinds of words they want. They signed Hüsker Dü because they liked Hüsker Dü and not because they think we will be the next Rick Springfield. And your guess is as good as mine as to what will happen into '86; I haven't got a clue as I'm too busy working on new songs and the next tour to stop and worry.

My last little tirade before I sign off: everyone lives in a big glass bubble. The bubble's lowest point rests on a mark on the center of a long line. That mark on the line signifies the status quo in today's world. If people inside the bubble make a concerted effort to move the glass bubble, it will. The lowest point of the bubble now rests on a new mark. I'll leave the rest for everyone else to figure out. Again, thanks to *MRR* and to everyone else out there who finds something of value in what we do, and please don't write us off yet. We're not that old; as a matter of fact, I think we're getting younger at heart. Just let us do what we've always done, get up and tell our stories to people. We hope you enjoy the new album. Take care, Bob Mould/Hüsker Dü.

In the almost quarter-century since *Candy Apple Grey*'s release, there exists a glaring line of demarcation separating an era when the "sellout" issue carried little weight, if any, from an era when it was a (usually deserved) mark for neutered albums by former underground torchbearers and sleazy major-label boardroom creations alike. There is no arguing what constitutes this line of demarcation: the release and freakish success of Nirvana's *Nevermind*.

Since most revisionist history relating to Hüsker Dü's major-label signing has been written post-*Nevermind*, there is usually little perspective of what it really meant for an underground band to sign to a major label in 1985.

"At that time [signing to a major label] wasn't really the taboo PC no-no it would become by the '90s," Tom Hazelmyer remembers. "A lot of us at that time remember that we had bought a lot of the first wave of punk rock on major labels back in the '70s when the majors thought punk would be the next big thing. For most to all indie bands of the '80s [signing to a major label] wasn't even an option so the majors hadn't become the boogie man they would once they started pilfering the best and brightest from the indies through the '90s. I remember the Hüskers being pretty excited about the deal, as I'm sure by that point they really did need the extra structure and support most indies just can't handle."

"It really wasn't that big of a deal. Really, what was the difference between Hüsker Dü and the Dickies?" Hart asks rhetorically.

Of course, there's a massive difference between a semi-novelty proto-hardcore band that was essentially formed to exploit punk rock's popularity, and thus get signed to a major, and a hardscrabble sonic blast-furnace that meticulously refined its sound over a six-year period until it pioneered a new form of pop. But when viewed from other angles, the two situations blur into one. Both bands correctly regarded a major label as the next logical step in development. Both bands put a major label's imprint on a sound that had yet to enjoy such treatment. Specifically, the Dickies were probably the fastest punk rock band around, let alone on a major label. In 1979 their sound was a direct link between first-wave punk rock of the Seymour Stein variety and the soon-to-be-termed "hardcore" of Black Flag, the Circle Jerks, and Middle Class. Likewise, Hüsker Dü brought a sound out of the early to mid-'80s and onto a major label at a time when their closest sonic cousin was the Replacements, who by 1985 and 1986 were too ensconced in folky, Americana leanings and thus sonically aligned with R.E.M. or the understood idea of "college rock," whereas only the thrash metal of Metallica, Megadeth, or Anthrax could approach the intensity of Hüsker Dü's *Candy Apple Grey* upon its release. (This would remain the case until Soul Asylum released *Hang Time* in 1988.) So in a weird fashion, *Candy Apple Grey* was the most sonically adventurous non-metal record to carry a major-label imprint since the Dickies' *The Incredible Shrinking Dickies*.

One claim that's usually tossed about in regard to Hüsker Dü's Warners deal is that the contract allowed the band one hundred percent creative control. This wildly misleading claim could be the subject of a lengthy examination on its own. There are myriad ways a major label can exert control over a band while perpetuating the claim that the band has complete creative control. There is no clause in a band's contract that says, "You will have one hundred percent creative control during your time on this label." Instead, the contracts typically are filled with countless "luxuries" that the label, in order to retain street cred, then misleadingly presents to the press as "one hundred percent creative control."

For instance, Warner Bros. had the final say in which songs would be released as singles. Also, Warners at first balked when informed that *Candy Apple Grey*'s follow-up would be a double album, but the label gave in for a number of reasons, "one hundred percent creative control" not being among them.

Hart is especially dismissive of the other oft-repeated claim that Hüsker Dü's contract, with its supposed artistic freedoms, became a pioneering model for other bands' transitions to majors: "The idea that our contract was used as a template or influenced how future contracts were negotiated . . . of all the things perpetuated in *Our Band Could Be Your Life*, that is one of the most questionable. Our contract was not a secret and most of the people in our grouping, if you will, knew what we were able to get from Warners. The later signings that ours supposedly influenced, I assure you that those bands would have requested the same things had our signing never happened. If other negotiations echoed what we were previously able to negotiate, well, perhaps by that point labels had gotten used to those types of demands."

Hart continues: "Do you see Sonic Youth signing a contract that says they have to use certain producers as chosen by the label? A lot of it is painfully obvious. Saying that Hüsker Dü negotiated a contract that opened the door for future bands to get signed to majors is like the sail-maker taking credit for what Columbus discovered. Back then, when a major label experimented with a band like Hüsker Dü, it was worth it. Hüsker Dü made money for Warner Bros. in ways that would still surprise us, ways that have nothing to do with record sales. The heightened credibility [for the label] alone."

Hart's reasoning on this point is arguable. After all, if the Hüskers had not proven that a major could be profitable with a true underground band, signings like the Jesus and Mary Chain (*Psychocandy*, 1985), Soul Asylum (*Hang Time*, 1988), the Pixies (*Doolittle*, 1989), Sonic Youth (*Goo*, 1990), fIREHOSE (*Flyin' the Flannel*, 1990), and Screaming Trees (*Uncle Anesthesia*, 1990) might not have occurred when they did, if ever. And when Hüsker Dü broke up in January 1988, Warners needed to fill the void and did so with R.E.M.

"I will say that the Hüskers being on Warners had almost everything to do with R.E.M. being signed," says Panebianco, who goes on to disagree with Hart's dismissal of their Warners contract as a groundbreaker. "The Hüsker relationship with Warners really transformed the idea of who could be signed by a label. When they got signed it was radical. When the Replacements signed, no one was saying 'Oh my god, I can't believe that!' but when the Hüskers signed, you did get reactions. Most of it was positive, but from the people that wanted to keep it as their own . . . that's where the negative commentary came from. The sellout backlash was actually much bigger with R.E.M. and the Replacements than it was with the Hüskers."

Sadly, there's only speculation as to how the Hüskers/Warners relationship would have played out had the band not dissolved at the beginning of 1988. It's important to remember that *Warehouse*'s follow-up would have been the band's eighth album, a point that few bands make it to with integrity intact.

"Let's just say that, at the time of our breakup, we were talking to producers. That's a little unusual for the great, free-thinking Hüsker Dü boys, don't you think?" asks Hart. ǂ

SOME THINGS DO FALL APART

12

Flip Your Wig was the final stop for the Hüsker Dü that fired on all cylinders, and whose members shared an unspoken but mostly agreed-upon sonic and aesthetic vision and could tolerate being in the same room with one another. It was also the last stop for the Hüsker Dü that made records for SST.

After June 1985, the band was no longer evasive about the major-label question during interviews, which were popping up in some high-profile publications. They still honored the requests of home-spun 'zines, while coverage of their first UK jaunt, which consumed almost the entire month of September that year, seemed to be the domain of *Sounds* and *New Musical Express*.

By late '85, Mould, Hart, and Norton found themselves on the receiving end of a new journalistic love affair with the louder, uglier representatives of the American underground. Unlike Americans, the British tend to take their music criticism with a healthy dose of irreverence that can include condescending commentary based on American redneck or suburban slob stereotypes. No *NME* or *Sounds* feature on Hüsker Dü reached the streets without at least one pointed jab about band members' choices in attire, for example. While running the obligatory spotlight on hot new bands, a British fashion magazine called *Blitz* reported, "There is, it has already been noted, absolutely nothing stylish about Minneapolis's HÜSKER DÜ. The only single thing about them that might be remotely considered so lies between the nose and the upper lip of Greg Norton."

But in magazines like the now long-defunct weekly *The Hit*, critics had a hard time finding enough superlatives to convey their feelings about Hüsker Dü's live show. Scribe Dave Henderson, in his review of the September 4 gig at London's Marquee, was no exception:

This was something of an event. The Jams were kicked out, the Ramones were out twanged and the lyrical prowess of everyone from the Byrds to the Beatles to the Monkees and back again was laid bare over a rough hewn web of noise which spiraled straight from the heart. Back in hometown Minneapolis they say everyone hates Hüsker Dü. But, they're only jealous. Sure enough, the sound was messy but the assembled hacks, John Peel and everyone from the long haired herberts to the spikey topped morons, were totally transfixed by this mangled music machine. Caring more for sound, power and down to earth performance than image, custom designed sweaters and tinted scalps, Hüsker Dü jumped several steps ahead. In fact, they jumped so high they pogoed. Hüsker Dü could be the next mega sensation to break from the American invasion. Their new single suggests that it's possible and tonight's performance confirmed that they're more than capable.

In the September 14 issue of the *NME*, on the other hand, writer Matt Snow penned a puzzling review of the same Marquee show, blaming technical problems on Lou Giordano and comparing the Hüskers to the Grateful Dead on the strength of an encore-placed "Reoccurring Dreams":

Hüsker Dü have forsaken the mixing talents of the notorious Spot, and hired Lou to enhance their clarity, vocal-wise. And from what I'm told of the new album, "Flip Yer Wigg" [*sic*] he's done a grand job, but live. . . .

As for the schreck-rock three-part harmonies, they were strained through an old sock, which even took a little edge off the primal screams that customarily greet the finding of the lost chord at the end of those magnificently cathartic choruses.

And as for their genuinely psychedelic rather than merely paisl-eyesque instrumental "Reoccurring Dreams", could it be a "Dark Star" for the '80s? If so, are Hüsker Dü hardcore's Grateful Dead, with all the hit and miss waywardness that implies?

And hark! What is this swimming out of the clenched shrillstorm as if to prove my point? Why, 'tis the very lovely and plangent theme tune from *The Mary Tyler Moore Show*!

Classifying the band as "hit and miss" after two shows and dismissing the final song as a tongue-in-cheek joke while misunderstanding its very real regional context, the review couldn't be any more perfectly British, or any more of a blueprint for the fickleness American underground bands could expect in the UK Bob's "usual symphonic fanfare of roaring harmonics" is framed as if Hüsker Dü had performed secret gigs in this writer's living room during the preceding two years. "The talents of the notorious Spot" were never utilized on the road, though it appears evident that this writer is determined to confuse the ownership of *New Day Rising* with loyal, never-miss-a-gig fandom.

The Hüskers returned from Europe and immediately set about recording *Candy Apple Grey*. Among peers, fans, and press, the cat was nowhere near the bag. This exchange published in an early-1986 issue of *Bucketful of Brains* magazine shows a typically frustrated response to the question repeatedly posed from August to November 1985 (the interview took place in September):

> B.O.B.: On a major label, given the opportunities that entails, what effect will there be on your approach to working?
> B.M.: None. It would give us a little more flexibility as far as taking time to do it; as far as what the end result is, with the labels we're negotiating with part of the deal is that we produce the records ourselves where and when we want and for how long. It's funny, the ones who're really interested do not want the band to change; they like us for the reasons everyone else does.

Mould elaborated in a January 12, 1986, issue of *Jet Lag* magazine:

> JL: Let's talk about your new contract. Why the big delay in signing. There were rumors . . .
> BOB: Basically, the rumor started because we reached an agreement in June of last year and a contract, there's a big gap and people interpreted the agreement as a contract. Fortunately, we didn't, and we waited until December to sign. Actually, Warners approached us around September of 84 when ZEN ARCADE came out.
> GRANT: 83.
> BOB: So we were going to approach them and every . . . you name a label and they called to make me an offer. So, we sat and waited to weed out who was honest and who was dishonest and it seemed pretty obvious that Warners was going to give us complete freedom to do what we wanted, so it's the label we chose.

Joe Carducci remembers how he felt about the band's decision: "In that period I was in regular contact with Bob about what they were doing. Most of the early major-label interest came in the form of requests for the records, beginning, in their case, with *Zen Arcade*. I sent it to someone at Mercury. [Major labels] often felt like they didn't know whether we would resent their interest but we encouraged it. In his case I assured him I respected Mercury because I was into Rush. He then said he thought of Hüsker Dü as the Rush of the 1980s."

Needless to say, tremendous pressure loomed over *Candy Apple's* recording sessions, which stretched from October 1985 to January 1986. For all of the making-albums-for-ourselves disregard of critical opinion, the two principal songwriters were up against a daunting task. The album could neither be a let-down for fans nor a reason for pessimists to issue a resounding "I told you so."

It's difficult to imagine that this was not a time of extreme stress. The band's trajectory had been soaring in one direction; they had made a very serious but logical choice; the competitive nature of the "Hart vs. Mould" songwriting dynamic continued and was perhaps ratcheted up by the Warners signing. All of these factors are often tossed about as reasons for the resulting greatness of the band's output. As Julie Panebianco notes, "That could be the beauty of Hüsker Dü is that those three guys were very different. The same thing that causes problems in a business and creative sense is the thing that sometimes inspired them to be great."

But this was a slippery slope to walk—things could turn real bad real quick.

It's very difficult to find a review of *Candy Apple Grey*, vintage or recent, that doesn't refer to opening track "Crystal" as immediately dispelling sellout worries. But while it is indeed a loud, discordant track with Mould's screaming, "Crystal" lacks propulsion, depth, intensity, sincerity, and anything remotely resembling a hook. Play "Crystal" after any Mould-penned track from side two of *Zen Arcade* and the net effect is that of a Top Fuel dragster giving way to a PT Cruiser with a blown head gasket. The song is paper-thin, but there was just enough going on to deliver the desired message to gullible reviewers.

Track two rights this wrong.

When Warners heard what Hüsker Dü brought to the table for *Candy Apple Grey*, they chose Hart's "Don't Want to Know If You Are

The best 7-inch of the 1980s American underground? If not, certainly close.

With legendary punk rock DJ Oedipus at Boston's WBCN, circa 1984.

© Kathy Chapman/kathychapman.com

■ Basement of Northern Lights
St. Paul, January 1985
The photo shoot wa
later used on the sleeve o
"Makes No Sense at All
© Greg Helgeso.

■ Caricature cover art from the *Lynndale's Burning* bootleg, recorded August 28, 1985, at First Avenue.

■ The band in 1985—and Bob with his ubiquitous American Wrestling Association shirt.
Lisa Haun/Michael Ochs Archives/Getty Images

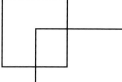

■ Mike LaVella of Pittsburgh hardcore outfit Half Life created this flyer for a show in the Steel City.
Courtesy Mike LaVella/ gearheadmagazine.com

■ "When Grant started to grow his hair out really
bad and started to walk around barefoot everywhere,
people took note of that," says Steve Albini.
© Daniel Corrigan/danielcorrigan.com

■ This flyer for a 1985 Seattle show featured
Hart's World Book Encyclopedia–derived
art from the sleeve of Land Speed Record.
Courtesy Minnesota Historical Society,
gift of Karl H. Mueller

KJET, KCMU & Time Travellers welcome

HÜSKER DÜ

THE DETONATORS

SOUL ASYLUM $7
Advance

Two Shows

Sat. Oct. 26 10PM

■ The Hüskers bed the bunny. *Lisa Haun/Michael Ochs Archives/ Getty Images*

HÜSKER DÜ
DON'T WANT TO KNOW IF YOU ARE LONELY

■ The March 1986 blueprint for a sizeable chunk of the indie- and alt-rock movements that would flip the music business on its ear just five years later.

■ Summer 1986 behind the Rossmor Building in downtown St. Paul where the band rehearsed. © *Daniel Corrigan/ danielcorrigan.com*

■ On the set of the *Warehouse* cover shoot, late 1986. © *Daniel Corrigan/danielcorrigan.com*

■ First Avenue, April 1, 1987. © *Daniel Corrigan/danielcorrigan.com*

■ First Avenue, 1987. © *Daniel Corrigan/danielcorrigan.com*

■ First Avenue,
September 7, 1987.
© *Daniel Corrigan/
danielcorrigan.com*

■ Mould around the release of *Workbook*, May 1989. *Paul Natkin/ WireImage/ Getty Images*

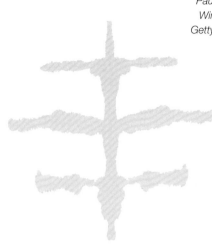

■ Hart in the Nova Mob days, circa 1990.
© *Daniel Corrigan/danielcorrigan.com*

■ Norton as sous-chef at the Table of Contents, St. Paul, early 1990s.
© *Daniel Corrigan/danielcorrigan.com*

Lonely" for the album's first special-release 12-inch treatment. The song equals or surpasses "Makes No Sense at All" as the best-known Hüsker Dü song and, for good reason, was many new fans' introduction to the band. This thrusting underground pop masterpiece stands as the catchiest, best-written song in the band's discography. Unfortunately, the world wasn't quite ready for the song's wall of guitar and unavoidable hook in the riffing, not to mention the hook awaiting listeners in Hart's soaring vocals. The track could easily have been "Smells Like Teen Spirit" five years early if not for the fact that the mainstream's tolerance was still wavering around U2, with a graduation to R.E.M. on the not-so-distant horizon. "Don't Want to Know . . . " distilled Hüsker Dü's pop-rooted repertoire up to that point—from its rawest form with "Everything Falls Apart" to the refined efficiency of "Makes No Sense at All"—and took it to the next level with heightened production values and the still-evolving songwriting aptitude of Hart.

Track three, "I Don't Know For Sure" is Mould's unapologetic rewrite of "Makes No Sense At All." (With source material as strong as "Makes No Sense At All," who can blame Mould for revisiting the track?) It's also Mould's strongest song on *Candy Apple Grey*, something that speaks to a new dynamic in the band.

One way that Warners differed from SST is that the major stood as a decision-influencing/making third party, while SST was little more than a label that let Hüsker Dü do whatever it pleased as a band, especially as perhaps the bestselling band on the label. This made for a major shift in band dynamics, since Hart was no longer subject to the veto process put in place by the previously dominating Mould. It's no mistake, then, that *Candy Apple Grey* featured two singles by Hart and none by Mould. The second of those is the album's fourth track, "Sorry Somehow," pulsing, organ-driven psych-pop with a foot in the future of hook-crazed indie rock.

"I guess it was fair for me to be singled out on *Candy Apple* because Bob had his songs singled out before," Hart says. "How come they changed horses in the middle of the stream with *Warehouse*, which was the beginning of my character starting to be attacked . . . ," he begins, before trailing off. "This sounds paranoid, but it does feel as though it all started right after *Candy Apple*."

Despite the spotlight shifting in Hart's favor, Mould's hand was still heavy enough that when the drummer learned that *Candy Apple*'s second single would be another of his compositions, he worried about the possible ramifications. "To tell you the truth, when I found out that Warners was going to go with 'Sorry Somehow' for the second track, I was not comfortable. I knew the shit was going to hit the fan," Hart remembers. "It was almost as if I was given enough rope to hang myself, but I was allowed to hold the rope. Let's put it this way: When you're dealing with two people and one of those people is Bob, and the other person starts enjoying some good luck, well, that luck is going to change."

Candy Apple's first side concludes with an acoustic gamble that pays off: Mould's "Too Far Down" segues nicely into his beautiful "Hardly Getting Over It," which opens side two and sonically predicts future solo releases.

Similarly, by never raising the intensity level past breezy pop-rock, Hart's "Dead Set on Destruction" predicts his future musical journeys, albeit to a lesser extent. Both this track and the following "Eiffel Tower High," aggressively average in its stylistic Mould-isms, exemplify the main problem with *Candy Apple Grey*: more than half of the album is Hüsker Dü on autopilot. That problem was bound to surface, and most bands can't stall it past their second or third album, much less hold it off until album number six. Hüsker Dü ripping off Hüsker Dü and falling short is better than many of the band's college-rock peers could muster, and in no way is this meant to imply that Hart and Mould had any intention of phoning in a ruling chunk of their major-label debut. It just happened that way.

Hart's entry into the ballad sweepstakes, the intimate and intense piano number "No Promise Have I Made," does well to break the monotony of "Eiffel Tower High" and "Dead Set on Destruction," but the album's closer, "All This I've Done for You," is Mould finally ditching the holding pattern he seems stuck in for much of the record. A solid semi-rager, "All This I've Done for You" hints at what would happen next in the Hüsker Dü discography.

Hart remained in charge of the band's visual presentation after Hüsker Dü signed to Warners. The number of promotional 12-inch EPs that each album required kept him busier than it did when the band was on SST. "My only restriction was what it had always been: I couldn't do anything that all three of us didn't agree on," Hart explains. "And with the promotional 12-inches, I would take my supplies on the road with us and work whenever I could. I never missed a deadline, and some of those deadlines were pretty quick."

SST, like most indies of the day, was not generous with promo releases. Only with their heavy hitters that they were trying to get onto college radio playlists did the label put out any sort of promotional releases. Major labels have a slightly different motive behind promotional titles: Increase exposure for newly signed unknowns (or what the label deems unknown). Majors sometimes issue cassette-only promos containing clips from songs and interviews. Usually, they also release 12-inches containing the focus track (A-side) backed with unreleased tracks or different versions of the A-side. Sometimes called "maxi-singles," these are basically EPs containing up to six unreleased or live tracks in addition to the A-side.

The March 1986 Guide was a cassette-only promo release that featured an interview with Hüsker Dü and excerpts from "Sorry Somehow," "Don't Want to Know If You Are Lonely," "Crystal," "Hardly Getting Over It," "Eiffel Tower High," and "Dead Set on Destruction." Warners also released a promo double 7-inch featuring two versions of "Sorry Somehow" backed by live versions of "Flexible Flyer" and "Celebrated Summer"; a 12-inch maxi-single for "Don't Want to Know If You Are Lonely" that had a live cover of "Helter Skelter" on its B-side; and a no-cover-art promo of the entire album that benefited from a much better mastering job giving it the clarity needed for radio play.

Critical and peer opinion of *Candy Apple Grey*, for the first time since *Land Speed Record*, was more evenly divided between negative and positive, with the latter winning out. A review in *New Musical Express* in May 1986 begins with something less than a ringing endorsement (complete with references to British television probably lost on most American readers): "Typical, bloody typical! Like one of those much-vaunted singing goldfish that mortify their owners by maintaining a dumb, glum silence when their big moment arrives on TV-am or *That's Life*, so Hüsker Dü, having been force-fed to the public by an adoring music press, deliver a first major-label LP that refuses to straightaway scream 'Classic!'"

Reviewer Danny Kelly goes on to assess the mood of *Candy Apple Grey*: "*CAG* also finds the band in disturbed, depressed mood. Apart from the single and Bob Mould's "Makes No Sense" retread, "I Don't Know for Sure," the record is disbelieving, unnerved, bleak and haunted throughout by snapshot shadows (nothing is plain here) of mirrors and hallucinogens—twisters of reality, inducers of doubt."

Conversely, Ralph Traitor, writing in the British weekly *Sounds* (later spun off as *Kerrang!*), can't figure out enough ways to praise the record: "While most American punk and hardcore stalled at the gates of accessibility, the prodigal Hüskers stormed through bullishly. Honing their skills ferociously and jealously guarding their artistic integrity in a display rare since the '80s icons peaked, Hüsker Dü reached their 'Revolver' period in record time."

Traitor continues, "'Candy Apple Grey' represents a watershed for American rock in that it negates popular wisdom about America's music industry and consumer care, bending no rules but its own en route to mass success. Many lesser lights are turning green or going out trying to emulate them, but Hüsker's sound is unique, an organic punk-pop blend."

The April 1986 issue of Andy Warhol's *Interview* magazine ran a section on "hardcore" in which Jack Rabid (editor of the long-running magazine *The Big Takeover*) interviews Mould:

> We may have just signed to Warner Brothers, but there is a difference between the way we do business and the way other groups do, because we choose to do it all ourselves! We're still self-managed, self-produced, self-car-driven, self-booked, self-promoted, and we still handle all arrangements for interviews, photos and other appointments. We don't hire middlemen. . . . And, in particular, we don't hire somebody to give the record company shit; we do it ourselves!

Mould goes on to offer a nice little pearl of wisdom and sign off with a prescient statement: "People want to think they're outside the norm, but in reality everyone is inside this pink balloon. Clusters of radicals are still part of society. All you do is influence the trends of the norms. You can just change where the balloon stands, you can't change what's in it." When Rabid presents the possibility that Hüsker Dü might "collapse with all the overwork, responsibility and basic exhaustion," Mould uncannily states, "Sooner or later it's going to happen. One of these nights it's all going to crack and that might be the end of it."

Neither *Candy Apple Grey*'s sales performance (120,000 units) nor its high of No. 140 on Billboard's Top 200 are things to take lightly. In fact, the album performed up to Warners' expectations on the strengths of "Don't Want to Know . . . " becoming a college radio hit and its video appearing in regular circulation on *120 Minutes*. Helping matters were the facts that the band didn't really lose any of its established fan base (nor temper their live attack), and the album was generally available in many more outlets than the average high-selling SST product.

"This was a time when independent sales were high," says Panebianco. "I remember finding out what Pavement sold at the height of their popularity [in the mid-1990s] and thinking 'Are you kidding me? This is a quarter of what the Hüskers or the Replacements sold.' People would say 'They're huge!' about Pavement. I was shocked. But the second wave of indie rock was a time when a lot of bands were coming out; there was a saturation. Obviously, this wasn't the case with the Hüskers."

Joe Carducci believes that *Candy Apple Grey* was ahead of its time, but not in an entirely progressive sense: "I like the work [SST] bands did with Spot better than anything they did afterwards, so I thought *Flip Your Wig* was soft-sounding, and *Candy Apple Grey* really sounded bad to me. Regular studios, engineers, producers, mastering engineers et cetera, still did not figure out the punk 'voice' until they had to after Nirvana got on the radio. In that sense Hüsker Dü was going to fail. But it's also true that Hüsker Dü was no longer functioning that well as a band by *New Day Rising*. They stopped practicing and started counting on putting the tunes together in the studio in a pop arrangement manner, rather than working them out in practice and live."

Perhaps it's appropriate to give the last word to the man who in many ways has become post-punk's figurehead. "I really like *Candy Apple Grey* but not as much as *Flip Your Wig*, though it seemed like a logical progression," says Mike Watt. "*Candy Apple Grey* in my opinion was not mersh [Watt-speak for "commercial"] or anything diluted 'cos of signing to a major label—not to my ears and mind. I believe that now and believed that then." ‡

YOU CAN GO HOME NOW

13

The notion that signing to Warners exacted no negative impact on Hüsker Dü's creativity was a reality as opposed to the idealistic fantasy it might have been for any other band in the same situation (not that there were any). Logistically, for dedicated fans, friends, repeated bookers, or others with whom the band had established a road rapport over the past several years, the (usually two or more) label handlers who met up with the trio in certain coastal metropolises were just part of the deal, as were the organized manner in which merch was handled and the in-store meet-and-greets sans performances that preceded gigs nowadays—all were harmless aspects of life on a major label compared to what a lot of other bands got themselves talked into. The Hüskers still drove themselves on tour, as they would until the very end. As Greg Norton was prone to exclaim, sometimes unsolicited, in conversations with longtime fans and friends, "I still drive the van!"

But something *had* changed, and it might have seemed easy to lay blame on the band's major-label status. During the second quarter of 1986, longtime fans noticed an obvious change at live shows, and it had nothing to do with the substantially larger crowds: Every song was recognizable (see sidebar, following page). A Hüsker Dü hallmark had long been set lists dominated by as-yet-unreleased material. While this might have been chalked up to Warners' presumed insistence that the band refrain from playing material planned for *Candy Apple Grey*'s follow-up (or the follow-up to the follow-up), the fact was that there was no new material. Unlike almost all of the band's tours before this one, no new material was worked out on the road; no new song ideas, aside from the occasional cover, were introduced during sound checks.

But was this really evidence of a problem? The band had been on the road, more or less, for five and a half years while managing a prolific release schedule that hadn't been seen since the days of the Beatles or the Byrds. If *Candy Apple Grey*, released during the first quarter of 1986, concluded an album cycle that began with *Metal Circus* in October 1983, this alone would have placed Hüsker Dü in a peerless position: one double album, three normal-length albums, an EP that could easily be considered an album (*Metal Circus*), and two landmark singles within three and a half years—and not just any three-and-a-half-year stretch, but one primarily lived on the road.

So, was the culprit creative exhaustion? If so, it would certainly be justified, but other issues played into it as well, issues that, given the aforementioned circumstances, would have plagued any band (not that any band could reach these creative heights or have this sort of influence on contemporaries and audience members who would go on to form bands). In an extensive interview with *Flipside* magazine for an issue that came out in the summer of 1986, Mould explained the plan for the rest of 1986, as well as for *Candy Apple Grey*'s follow-up:

> We have a lot of songs as always. But we haven't gotten together to figure out what we're going to do yet. We're too busy touring. Then we're going to take the summer off and do some work on the next record. Maybe the album will come out early next year. It's really up in the air. We're one of those bands that have lived and died by a timetable for the last five years. I just tore the damned thing off the wall when we started this tour. I said, "This is silly." I looked at it and there wasn't but five days off and I said, "I can't do this anymore." I was not going to kill myself. We're just going to go home and cool out and work on some tunes.

It could be speculated that this act was not entirely personal and that Mould was concerned with the fate of the band. Or maybe he'd had enough nights like the following, recounted by Richard Abowitz in *Gadfly* magazine in 1998 and put on by Abowitz's friend (Chuck) at a dilapidated Elk's Lodge in Philadelphia, February 1986:

> The concert was packed and rumors were running through the audience that local Neo-Nazi skinheads might be showing up to attack. The Warner people traveling with Hüsker Dü were being assholes behind the scenes and Chuck's staff was getting sick of them. When Philadelphia's thrash legends F.O.D. (immortalized in songs by the Dead Milkmen and Green Day) opened the show the Warner's people went ballistic. "We told you not to put a punk band on the bill. We're trying to get them away from that," one said. Another Warner representative tried to confiscate a soundboard tape, which F.O.D. hoped to use for a live album. Soul Asylum, who at the time was derisively referred to as Hüsker Dülite, was on the tour. About halfway through their set the power in the old building went out for an hour.
>
> When Hüsker Dü took the stage the restless crowd surged forward and many broke into wild slam dancing. Then they literally brought the roof down. It started out a drizzle, so slight you're not sure if it's raining: a flake of dust and then a little plaster. Soon, however, chunks of ceiling tile were landing on the band, the audience, and on all the Warner Brothers handlers who were gathered at the bar. Somehow Hüsker Dü made it through the show. They finished with covers of "Ticket to Ride" and "Love Is All Around." . . . The Warner's people told Chuck it would be their last time working with him and it was.

The band took eight months off from playing live, even locally. Mould and Hart, who wrote separately and outside the studio, became so competitive about their respective songwriting presences on the next album that when they finally arrived to record, each had too much material. At some point, Warners (Mould and Hart were communicating with the label separately) was informed that the release would be a double. Because Mould would not allow Hart to have an equal billing, the score was settled at Hart nine, Mould eleven. Remarkably, with much of the album, Hart's songs sound like they could be Mould's, and vice versa.

"Warners did not want to release a double album," Hart recalls. "It was stupid. It was an excuse for Bob to flex his muscle and prove to everyone that 'the contract says we can do whatever we want!' It needed to be a single album."

"Keep in mind that Bob had stopped drinking by this point, and Grant was seeing Ivan, who was a drug user and I know that it was just another barrier between Grant and Bob," Norton explains. "There were a couple of tours, right before the final one, in which Grant and Bob both took separate flights back to Minneapolis and left Lou and I to drive the van across the country."

The wheels had fallen off, but not completely. *Warehouse: Songs and Stories* is the low point of an extraordinary discography (i.e., it's the album that countless lesser bands didn't even have in them to begin with).

The circumstances that drove Grant Hart and Bob Mould apart are not special in any way, except for the fact that this was Hüsker Dü. Somewhere, a band breaks up every five minutes for the exact same reasons. But one uncommon situation that accelerated the breakup was the suicide of David Savoy on the eve of Hüsker Dü's first tour in support of *Warehouse*. "Later on, we found out that, all of his life, David was prone to disappearing for long periods of time, in which he'd live in abandoned warehouses," says Hart. "He had a long history of unstable behavior and depression."

Shock reverberated through the Hüsker camp, and the tour was postponed for a short time, which did nothing to help an already sinking ship. According to Hart, it was Mould's idea to play *Warehouse* from start to finish each night without hitting any of the back catalog. "And that's what we did during the first half of 1987," he says, "because the way it was presented to the band, well, it was obvious that Bob wasn't asking."

"Many of the songwriting people were attracted to Hüsker Dü through Grant's songs and songwriting, and I think that that really put Bob off," remembers Julie Panebianco. "But this type of competition and friction is the kind of thing that makes bands really exciting, then, at a certain point, it becomes bad. Then, when David died, things got really bad."

In the songwriting department, the album is solid and features some of Mould and Hart's catchiest songs. Comparing the album to *Zen Arcade* based solely on its length, however, is ridiculous. The two albums have very little in common. *Warehouse* feels like a Bob Mould solo album fused with a Grant Hart solo album.

Because *Candy Apple Grey* was notable for two singles that both happened to be Hart's, it's perhaps no surprise that Mould pushed hard for control over which *Warehouse* songs would get the same treatment. "*Candy Apple Grey* was Grant's record, but Bob obviously made a serious play for *Warehouse*," says Panebianco.

"It boggles my mind how Warners would have chosen what they chose without some sort of push," Hart says of the decisions behind the *Warehouse* singles. "And it was kept from me. I remember asking Bob which songs were going to be chosen as singles, and he said he didn't know. A couple of days later, I was in the back of the van while Bob and Lou were up front, and they thought I was asleep. I heard Lou ask Bob the same question, and the answer was 'Could You Be the One?' and 'Ice Cold Ice.'"

Plotless live-performance videos were shot for both songs, and despite the fact that neither took off, the band's profile increased steadily, though the members had reached a creative plateau within the band context. Hüsker Dü performed on NBC's *Today Show* when the show spent a week in Minneapolis, and, in a famously awkward appearance, on the *Joan Rivers* show. Also on the promotional front, an entirely different version of *Warehouse* was manufactured as a promo, featuring half of the original song list interspersed with an uncomfortable and one-sided "interview" with the band that finds Mould disagreeing with much of what Hart has to offer. This promo also features Norton's "Everytime," a song that didn't make the album proper but that also showed up as a B-side on the 12-inch version of "Could You Be the One?"

When Hüsker Dü took another break after touring, studio jam sessions failed to produce anything worthy of the follow-up record that Warners was pushing hard to get out of the band.

"I started to get the feeling that neither [Mould nor Hart] were putting forth their best effort when it came to someone else's material," says Norton. "I was starting to write more material at this time, and with Bob stating that Grant would never have more songs then he did [on an album], blah, blah, blah . . . it was pretty bad timing for me."

Because it had worked in the past, the band hit the road again during the second half of 1987 in hopes of rejuvenating some of the collective creative impulses that had served them so well in the past. The stage had become one of the only places that the band still communicated in a harmonious fashion.

"During that last year, not only are we trying to hire new management, but we were under pressure from Warners to use an outside producer, so we're interviewing prospective producers and managers at the same time," continues Norton. "We're trying to write new material, and we were trying to do it on the road. There was a fair amount of frustration on my part and Bob's part, and quite possibly Grant's part, because the material was not coming together like it used to."

It was on this tour that Hüsker Dü revisited its back catalog in an attempt to spark inspiration for new material. "I know that Grant and Bob have said the last year or year and a half of the band was miserable for them, and there were some bad times," says Norton. "David Savoy dying right as we were to leave on the *Warehouse* tour . . . that certainly wasn't positive for anyone in the band. So we're on the road with new management, we're all staying in separate rooms, there's not really any hanging out together, but we played some great shows during that last year. So I wouldn't say that everyone was so goddamned miserable one hundred percent of the time."

In fact, during the band's final year, the stage could be counted on to provide a respite from any negativity for at least an hour or more each night. As Horton recalls:

> The last handful of shows we did, the night we played in Madison, that was a fucking brilliant set." We had a great time. We dug in and pulled out all of these tunes we hadn't played in a while. We even went back to the other set of songs that didn't make it onto *Land Speed Record*, and we were actually discussing taking some of them into the studio for the next record. The next night, we were in Green Bay, and that's the night Grant spilled his Methadone. The next night we're in Champaign-Urbana, and things are okay but a little shaky. Then in St. Louis, Grant had this woman flown in to meet him when we rolled into town. She was pretty distinctive-looking and everyone knew what was up. She was not replacing the Methadone. That night, Grant played his ass off . . . it was a great gig. Then it was the Columbia, Missouri, show at the Blue Note and Grant's so dope-sick he's barely hitting the drums, so that one was cut short. Lou pulled him out of the mix. And that was the last show, ever. Bob called ahead and canceled Omaha.

The question as to who actually quit the band first has been beaten into the ground by band members and the press. The truth is that an event as random and mundane as a flat tire could have led to Hüsker Dü's breakup during the band's last year and a half. *Warehouse* is far from an embarrassment, but given the climate within the band, the next album probably would have been another story. "We had a lot of things leaving our control and becoming the responsibilities of the handlers," Norton explains. "While this should have freed up more time for us, we actually had less time because the band's profile was increasing, so we had interviews, photo sessions, college radio IDs, promo IDs filling up our days, and I think that the pressure and lack of free time from this is what may have contributed to Grant's drug use. We had always said, 'Hey, as long as we're having fun, we're going to keep doing this.' We were still having fun when we were playing live, but everything else wasn't very much fun. It was like a job."

At the time, Hart's long-term boyfriend, who worked at a local screenprinter that manufactured band merchandise, was often regarded by those close to the band as one half of a relationship in which drugs accounted for much of the dynamic. Norton believes that Mould saw the boyfriend as the reason Hart fell into drugs.

"So when we got back to Minneapolis," Norton continues, "the whole thing with the intervention didn't happen. When the band actually did break up, I kind of felt like I was the only one in the band that actually wanted it to stay together. Bob had told me at the time that he was sick and tired of letting Grant control his life, and he had written a letter to have himself removed from the contract. We had a discussion about continuing on without Grant, and then a couple of years later, Grant tells me that Bob approached him about continuing the band without me, so I still, to this day, don't know who to believe."

"Our two confirmed albums had been made, and our contract was being looked at again with one insistence being that we use an outside producer for the next record," says Hart. "Imagine that—the DIY one-hundred-percent control Hüsker Dü having to use an outside producer against the band's will."

Jim Crego, one-third of popular (and loud) Minneapolis mainstays God's Favorite Band recalls the news of the split back home. "I don't think that anyone was that surprised. No one walked around, hanging their heads with armbands on," he says, adding, "nor did anyone say 'Oh, I saw that coming.'"

Crego continues, "I think that a lot of people were thinking that Bob was going to be huge again, and that Grant wouldn't be, mostly because of personality and lifestyle issues."

Chris Benson, one of Crego's mates in God's Favorite Band, down-plays Hart's "lifestyle" issues in the context of the contemporary Twin Cities rock 'n' roll zeitgeist. "At that time, the latter part of the '80s, with the music scene here, the heroin use was just out of control," he says. "There was a whole scene of bands into that. It's not like Grant was the sore thumb sticking out doing heroin. At that point, I'd say seventy percent of the people in the Minneapolis music scene were doing it."

■   ■   ■

"It was really different from what I was used to with bands," Panebianco says, looking back on the band's last days. "It wasn't any-thing overt. It did seem like a bit of a popularity contest. I didn't really think about it until later . . . it wasn't obvious on the outside. I did go on the tour when everything fell apart, though, even then it was only really things like 'This one likes to do this and that one likes to do that,' and that Grant and Bob would go to Karen indi-vidually with concerns, but they never approached us together. They wouldn't even travel to New York together when meeting with the label, but they were two different, highly creative people."

In hindsight, Hüsker Dü's situation was a perfect example of an enigmatic, groundbreaking, and inhumanly prolific block of new music being created for the world, and the world responding with inhuman expectations of the three very human guys who created it. Two band members are no longer on friendly terms? Some dabbling in drug use? No unreleased material being written or performed live? What did the world expect?

In the almost quarter-century since Hüsker Dü's breakup, there has been an incredible amount of musical output that can be traced with confidence to the ground broken by the band between 1980 and 1988. But in an abstract and mostly unwitting fashion, Hüsker Dü has leveled a decidedly counterproductive impact on an altogether different form of expression: music journalism.

Though a few issues among band members have mellowed over the years, energy has shifted to different topics, and Mould, Hart, and Norton still harbor discontents that easily rival, if not surpass, the cloud that hovered over the band six months after the breakup.

After all, very few influential bands remain broken up for more than twenty years, as the past decade's trend toward reunions (many of them wildly dubious) has shown over and over.

Except for the occasional review of a solo Mould album, no piece of posthumous Hüsker Dü–related coverage, long or short, exists in which the writer does not expend an inordinate amount of wordage ensuring that, at the very least, open wounds stay open. Not only do these pieces stretch out for another year or more the cynicism, distaste, confusion, and miscommunication that have plagued the three band members since the bottom fell out in 1988, they usually make things worse. Much worse.

Naturally, the incendiary qualities of the Hüsker Dü story can't be ignored when profiling the band or its members. But dwelling on them until a band member gets upset during an interview? Probing until a band member says things that he will undoubtedly regret once it's too late? Presenting a quote so far outside of the intended context that it basically becomes a fabrication on the writer's part?

"I've read so much about Hüsker Dü that simply was not true," Crego says. "I think what started happening—and I think one of the biggest problems between [Mould and Hart]—is that everything they say to one another is said through various media outlets. They've each said the words, but they haven't said the words to one another."

The problem between Grant Hart and Bob Mould would never have approached the intensity it did had the two not previously experienced an equally strong, if not stronger, bond of a positive nature before things went south. And that was a bond completed by Greg Norton, not by any alleged romantic involvement between Hart and Mould. In the late '70s, being a kid like Greg Norton, Grant Hart, or Bob Mould guaranteed personal conflict, grating loneliness, fear, condescension, disrespect, misunderstanding, and social misfires with prospective friends or lovers. It was not cool. It was not fun. Of course, such adolescent discomfort was by no means unique to these three, but it certainly was symptomatic of the exposure given punk rock and post-punk at the time. Norton, Hart, and Mould's gravitation toward the music and culture was driven by the need to expand their frames of reference to accommodate growing intellects and discriminating tastes in pop culture, and, most importantly, to harness their creative drive. Simply put, it was a personal choice to add "get my ass kicked" to their daily schedules.

Today, Minneapolis/St. Paul effortlessly puts most American cities to shame on any number of levels. The area is an amalgam of artistic tolerance, civic efficiency, "green" progressiveness, and subtle but frequent reminders that it's a place whose residents care for their cities. It's also a sure bet that today no musical culture or genre compares to how punk rock and post-punk felt to intelligent loners in the late '70s and early '80s, and it's laughably obvious that no music today leaves a similar mark on pop culture at large. Today, the teenage or college-aged equivalent of a Norton, Hart, or Mould seems impossible among a peer group that, by and large, often makes creative decisions for an audience of some size. "Hey, that sounds like something I'd like!" has been replaced by "Hey, do the right people like it?" After rifling through seemingly endless used bins and thrift shops and continually experiencing romantic rejection and a lack of common ground with anyone, someone with a passionate interest in punk rock, post-punk, or early industrial music (like Throbbing Gristle) back in the '80s didn't waffle over such details when he or she found a like-minded soul. Strange friendships formed between older folks whose eggs had been thoroughly scrambled by Vietnam and high school– or college-aged music fanatics. The four-hour monologue about listening devices hidden in the cat litter was worth it so long as the conversation drifted toward Pere Ubu.

The "we did it for the band" platitudes can be tossed about until faces turn blue, but the truth remains that it takes an extra-musical commitment to tackle what Greg Norton, Grant Hart, and Bob Mould collectively faced during the first two years of Hüsker Dü. Starting an imprint in the face of Twin/Tone's rejection, practicing every night, getting in a van and playing to five people in a terrifying shithole nine hundred miles from home, living off of a five-dollar per diem, surviving the Children's Crusade tour on speaking terms—these are not achievements accomplished with casual acquaintances. They required something exponentially deeper than mere teamwork. ǂ

REAL REAL WORLD

14

There are at least two good reasons why this chapter doesn't go deep into the post–Hüsker Dü lives of the band members. First, each man's story deserves full-book treatment. Second, this is a book about Hüsker Dü, not a book about Nova Mob or Studebaker collectors (Hart), Sugar or professional wrestling scriptwriting (Mould), or successful chefs or golf enthusiasts (Norton).

After the band's early-1988 demise, Grant Hart was recording new music and playing out live within six months, making the move from drums to guitar (though he provided drums on the 12-inch single released in 1988 by New Alliance band the Yanomamos). Bob made a quick and permanent exit from Minneapolis, returning only when the city popped up on a tour itinerary. Norton was forced to keep a low profile in order to deal with the breakup's financial impact on his life.

In October 1988, Hart rebounded with the *2541* EP, named after the Nicollet Avenue address shared by the band, Twin/Tone, and Nicollet Studios. This three-song affair is carried by the perfect pop of the title track. The lyrics explicitly and nostalgically recall the harmonious days in Hüsker Dü. Hart was playing with a band sometimes known as Toadstool, followed by a handful of gigs as Grant Hart and the Swallows, or just the Swallows. In fact, the Swallows were already together (albeit very loosely) before Hüsker Dü's last gasp. Mould apparently held some animosity about this, and Norton speculates that it may have helped fuel the breakup.

Hart's debut full-length as a solo artist was released on SST in early 1989. *Intolerance* was performed and recorded by Hart alone and has never been deservedly acknowledged for beating the first major home-recording trend ("lo-fi") by four or five years. It's also a fine pop record that definitely silenced an unknown percentage of Hart naysayers. Marshall Crenshaw and Robert Forster of the Go-Betweens both would cover the title track in coming years.

Desiring to lead a proper band, Hart formed Nova Mob in early 1989. Michael Crego remembers getting the offer from Hart to join his new band. "I was about twenty and I thought it was a prank call," Crego says. "I was running a Dairy Queen in the Minneapolis area, and I got a phone call from someone saying they were Grant Hart and asking me to drum for his new band. I said, 'Whoever this is, leave me alone' and hung up, and he called me right back, and said that Tommy Merkl was playing bass. Tommy was a high school friend of mine. I thought, 'Are you out of your mind' as I had a huge case of stage fright at the time.

"I went and practiced with them for a little while," Crego continues, "then there was this Halloween party at this warehouse in downtown Minneapolis, and my brother's band Dragnet played, and Grant decided that he'd take his Hüsker status up on stage, and after a few drinks we played a few songs and trashed about a thousand dollars worth of equipment Who-style, and that's how I ended up in Nova Mob. That was two days after we practiced for the first time."

The band played out for the first time in April 1989. The set list for that show (as well as earlier Toadstool/Swallows dates) is notable for the inclusion of Mould's "Hardly Getting Over It."

Nova Mob's debut album, *The Last Days of Pompeii*, was released by Rough Trade in 1991 on the same day the label declared bankruptcy. This dense, multi-concept song cycle confused the living hell out of critics. As a result, *Last Days . . .* did not attract the same amount of positive attention as *Intolerance*, to say the least.

Minneapolis *Star Tribune* pop music critic Jon Bream recalls one incident in particular. "Grant once came up to me at First Avenue and asked how come I didn't write about him and Nova Mob," Bream begins. "He asked was it 'because I'm a junkie homosexual?' Or maybe a homosexual junkie, I don't remember the exact order. I was rather taken aback by what he said. . . . And I didn't verbally respond. What I really wanted to say was that the last time I'd seen Nova Mob I thought they sucked, especially the guitarist du jour. And I saw no constructive purpose in writing a piece, or even an item, about how and why Nova Mob sucked—because other times they did not suck."

Crego, who also says Hart would never talk to him about Hüsker Dü, recalls one incident, at a *CMJ* Showcase in New York, when Hart apparently did think they sucked. "We were supposed to play for a half hour before the Buzzcocks, and we were looking for a record deal, as were the Buzzcocks," Crego explains, "and two songs in Grant gets pissed off about my playing and he stormed off stage and didn't come back." Stating that Hart questioned his playing not infrequently, Crego turns philosophical: "I put up with it—I mean, I was playing with Grant Hart for Christ sakes. . . . In Hüsker Dü, he wasn't just singing and playing drums at the same time. That wasn't Don Henley doing ballads—that was Grant Hart singing and ripping the head off of it."

While on tour in Europe in the summer of 1992, the band weathered a freak van accident that, along with other factors, instigated the demise of that particular lineup and put things on hold for a while.

Hart exhumed Nova Mob as a four-piece band and recorded a self-titled album for Restless Records in 1994. A much more straightforward affair, this album suffered from promotional and distribution woes that added to the internal strife infecting the band, and everything came apart on tour.

Steve Sutherland, who replaced Crego behind the kit in the reconstituted Nova Mob after answering an ad in *City Pages*, experienced some of the same difficulties as his predecessor. "Being in a band and being on the road can be diffficult even in the best situations," he says, "and being in a band that has two drummers, for me, it was timo to test new waters."

Which is not to say Hart couldn't be warm and generous. "The first time we played together, it went pretty well," Sutherland says, "and then Grant took me into this room that was full of vintage drum sets—he's a collector—and he asked me which set of drums did I want to bring to Europe. So that's how I knew I was in the band."

Sutherland also offers an interesting take on Hart's reception in Europe. "I think that prior to the recording of the self-titled album, the first one I was on, and right after, and during my first two-week tour of Europe, I think the momentum was there, moral was high, it was an exciting time, and Grant was seen by the Europeans as maybe the stronger of the two between Bob and Grant as far as Hüsker Dü was concerned . . . and I think that by his nature, he really fights some of that, so by the time I left, I'd say the morale wasn't necessarily that high."

After the demise of the four-piece Nove Mob, Hart kept up his end of the deal and arrived solo to each booked date, playing intimate, career-spanning sets. One of these gigs featured music from Hart's next solo album, the solid but largely overlooked *Ecce Homo*, released in 1996 on World Service.

As the year 2000 approached, *Good News for Modern Man* (Pachyderm) gave patient Hart fans the record they always claimed the songwriter was capable of. Sounding like every minute of the previous three years was spent buried in meticulous songcrafting and mood-perfecting, *Good News* was easily Hart's best post-Hüsker work to date. In an uncanny display of repeated bad luck, label mismanagement and more distribution nonsense severely injured this album's chances of reaching the larger audience it surely could have won over.

Hart, age forty-nine and a decade removed from the release of *Good News*, managed to surpass that album three times over with *Hot Wax*, released by MVD on CD in late 2009 and on vinyl by MVD/Con D'Or in early 2010. Backed by three core members of Montreal bands Godspeed You! Black Emperor and A Silver Mt. Zion, Hart made what at first feels like an especially charming and solid nod to the breezy psychedelic fare that he's gained so much from in the past, but after one gets to know the record, it reveals itself to be a timeless pop album.

Hart has covered a great deal of ground in support of *Hot Wax*, touring New Zealand, Australia, the UK, Eastern Europe, and the United States (including Norton's Lucky Cat Lounge in Red Wing, Minnesota).

I   I   I

After the band's breakup, Norton made his way up through the nooks and crannies of the restaurant business, working at several area eateries, such as Faegre's, the Minnesota Horse and Hunt Club, Harbor View Café, the Loring, and Table of Contents. During this time, he gained a friend and mentor in a chef named Lenny Russo, the catalyst in Norton's decision to start cooking. "I followed him around to a couple of different restaurants, and he talked me into moving from the front of the house to the back of the house and started teaching me how to cook," Norton told *Magnet* magazine. "I had some natural ability and a good palate, so I dove into that. My only training was just on the job."

In 1995, Norton was offered the chance to facilitate the opening of Staghead in Red Wing, where he would also serve as head chef, a first for the culinary up-and-comer. In 1997, Norton and his wife divorced. He started dating the Staghead sous chef, whom he would wed in 2000. Greg and Sarah Norton left the Staghead in 2003 without a definite strategy for the future and promptly put together plans for their own restaurant. Choosing a hidden location in Bay City, Wisconsin, about five miles outside of Red Wing, the couple opened The Nortons' in October 2003. In an August 2007 interview with *Mpls. St. Paul Magazine*, Norton explains, "After checking out a couple of different spots, we decided [it] was the location we liked, even though it's in the middle of nowhere, we're a mile off the highway and we're in an old pole barn. I think people pull up and say, 'You gotta be kidding me—that place is a great restaurant?'"

Still thriving (not an easy task in the restaurant business), The Nortons' has grown an excellent reputation through the couple's prowess in the kitchen and the former bassist's interest in wine. The restaurant's wine list has won three consecutive awards from *Wine Spectator*. In June 2008, The Nortons' began moving operations from Bay City to the heavily trafficked main drag of Red Wing, changing its name to Norton's Downtown and Lucky Cat Lounge. Nearby, the couple opened the Lucky Cat World Wine Market. (The names are in tribute to the restaurant's two adopted cats, the beloved Stanley and Cooper.) In Red Wing, Norton's expanded to occupy a commercial space that at one time housed a department store. Very quickly, Norton's became a restaurant with more than sixty employees, but instead of it spelling eighty-hour work weeks for the owner and founder, Greg Norton suddenly found himself without many of the duties that ate up his days before the move.

Norton now oversees the entire restaurant while Sarah holds the title of head chef. With a green agenda in mind, the menu items are primarily made from organic ingredients, and the business utilizes recyclable goods whenever possible.

Music has not remained entirely absent in Norton's life. In 1989, he formed Grey Area with Jo Jones on drums and former Northern Lights record-store cohort Colin Mansfield on guitar. Grey Area recorded two albums, neither of which was finished, played frequently in the

Minneapolis/St. Paul area, and toured the Midwest and the South. Nobody seems to remember what the band sounded like. Longtime *Minneapolis Star Tribune* music critic Jon Bream recalls, "Even in Grey Area, sure, he helped spark interest because it was his first post-Hüskers group, but so did Colin Mansfield from Fine Art, another respected band from the Minneapolis scene. Grey Area never got much bigger than the middle act on a three-band bill at the 7th Street Entry." Though Bream saw Grey Area in a live setting, he doesn't have any "vivid recollections." Grey Area broke up in 1991. It would be another fifteen years before Norton would return to making music.

The consummate avant-jazz enthusiast, Norton became a fan of the Bad Plus, a Minneapolis trio featuring drummer extraordinaire Dave King (also of Happy Apple and Halloween, Alaska), who happened to be a former restaurant coworker of Norton's. After a Minneapolis gig by the Bad Plus in 2003, Norton reintroduced himself to King, and the two batted around the idea of playing together. The project came together in 2006 when they formed the clumsily named the Gang Font feat. Interloper, along with Erik Fratzke on guitar and Craig Taborn on keyboards. The band debuted in August at the 7th Street Entry. Progressive jazz label Thirsty Ear took a liking to the band's skronking and in early 2007 released its self-titled debut. The album was recorded in just under twenty-five hours over the previous holiday season. The Gang Font's sound is an abrasive one owing a large debt to the jagged, rock-influenced approach of Ornette Coleman's late-'70s band, Prime Time, and perhaps unsurprisingly, the Minutemen.

As 2009 drew to a close, Norton co-founded a trio called Con Queso with Berndt Evenson on guitar and vocals and Seth Mooney on drums and vocals. Like many bands comprising co-workers, this one started purely as a recreational concern. Still active as this book went to press, Con Queso has toured regionally and opened for the Meat Puppets. Sounding like the Minutemen (but about as loose as the Minutemen were tight), Con Queso's sound also recalls an equally loose version of Ornette Coleman's Prime Time Band and vintage Cream. And they cover Blur.

One thing has remained constant throughout Greg Norton's careers in music and the culinary arts: He still has the head-turning mustache, with its ends styled into careful angles. One can't help but envision Norton twirling a curl as he devises a fiendish crime or revels in the act of tying a helpless woman to a train track.

Hüsker Dü album covers adorn the walls of Norton's restaurant, and a band photo can be seen behind the bar. The Norton's website even has a special "Mr. Norton's Music Page" in which Norton simply writes, "As most of you know, I was in a band called Hüsker Dü, along with Bob Mould and Grant Hart. The band was together from 1979–1988." Norton's may always get more coverage from the music press than from culinary magazines, as Norton has mock-complained, but as Hart puts it, "I really have to take my hat off to him . . . he jumped into a completely different art form and has succeeded. He is to chefs now in the area what Hüsker was to bands twenty years ago."

I　　　　　I　　　　　I

Shortly after Hüsker Dü packed it in, Mould moved to rural Minnesota an hour or so north of the Twin Cities to regroup and work on his first solo album. Bream explains the local reaction to Mould's departure: "Locals are always disappointed when established people leave us. We're kind of provincial that way. But then I think people came to understand. No one really understands the breakup of Hüsker Dü."

Today, according to Bream, "The Minnesota music community seems to have the utmost respect for Bob Mould, even for his lesser projects. He is revered here in both the music community and the gay community."

After woodshedding, literally, his new songs in rural Minnesota, Mould inked a deal with the newly formed American branch of Virgin Records and started looking for a rhythm section, landing one with a couple of interesting resumes. Tony Maimone was an early member of preeminent post-punk band Pere Ubu, playing bass on all of the band's ingenious late-'70s and early-'80s albums. He then worked with They Might Be Giants during the mid- and late '80s. Drummer Anton Fier was a founding member of the Feelies, commanding the kit on that band's 1980 debut, *Crazy Rhythms*, one of the more criminally underrated American post-punk albums. He was also part of the first Lounge Lizards lineup and went on to lead the Golden Palominos. "Bob was originally interested in talking to me about co-producing his record," explains Fier. "That obviously didn't work out. Then he asked me if I wanted to play drums on the record. I said yes. I was a Hüsker Dü fan and Bob was somebody that I was very interested in working with."

The resulting album was *Workbook*, released in 1989 to a favorable response among fans and critics. Mould's sensitive side had been advertised on many Hüsker Dü albums, with a wall of volume in tow. This time, it was accompanied by string arrangements, twelve-string acoustic strumming, and a lush agenda that was assembled like an engine. "See a Little Light" was pleasantly inoffensive jangle pop tailor-made for college radio, where it did well. "Compositions for the Young and Old," "Brasilia Crossed with Trenton," and "Lonely Afternoon" didn't stray far from this formula. The subject of the slightly louder and gloomier "Poison Years" should be obvious. *Workbook* is well-written, introspective college rock that fit the era with ease, but timeless it is not. "I'd say *Workbook* is my favorite of the two [Mould] albums I was on, but only because it was better conceived," says Fier.

While most of the *Workbook* tour saw smaller crowds of three hundred to five hundred fans, with Mould, Maimone, and Fier performing as a trio, a short, two-week promotional tour featured power-pop workhorse and dB's main man Chris Stamey on rhythm guitar.

Mould's days of flirting with the good-natured jangle were limited. *Workbook*'s follow-up, 1990's *Black Sheets of Rain*, was a decidedly angrier, coarse affair, though the album in no way warranted the overblown reaction of critics who were expecting another *Workbook*. In the *All Music Guide to Rock* Stephen Thomas Erlewine called *Black Sheets* a "scalding, monolithic collection of soul-baring lyrics and primal guitars," while David Sprague in *Trouser Press* compared the album to an "overheard session of extremely bellicose primal scream territory." *Black Sheets* is certainly a more exciting listen for diehard Hüsker fans, but the past eighteen years have tamed these songs considerably. The opening title track is seven minutes of paper-thin distortion and plodding riffs built around a serviceable hook. "It's Too Late," which briefly poked its head into the college charts, sounds like Cheap Trick (Mould, in fact, included "Surrender" as an encore on *Workbook* set lists) backing Mould while he plays something too weak to make the *Warehouse* cut.

With Maimone, Fier, and Virgin Records no longer in tow, Mould did a few intimate solo dates in 1991 before cooking up a new plan. Having moved from Tribeca to Brooklyn, he wanted a band again—not hired players, but a tight, harmonious power trio that would appeal to his established fan base while not alienating that new, monstrous demographic whose buying habits were now dictating the industry: the alternative rock audience.

Sonic Youth famously tagged 1991 as "The Year That Punk Broke." A multifaceted comment that had nothing to do with punk rock as a musical style, it was a tongue-in-cheek reference to the unprecedented attention that major labels were giving to the indie underground and anything that even remotely sounded like the indie underground. Long-toiling bands like Sonic Youth and Dinosaur Jr were now on the majors and finally able to make a living playing music (albeit with minor compromises), while godawful hacks and opportunists (e.g., Paw, Candlebox, Collective Soul) were getting signed with little foresight. Of course, most of this was a result of September 24, 1991, the day that Nirvana's *Nevermind* hit stores, an event traceable to Hüsker Dü's major label relationship half a decade earlier.

Mould home-recorded a demo tape of almost thirty songs and started looking for an appropriate rhythm section, which he soon found in Boston music scene stalwart Malcolm Travis and Athens, Georgia, fixture Dave Barbe, who had just retired his own band, the Hüsker-influenced Mercyland. With about ten years on Mould and Barbe, Travis had already hit the kit for underrated post-punk/new wave oddity Human Sexual Response and then the Zulus, a band that fit a little better into the American indie underground of the 1980s. The Zulus' sole album, 1988's *Down on the Floor* (Slash) was produced by Mould.

Sugar's first live show was at Athens' legendary 40 Watt Club on February 20, 1992. In September, the band's debut full-length, *Copper Blue*, was released by Rykodisc in the United States and by Creation Records in the UK They quickly established themselves as a notoriously loud live band. "At that time, standard PA power equip-ment requirements on a band rider was eight watts per projected audience member, eight watts per capacity. Sugar's rider was thirty watts per projected audience member," remembers Barbe. "The thing that made that big swirling, encompassing guitar sound was a big loud amp."

Copper Blue rests in a perfect middle ground between experi-mental indie rock and more traditional alternative rock. It was an advantageous year for an underground legend to release an album like *Copper Blue*. The grunge-hungry climate helped open ears to all things louder, faster, and heavier, though Sugar sounded nothing like Soundgarden, Pearl Jam, or Nirvana. "Helpless" and "If I Can't Change Your Mind," two tracks of inviting, modern power-pop, climbed the college/alternative charts, and their respective videos got mileage outside of MTV's specialty programming like *120 Minutes*. As a result, *Copper Blue* went gold, making Sugar Mould's most commercially successful venture to date. The building, ethereal layers in songs like "Changes" were similar to the beauty-through-noise, shoe-gazer rock of Mould's Creation labelmates Ride and My Bloody Valentine, both of whom undoubtedly spun their fair share of Hüsker Dü albums in younger days. Sugar's success, based on a sound that maintained creative integrity and underground credibility, was a ticket to a wider audience. There is some truth to the common claim that Sugar is what Hüsker Dü would have sounded like had Mould continued with the name but without Norton and Hart.

As for Nirvana, Barbe downplays their impact on Sugar's success: "My memory is that people were just really excited about the fact that Bob Mould was in a new band, that it was a rock and roll three piece. Nirvana selling however many millions of records they did, I'm sure that didn't hurt, but the Sugar appeal and the Nirvana appeal was probably a little bit different."

Copper Blue was followed a year later by the more discordant *Beaster* EP, a sonically colossal song cycle loosely based around a religious concept. "The only problem with *Beaster* is that it was marketed as an EP instead of an album," Barbe says. "People would have taken it more seriously. It's probably as long as *Pet Sounds* or *Revolver*."

Barbe also explains that *Beaster* was not written as a concept EP, but that its six tracks were, in fact, recorded during the same session that produced *Copper Blue*. "JC Auto" and the furious "Tilted" (the most aggressive song Sugar would ever release) found their way into the regular Sugar set, though the entire EP was played live shortly after its release, even the drum-less ambient outro, "Walking Away."

As Sugar became a touring machine with members living in different cities (Mould moved to Austin, Texas, in 1993), the band made do with the U.S. postal system and efficient practice sessions. "We would practice in Athens and use Athens as our springboard before we went out on tour," Barbe continues. "I was married and living in Athens with two small children, and that was not a situation that applied to the other two members. My experience was that Bob had an extremely loyal fan base. There were Hüsker people that grew up and got jobs and got married and had stopped going out to see bands six nights a week, but would go out and see Bob when he came to town."

Sugar's final album was the somewhat disappointing *File Under: Easy Listening* (also known by the silly anagram *FU:EL*). Ironically, its sarcastic title held some truth. *File Under* didn't pack the energy or the songwriting chops that made *Copper Blue* and *Beaster* special, and the band's swansong seemed to suffer from a need to be too eclectic, incorporating faux roots rock ("Believe What You're Saying") and sappiness that should have been saved for a Mould solo album ("Panama City Motel"). *File Under. . .* is rescued by a handful of Mould classics, such as the should-have-been-huge "Gee Angel" and the immensely heavy "Company Man."

Sugar is also notable for what must have been the most amicable breakup of Mould's career. When Barbe put his family before rock, Mould was accommodating.

Sugar's final show was in Japan in the spring of 1995. The band had lasted exactly three years. And it was a band—Mould always found room on each release for two or three of Barbe's compositions. "I remember getting a call from someone at *SPIN* after I was done," Barbe recalls, "and I told them that I was just taking a break, I didn't see the point in announcing it. . . . I was aware that if I said 'We're not playing anymore because I have to be at home with my family' that Bob was going to get five hundred phone calls."

Rykodisc posthumously released the sprawling *Besides* collection in the summer of 1995: seventeen tracks of alternate versions and unreleased songs, including a cover of the Who's "Armenia City in the Sky." The first 25,000 copies of *Besides* came with a second disc documenting a suitably representative live set recorded on November 2, 1994, at an old Hüsker haunt, Minneapolis' First Avenue.

Sugar had a good run and dissolved with all pistons going, something not all bands can claim. "Nobody remembers going to see us with nobody there. Nobody remembers us putting out a weak, disappointing record, or playing a bad show. I think that the short run of the band is something that makes me look back on it in a positive light," concludes Barbe.

Bob Mould is one of those rare ex–punk rockers who have remained prolific into their mid-thirties without releasing a real dud. S ticking with Rykodisc, Mould wasted no time after disbanding Sugar, recording his self-titled third solo album in September and October 1995. He plays every instrument on the album, and even though Mould had publicly expressed adoration for the four-track revolution then taking over indie rock, *Bob Mould* (1996) is no low-fi adventure. Often referred to as the "Hubcap Album" (despite the cover art's greater resemblance to a telephone receiver), some of the songs could be leftovers from the Sugar days, scrapped due to their downbeat, highly personal nature. "Anymore Time Between" is a soaring ballad that lyrically references a grown man (Mould?) crying. "Fort Knox, King Solomon" and "Next Time You Leave" are similarly down numbers that occasionally burst into Mould's signature walls of distorted treble. The call of rock couldn't be ignored, however: "I Hate Alternative Rock" veers close to the genre referenced in its title to express discontent about something that Mould laid the groundwork for. "Egøverride" is another state-ment about an industry Mould so fervently loathed but needed for survival. Indirectly, the album would become Mould's biggest money-maker to date. Written for this album but scrapped, a song called "Dog on Fire" was covered by They Might Be Giants and became the theme to Comedy Central's *The Daily Show*.

Mould's next album, *The Last Dog and Pony Show* (Rykodisc, 1998), was preceded by an announcement that he would cease to play with a full band and essentially abandon rock music alto-gether once the album's support tour had concluded. Mould's time in New York had inspired what would become an ongoing interest in dance music. None of that is immediately apparent on *The Last Dog and Pony Show*, however, aside from a few metronomic tem-pos and an embarrassing foray into novelty hip-hop ("Megamanic") that is hilarious in hindsight. Album opener "New #1" could easily rank among the top five catchiest songs in Mould's solo career, car-ried along by a somber twelve-string riff and a towering signature Mould hook. As one might expect of a farewell to rock, *The Last Dog and Pony Show* features more varied and harder material than its predecessor. Some versions of the album came with a second CD featuring Mould's twenty-four-minute interview with Jack Rabid that subsequently aired on National Public Radio. As he did with *Beaster*, Mould wrote an essay to accompany the album, though it only partially explains his decision to divorce his chosen genre of twenty years:

> I feel this one is more for the general listener, and I came to that conclusion much sooner than I normally would. Last electric band tour—Maybe I should be putting that in gigantic bold flashing neon letters, like LOANS or WE BUY GOLD or something. I've been doing this (electric band touring) for the better part of 19 years, and I'd like to move toward something that doesn't disrupt my attempt at having a life, separate from my career, for chunks of 4 months of time. So, this will be the final time around with an electric band, and then I'll figure out other ways of performing live. Don't know what they are yet.

The more than three-year hiatus from performing and releasing the style of music for which he'd become known coincided with Mould's time in the field of electronic music. This was partially if not entirely born of the socially active lifestyle he began to embrace in the late '90s and which came to fruition in Washington, D.C., during the first five years of the new century. He made an electronic-rock album, *Modulate*, and delegated his even more electronic/techno-based creations to the moniker Loud Bomb (an anagram of Bob Mould) for the *Long-Playing Grooves* album. Both were released simultaneously in early 2002 on Mould's own Granary Music label. His career as a club DJ and party promoter (the Blowoff series of dance parties) was not a fleeting distraction or impulsive career detour. In fact, Mould has found much success with this facet of his career. So that his fans wouldn't forget the guitar rock that had defined his solo career up to this point, a live album, recorded in 1998 during the *Dog and Pony Show* tour, was released as *LiveDog98* on Granary (the label's first CD) in 2002.

The rock 'n' tour lifestyle called, though, leading to a prolific spurt of rock-based albums from 2005 to 2010. Mould brought some electronic concerns with him when he made 2005's *Body of Song* (Yep Roc), but *District Line* and *Life and Times* (both on Anti- and released in 2008 and 2009, respectively) marked a return to the guitar-focused sound that's now synonymous with Mould's solo career. For the two former records, the Bob Mould Band featured Fugazi drummer Brendan Canty, and it was announced that the band's live sets would be much more Hüsker Dü–friendly than previous post-Hüsker outings. Aside from an occasional hit or two ("Makes No Sense at All" or

"Celebrated Summer," for instance), Mould had more or less avoided the Hüsker catalog when playing live. The announcement of this change in policy led to incorrect speculation about a reunion, but it also paved the way for Mould's 2009 All Tomorrow's Parties collaboration with the duo No Age in New York. The two younger musicians backed Mould for a set split between Hüsker and No Age material (and a cover of Dee Dee Ramone's "Chinese Rocks"). In 2010, the Bob Mould Band's limited-edition CD, *Live at ATP 2008*, was released by Mould's latest imprint, BMD.

Peripheral to music-making, Mould co-conceived S.O.L. (Singles Only Label) in the years immediately following the Hüskers' breakup. S.O.L. released 7-inches by Scrawl, Concussion Ensemble, the Shams, William S. Burroughs, Springhouse, and, of course, Sugar. Many of the releases were packaged in quasi-jukebox sleeves and were pressed in limited editions. The label was run and managed on a day-to-day basis by Nick Hill, with Mould and Steve Fallon (then the owner of Hoboken's infamous Maxwell's) providing conceptual and financial guidance.

In 1994, Mould was interviewed by fiction writer and performance artist Dennis Cooper for *SPIN*. The interview would become infamously known as Mould's "public outing" due to Cooper's allegedly unscrupulous handling of certain subject matter. In a March 2010 interview with the film website smellslikescreenspirit.com, Mould commented, "I think [my sexuality] was pretty much an open secret. Yeah people knew. I never really felt like it was an important part of the music. I felt like I'm a musician and this is what I do, these are the stories I tell. My unique perspective was in there, but yeah, in '94 *SPIN* magazine made a big hullaballoo about me being gay, and that was that. Sixteen years later, I look back and laugh about the whole thing. Sort of an uncomfortable public coming out."

During an early-2000s intermission not just from rock music but from music in general, Mould landed work as a scriptwriter for World Championship Wrestling. Though this stint lasted less than a year, it is sometimes an undeserved punch line that often seems to be delivered in a curious if not condescending tone when covered by the press. Worse, it's been alleged that the move was related to Mould's sexual preference. In fact, Mould is a walking encyclopedia when it comes to professional wrestling, a subject for which he has had a lifelong love. Early Hüsker Dü photos show him wearing a sweatshirt bearing the logo of the AWA, a hugely popular Minneapolis-based pro-wrestling circuit from the 1950s through the 1980s. As Mould explained in a 2008 interview with *SPIN*'s Steven Kandell, "I grew up watching wrestling and went to matches at the Montreal Forum. It was huge in the Twin Cities, too. I got to know people in the business, like [former AWA star and future Minnesota governor] Jesse Ventura, and eventually weaseled my way into hanging around it. Once I knew how it worked, I became a real student. I'm a quick learner. I had friends at WCW in Atlanta who used to ask me for ideas, and in the fall of '99, they asked me to take a job." If anything, the brief career deviation was an example of a creatively restless person following what probably seemed (to Mould, at least) like a perfect fit at the time.

Another non-music gig ensued on April 5, 2007, when *Washington City Paper* debuted the "Ask Bob Mould" column in the opening spread of the arts section. It was exactly what the title suggests. Arts editor and diehard Hüsker Dü/Sugar fan Mark Athitakis explains:

> Bob and I agreed that the column shouldn't be a "quiz Bob about the Hüsker Dü/Sugar days" kind of thing, and there were some questions like that. But most of them weren't. Thing is, in some ways Bob became a victim of his own humility—he never pretended to be a sage expert on anything, so there's no natural impetus to pepper him with questions that aren't about himself. So over time the column tended to stick to "Bob themes": music, wrestling/athletes, homosexuality. Which was fine, but the fun weeks were the ones where he'd tackle stuff like grilling or whether the moon landings were faked. My favorite ones were the ones where he let loose a little, being sort of willfully arch about [Guns N' Roses' long-delayed] *Chinese Democracy* and stuff like that. I wish more questions like that came in, because those were the ones he clearly enjoyed doing the most. I should add that Bob was never a difficult edit. He's an articulate guy who knows what he wants to say and was good with hitting deadlines.

Each week, Mould's answers were reliably heartfelt, concise, and, as Athitakis implies, sometimes quite humorous:

> I have always wanted to ask you about what it is like to become famous without seeking it. How did you deal with that when you were younger,

and what would you recommend to talented artists finding themselves in an awkwardly "famous" spot?

—Michael King, New Jersey

[Mould] You are the company you keep. I have noticed, during busy or high-water periods in my career, that I am approached by people who may be interested in associating with me; to what end, sometimes I can't discern. Usually, we share nothing of interest or value. It's good to remember who your true friends are and to try not to let notoriety or fleeting success interfere with those friendships. There is a big difference between friends and sycophants.

As the summer of 2008 came to a close, Mould issued a press release stating that he had begun work on his autobiography, to be written with the help of Michael Azerrad (*Our Band Could Be Your Life*). One year later, for an interview with *The Big Takeover* magazine, Mould mapped out the dynamics as they were at that point:

Michael is directing traffic. That's the term that I would use. I'm doing all of the writing and sending chapters off to Michael and he's doing old-school line-editing as well. He's cleaning up grammar, which I'm usually pretty good at, but sometimes it's better to have someone else look at it and find a quicker way to say something. I'm definitely doing the writing, the lifting. It's coming along pretty well. There are two different levels I'm writing at right now. One is purely chronological with all of my notes and thoughts and that's up through *Beaster* right now, so I've got to pick up the pace. In addition to that, I'm doing the full writing and that's up to just signing with Warners in 1985. So the short writing is up to '93 and the real writing is up to '85.

When asked if he found it harder to write a book about himself than it was to write autobiographical songs, he replied, "It's much harder than writing songs. That's why Michael is that other voice who can go 'what are you really trying to say here?' It's good to have someone say 'I don't understand what you're talking about here' because I'm too close to it. With autobiographies, I don't know if they're easy or harder to write in general, but it's hard for me. You write it once and maybe you start writing memoirs."

In March 2010, Mould spoke to smellslikescreenspirit.com about his appearance in *Bear Nation*, a documentary about the bear subculture within the gay community, and in the process provided a nice wide-angle look at his life during the past decade:

> It was sort of a happy accident. I moved from New York City to Washington, D.C., in the summer of '02, and started DJ'ing in D.C. in early 2003. I started up a party with a friend of mine, and the party [was] called Blowoff. As time went on and I started meeting people and getting out, I started seeing this trend of people who were really heavily into newer music and sort of edgier music, and everybody was more masculine and sort of furry and not so body-conscious, and I was like, I heard about this "bear" thing, but is this what it is? I guess my entry point was about six years ago, coming to understand the bear culture and getting embraced by it a little bit. It's really funny, because it's just sort of a natural fit for me. And as time went on and Blowoff became more of a thing, and we started going to other cities and gathering sort of a bear following, then all the music guys started coming out of the woodwork, and all these guys in their thirties and forties would come up to me when I was on break when I was DJ'ing and say, "I saw Sugar at the International Ballroom in Atlanta in '93," and I was like, what? I didn't know you people were out there in the audience back then. So it's this sort of crazy full-circle thing that I didn't see coming. ⚌

DÜ HÜSKERS: THE LEGACY

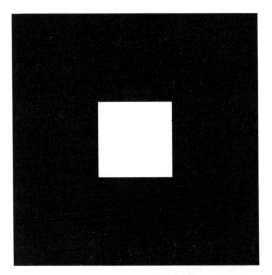

Epilogue

At different times in the '90s, Hüsker Dü was referenced as an influence by anybody that wanted to have a pedigree. I don't mean that immodestly, but if you wanted to be cool, you dropped the name Hüsker Dü in 1995 or whatever.

—Grant Hart

When it comes to their influence on underground music, Hüsker Dü's first and most overlooked legacy is their role in helping create the hardcore genre. The trio's velocity and volume left a major mark on audiences and the bands with which they shared stages. If Hüsker Dü was not the fastest hardcore band in the country at the time, they were certainly one of a handful. In terms of volume, the competition shrinks even more. It could be argued that the Hüskers were merely paying forward the influence that bands like Discharge, the Fartz, and, initially, the Dickies, had on *them* if not for the fact that Hüsker Dü were *the* DIY pioneers of the Midwest.

There's an almost unanimous ignorance about Hüsker Dü as the entity responsible for laying the lion's share of DIY groundwork across the upper Midwest through their touring, running Reflex Records, and offering reciprocity to the increasing number of contemporary bands from nearby cities that toured through Minneapolis. If Black Flag provided the spark—the reassurance that, yes, you too could "get in the van" if you really wanted to—the Hüskers kept the resultant flames fanned in the northern tier during hardcore's 1981–1982 heyday. A considerable amount of this credit is due to the "weekenders" that Mould repeatedly booked beginning in the winter and spring of 1981, before the cross-country Children's Crusade tour and in the time between that tour and the next nationwide excursion booked around the recording of *Everything Falls Apart* in mid-1982.

Hüsker Dü built themselves into a reliable, decent draw in Chicago before any other city, it being the site of their first out-of-town gig in March 1981. At the time, Chicago was nurturing its own soon-to-be legendary hardcore scene with the Effigies, Naked Raygun, Articles of Faith, and, for a short time, Strike Under. These bands became quick friends and colleagues of the Hüskers because of Mould's hospitality when these bands passed through Minneapolis. For a time, Mould was second only to First Avenue and 7th Street Entry's Steve McClellan as the go-to guy for a gig and a floor to crash on. "They sort of wrote the template for how to get people to recognize you," remembers Santiago Durango, who was then the guitarist for Naked Raygun and would go on to much more underground acclaim, filling the same slot in Steve Albini's seminal Big Black before moving into his eventual career as a rather high-profile music lawyer (he won the Cynthia Plaster Caster case, helping the famous groupie recover her bronze casts of Jimi Hendrix's genitalia as well as those of other rock stars). "The constant touring, the constant recording, and the putting out of the vinyl—up until that time, bands weren't doing it for themselves. Hüsker Dü sort of showed everybody how to do it. They carved out a road for everyone else."

Although the Hüskers didn't confine their DIY ethos to the Minneapolis city limits, there's really no way to express how important the band was to the explosion of underground talent that the Twin Cities would export in the late '80s and early '90s. "I admired Hüsker Dü from the very beginning because they had a great DIY ambition about them," recalls Twin/Tone cofounder and former Replacements manager Peter Jesperson. "And despite whatever feelings Westerberg or the rest of the Replacements had, I think they also admired the fact that Hüsker Dü were able to put one foot in front of the other and make things happen."

I   I   I

Hüsker Dü wasn't a genuine hardcore band for very long, especially compared to some of its contemporaries. (The band's friends in D.O.A., for example, continue to create music that's at least audibly similar to their first hardcore blasts of energy three decades ago.) The difference between *Land Speed Record* and *Flip Your Wig*—that is to say, the difference between 1982 and 1985—is akin to the difference between Lou Reed's *Metal Machine Music* and the soothing sounds of Mannheim Steamroller, which is precisely why Hüsker Dü's major contribution to the underground, indie rock, and then alternative music can be traced back to the period when *Flip Your Wig* dominated the underground scene. This was also the period when the Hüsker Dü influence began to spread courtesy of musicians who were not named Bob, Greg, or Grant.

By the time their third or fourth album came out, the great majority of early hardcore bands were something else entirely, so the Hüskers were not unique in that respect. It's just that the vast majority of these sonic shape-shifters became crossover thrash-metal or pop-punk bands. In the latter case, bands usually proudly referred to themselves as "hardcore" throughout their entire careers. This pride in hardcore roots didn't become common until New York City became the epicenter of the genre, which was, counter to typical fashion, after the first wave had played itself out everywhere else. When Hüsker Dü was playing hardcore that one could be proud of, the term was not yet common; in fact, if uttered among practitioners, it was usually done so in a derogatory fashion.

Essentially, two other hardcore bands in addition to Hüsker Dü incorporated pop melodies, and in doing so, both inadvertently created a separate and still-active genre of underground guitar rock. The Descendents and Bad Religion used melody in different ways, but their efforts spawned what is known as the "South Bay sound" or "SoCal pop punk." In fact, it's what Bad Religion's label, Epitaph, built much of its name on. The Offspring is a good example of the influence being picked up to successful ends by a second-generation band.

It's debatable whether the Descendents were influenced by Hüsker Dü or if they followed their own creative path. Regardless, the former's *I Don't Want to Grow Up* (1985) is an essential example of a former hardcore band mastering the wonders of pop, as well as the barometer by which credible pop-punk is measured to this day. By the time of this release, Hüsker Dü was leaving a massive wake behind their pop-core hybrid, but it is plausible that the Descendents' 1982 debut long-player, the stone-cold classic *Milo Goes to College*, informed the Hüskers' turn toward pop. *Milo* immediately predated the recording of *Everything Falls Apart*, and while the Descendents rocked looser, goofier lyrical themes, they can especially be heard in the title track to the Hüsker release in question.

As for his band's influence, the Descendents' Bill Stevenson is customarily dismissive and self-deprecating when asked. "We were fifteen and really did not know much about how to play music, so we just did what we could do," he says. "The biggest influence on the Descendents was a band called the Last, who were from our hometown, Hermosa Beach, and who went to our same high school. The Last were doing what I guess at the time was considered 'powerpop,' but there was nothing like it anywhere, and has never been anything like it since. The Last is how you get from the Kinks to the Descendents. Songs by the Last were the blueprints of the South Bay pop punk sound. The Descendents got the credit for it, but the Last did it."

Hüsker Dü's own precursor, but certainly not their sole melodic influence, was Mission of Burma. One can hear strains of future indie rock in the Boston band's sound. But in songs like Hüsker Dü's "Chartered Trips," "First of the Last Calls," "It's Not Funny Anymore," "If I Told You," "Private Plane," "Green Eyes," "Don't Want to Know If You Are Lonely," and many more, listeners need not strain to hear the future of underground guitar rock lurking right around the corner.

As 1985 turned into 1986, the Hüskers' influence had rippled across the country and played a hand in the sonic shift that was taking place in the underground. After processing the one-two punch of *Metal Circus* and *Zen Arcade* (released October 1983 and summer of 1984, respectively), plus witnessing one or more live show by the trio, many existing bands made a Hüsker-informed shift in their sound while many new bands formed with *Metal Circus*, *Zen Arcade*, or even *New Day Rising* fresh on their brains. By the release of *Flip Your Wig* in August/September 1985, there were already other records and bands that sounded like Hüsker Dü. Of course, all credit shouldn't go to the Hüskers; they were part of a small handful of bands that either informed an overall melodic detour in more discordant music or influenced new artists to layer noise over hooks, still a fresh concept in 1985. Other established or already broken-up bands that had tread this path included the Descendents, Bad Religion, Mission of Burma, Naked Raygun, the Wipers, the Embarrassment, early Dream Syndicate, and the Meat Puppets.

The first obvious example should come as no surprise. Soul Asylum was not afraid to put the occasional Hüsker nod, or flatout interpretation, on any of their early albums, beginning with *Say What You Will, Clarence . . . Karl Sold the Truck*, or even on the band's first hit, 1992's "Somebody to Shove." But by 1992, Soul Asylum sounded like a lot of bands (or vice versa). Soul Asylum also had the obvious Minneapolis connection and Mould even produced the band's first two LPs as well as the odds 'n' sods collection, *Time's*

Incinerator. When Louisville's Squirrel Bait released their self-titled debut in 1985, they became one of the first—if not *the* first—non-Minneapolis group to be compared to Hüsker Dü. Along with Squirrel Bait's first album, several other debuts of 1985 and 1986 displayed an undeniable Hüsker Dü influence, so much so that a few could be regarded as blatant copycats. This is not meant as a derogatory statement. After all, there was no better band to emulate at the moment, and the phenomenon itself says volumes about the power and appeal that Hüsker Dü's music amassed in a short period of time.

Outside of the Midwest underground communities, Hüsker Dü may have left their biggest real-time creative footprint on the Boston scene. They had played Boston and the surrounding area numerous times since April 1983, and resident board-jockeys Lou Giordano and Josiah McElheny had become the band's traveling tag team of sound-men. The Brookline-bred quartet Sorry remains sorely overlooked in Boston's fertile punk rock/hardcore/post-hardcore scene of the early to mid-1980s. Like Squirrel Bait, the band released just two albums and benefited greatly from an association with Gerard Cosloy, whose legendary *Bands That Could Be God* compilation begins with the Sorry single "My Word." Sorry's 1984 full-length debut, *Imaginary Friend* (Radiobeat), draws on the Minutemen, Mission of Burma, Hüsker Dü, and fellow Boston band the Proletariat. With its increased tunefulness, Sorry's second full-length, *The Way It Was*, displays a night-and-day difference from its predecessor, a change similar to Squirrel Bait's shift toward more melodic and anthemic tunes with that band's second release, *Skag Heaven* (1986). Members of Sorry would go on to join the post–Mission of Burma outfit Volcano Suns, where Hüsker Dü-isms were less frequent but occasionally noticeable.

Moving Targets, who released their brilliant debut, *Burning in Water* (Taang!!), in 1986, had spent several years honing their melodic amalgam of hardcore and Mission of Burma and Hüsker Dü influences. Like their Boston neighbors, Sorry, with whom they share a gross lack of posthumous attention, Moving Targets' introduction to a wider audience also came via *Bands That Could Be God*. The trio's two follow-up LPs do not display a major drop in quality, but *Burning in Water* stands as Moving Targets' only through-and-through classic.

Also in Boston, Salem 66 was an all-female trio formed in 1982, a fairly uncommon situation in the American underground of the time. Rather than adding melodic elements to a hardcore blueprint,

Salem 66 presented a darker, noisier take on the college-rock jangle aesthetic pioneered by R.E.M. Nonetheless, Hüsker Dü was a very big reason that a middle ground existed for this to occur because the band's influence helped add teeth to the otherwise gentle and overtly quirky nature of college rock. (If anything, Hüsker Dü was thankfully averse to quirkiness, an underground rock byproduct that Hart can spend hours hilariously bemoaning.) Salem 66 released two excellent albums, *A Ripping Spin* (1985) and *Frequency and Urgency* (1986), in which the punch of garage rock and pop-savvy Hüsker Dü moments mingle with more accessible, folk-tinged college rock, not unlike what the Hüskers would dabble in on *Candy Apple Grey*.

Also out of Massachusetts, Dumptruck might have been nothing more than a third-rate R.E.M. had they not turned an ear toward the more sonically adventurous efforts of Hüsker Dü, the Embarrassment, the Feelies, Mission of Burma, and the Minutemen. Their 1983 debut, *D is for Dumptruck*, is a brooding masterpiece of art-damaged punk jangle as essential as any album carrying the SST logo from the same year.

In western Massachusetts, the teenage J Mascis and Lou Barlow outgrew their pummeling hardcore band Deep Wound, cobbled together all of their sonic interests (which were not limited to hardcore or even indie rock), enlisted drummer Emmett "Murph" Murphy, and recorded a self-titled debut album under the name Dinosaur (the band later added "Jr" for legal reasons). Told by Gerard Cosloy that Homestead would release whatever the band submitted, the 1985 album is a fascinating love letter to everyone from the Cure to Neil Young to, yes, Hüsker Dü. The band's sophomore effort in 1987, *You're Living All Over Me* (SST), is much more singular, but Mould's playing left a definite mark on Mascis as the latter developed into an underground guitar god in his own right.

Following in the shadow of Dinosaur Jr but with more of an emphasis on pop punk was Boston's Lemonheads, whose first five full-lengths (from 1987's *Hate Your Friends* to 1992's, *It's a Shame About Ray*) map a move from melodic but sometimes harsh post-hardcore to polished fuzz-pop and never fail to reference some point in the Hüsker Dü discography.

Finally, when looking to Boston, mention must be made of the Pixies' debt to Hüsker Dü. Partially (and famously) coming together in 1986 around a classified ad seeking musicians who were "into Hüsker Dü and Peter, Paul, and Mary," the Pixies would go on to give repeated,

234

if not more abstract, nods to the Hüskers as they picked up the alt-rock torch and laid further groundwork for Nirvana and Sonic Youth.

Down in D.C., not even Ian MacKaye's staunchly insular Dischord camp could avoid the innovations leveled against hardcore by Hüsker Dü. Both Dag Nasty and the short-lived but legendary Rites of Spring echoed a not-dissimilar pop-meets-hardcore approach. Minor Threat had released the *Salad Days* EP, their swansong, in mid-'85, another example of a new era dawning all over the national underground scene as a whole.

Back home, the Hüsker Dü influence carried on by bands such as Soul Asylum and Arcwelder, both of whom wore the Hüsker sound on their sleeves, especially the latter. As Tilt-A-Whirl (before the carnival-ride manufacturer threatened a lawsuit), Arcwelder released a lost classic with their 1990 debut, *This*, the perfect meld of Hüsker Dü influences and the emerging aggro-rock genre that would find a home on Tom Hazelmyer's Amphetamine Reptile label. After a second strong album, *Jacket Made in Canada*, Arcwelder was picked up by Touch & Go and released four albums over the next decade, all featuring a pronounced Hüsker Dü influence (especially thanks to singer/drummer Scott McDonald's pronounced Mould-like vocals).

The indie rock explosion of the early '90s and its big brother, the alternative-rock movement, saw repeated nods to Hüsker Dü. "Taking inspiration from Hüsker Dü/We're a new generation of electric, white-boy blues," Lou Barlow sang sardonically on Sebadoh's single "Gimme Indie Rock." After Mascis ejected Barlow from Dinosaur Jr, the latter made a full-time endeavor out of Sebadoh, and Hüsker Dü was a constant sonic touchstone. Dave Grohl's post-Nirvana success story, the Foo Fighters, have brilliantly and repeatedly assimilated Hart's "Don't Want to Know If You Are Lonely" into many of their best (and biggest) moments. Superchunk, the venerable Chapel Hill, North Carolina, band that basically defined straight-up indie rock before growing Merge Records into one of the most respected independent labels in the country, owed a considerable amount of its sound to mid-period Hüsker Dü.

The list goes on, proving one indisputable fact: There are not too many degrees of sonic separation between the Hüsker Dü sound and much of 1990s indie rock, not to mention whatever flashes of integrity appeared in the alt-rock sweepstakes of the same decade (Foo Fighters, Catherine Wheel, Smashing Pumpkins, Nirvana, etc.) or the emo movement of the last decade.

As Hazelmyer sums up, "In a nutshell, the rulebook hadn't been written yet, and the Hüskers weren't unique in that they took the basic premise in a new and different direction. What was unique about the Hüskers was that there was huge songwriting talent buried in an initial blast of noise and speed, that over time crept to the fore, while never completely shedding that urgency that first launched them."

I   I   I

Interesting or unpredictable instances of praise say volumes about a band's legacy. On VH1's *100 Greatest Hard Rock Artists*, Hüsker Dü ranked number sixty-eight, ahead of Megadeth and behind the Rolling Stones. Not bad considering the breadth of competition and intended mainstream audience. But Kirk Hammett's appearance on screen as the talking head praising the Hüskers during their two-minute overview proved a vital truth: Hüsker Dü's music transcends the hardcore, punk, indie, and alternative ghettos, commanding respect from a wider variety of mindsets and holding its own in a class of high-quality "heavy music" for which genre and aesthetic boundaries have little to no bearing. This is a loose royalty in the grand scope of rock that includes but is not limited to Led Zeppelin, Slayer, Black Sabbath, Black Flag, Sonic Youth, Queens of the Stone Age, and Hammett's own band, Metallica.

But perhaps the ultimate testaments to Hüsker Dü's influence are the history, scope, and sheer number of Hüsker Dü covers that have been recorded as well as notable tributes and references to the band in song. Taken as a whole, the list resonates deeper than any surprising or high-profile endorsement, written or broadcast piece of journalism, or sonic similarity found in the discographies of bands from the past quarter-century.

Opinions differ on the sentiment behind the Replacements' "Somethin' to Dü," though it's easy to see how it could be read as a comment—positive, negative, or indifferent—on how seriously Hüsker Dü, with Mould as the obvious target (i.e., Westerberg's last-line wordplay, "Breaking the Mould"), took their craft. If the Hüskers' drive and determination were commanding the attention or raising the ire of local bands at such an early stage in the trio's development (1981), the song is certainly a positive comment.

There are no known mentions of Hüsker Dü in another artist's work between "Somethin' to Dü" in 1981 and the Dead Milkmen's "The Thing That Only Eats Hippies," released in 1986. As its title suggests, the song relates the story of a beast created to consume hippies and admonishes, "So, Bob and Greg and Grant you should beware." Presumably the song's subject matter riffs on the title of the album from which it came, *Eat Your Paisley*, which, in turn, is presumably a reference to L.A.'s Paisley Underground movement. Perhaps the lyric is a reference to the Hüskers' move away from their hardcore roots. Even so, the sentiment is misguided, given the dismissal of the Paisley Underground heard in Mould's monumental treatment of the Byrds' "Eight Miles High" and read in a handful of 'zine interviews of the era.

At the height of his popularity, nattily attired singer Robert Palmer was known to perform thirty seconds or so of "New Day Rising" as part of an encore medley. Neither Hart nor Norton has heard any recordings of these performances, but Paul Hilcoff's tremendous online Hüsker Dü database (thirdav.com) cites the Robert Palmer *Superstar Concert Series* triple-LP from Westwood One Radio Networks as including a recording of the medley performance from 1987; other sources indicate that a Palmer cover of "New Day Rising" was featured on a Westwood One radio broadcast of a San Diego concert recorded in July 1986.

The first band to record a Hüsker Dü cover in a studio for the intention of commercial release was possibly fellow Minneapolis act the Blue Hippos, a band formed when Otto's Chemical Lounge dissolved. With Terry Katzman as producer, the group recorded a version of "Drug Party" for their self-titled 1987 debut on Twin/Tone records.

Not surprisingly, the number of commercially released Hüsker Dü cover versions gradually increased with recognition of the band's influence. The year 1988 saw the commercial release of two covers, while four were released in 1989. Only one reached the public in 1990, then four popped up in 1991, and five in 1992. Most were done by very obscure bands, with Coffin Break, Mega City Four, Big Dipper, Drunken Boat, and the almost-huge shoegazers Catherine Wheel being the best known, relatively speaking. Many of the unmentioned bands were from Europe, where appreciation for Hüsker Dü always ran a little deeper than it did in the States. One of the first covers released after the Hüskers' demise was by the German band the Strangemen, which included a version of "Diane" on a covers album. "Diane" and "Don't Want to Know If You Are Lonely" would go on to be the most covered Hüsker Dü songs.

In 1993, due in no small part to the popularity of Sugar, the Hüsker Dü cover floodgates opened.

Minneapolis alt-rockers Trip Shakespeare, featuring future Semisonic front man and Grammy-winning songwriter Dan Wilson, included their version of "Dead Set on Destruction" on their covers-only *Volt* album. The same year, the Minneapolis underground banded together to provide a song-by-song tribute to *Zen Arcade* entitled *Dü Hüskers: The Twin Cities Replay Zen Arcade*. The seventy-seven-minute release featured some brilliant contributions, several of which were turned in by members of the then-flourishing Amphetamine Reptile stable: Hammerhead contributed a hair-raising take on "Something I Learned Today," Vertigo tackled "Masochism World," Teenage Larvae (an AmRep supergroup of sorts) giggled their way through "The Tooth Fairy and the Princess," and Janitor Joe did "What's Going On." The likeminded Arcwelder and Muskel-lunge knocked out "Whatever" and "Chartered Trips," respectively, while indie psych-pop rockers Walt Mink offered up a brisk version of "Somewhere." God's Favorite Band, the Hang-Ups, ZuZu's Petals, Flour, and the Mighty Mofos, among many other Twin Cities stalwarts, also checked in.

The Hang-Ups and Vertigo released a split 7-inch of their respective *Dü Hüskers* covers; the former, often cited for a penchant for catchy melodies (strange bedfellows with Vertigo), turned in "Eight Miles High," making for a nice spoof of the original SST 7-inch. The sleeve is the same as the SST release but with the less-than-subtle addition of a superimposed jet engine sucking up seagulls.

On the hyper-obscure but no-less-interesting side of things, New Jersey home-recorder Apollo DeLucia, recording as Apple-O, covered *Land Speed Record* in its entirety and released it as "bonus" material on his *Search for Terrestrial Intelligence* cassette in 1993. The covered album stretches to twice the length of the original because Apple-O favored the quant lo-fi pop of most bedroom artists of the early '90s and even included polka and reggae versions of *Land Speed* tracks.

In 1994, Bay Area "homocore" pop-punk band Pansy Division covered "The Biggest Lie" for their hilarious *The Nine Inch Male*s EP, released on Lookout! Records. That was followed the same year by a second Hüsker Dü tribute album, *Case Closed? An International Compilation of Hüsker Dü Cover-Songs*, on Germany's Snoop Records.

Again, most of the artists featured have been somewhat lost to obscurity, but the most notable contributors include Sick of It All ("Target"), Motorpsycho ("New Day Rising"), Big Drill Car ("Celebrated Summer"), D.I. ("The Biggest Lie"), Gigantor ("Green Eyes"), Balance ("Makes No Sense at All"), Alloy ("Out on a Limb"), and Only Living Witness ("Hardly Getting Over It"). The latter, who also subsequently released the same version of "Hardly Getting Over It" on their sole full-length for Century Media, proved, along with Sick of It All and a few of the other bands mentioned, that Hüsker Dü had made a particular mark on the underground metal/hardcore community.

Case Closed? was put together to benefit the awareness of rainforest depletion, though exactly how is unknown. Grant Hart does contribute a liner-note blurb, though it clearly voices his own frustrations with the Hüsker Dü copyright and royalties situation in 1994:

> I have stared at this blank page a while now. I want to tell you how the "tribute" album makes me feel. I want to tell it in a way that re-affirms my worthiness of such a tribute, but I find it impossible to do so. If I were writing a song, this would be a good place for the guitar solo. It came as a disappointment to hear about the limits placed upon bands covering other people's songs. As far as I can tell, these laws that protect songwriters have made it impossible for musicians to interpret existing songs freely.

The initial sign that the first-wave thrash-metal legends of Anthrax were unapologetic Hüsker Dü fans came in late 1994, when a bootlegged live performance by the one-off tribute band Dü Hüskers (no link to the aforementioned Minneapolis tribute) began circulating the underground. The band consisted of musician/actor Zach Throne on guitar/vocals, Jimmy Ilario on bass, and Anthrax drummer Charlie Benante. The set covered Hüsker Dü's entire career with an emphasis on later material, and with Anthrax guitarist and spokesperson Scott Ian doing guest vocals on "Punch Drunk."

The third known Hüsker Dü tribute compilation is the *There's a Boy Who Lives on Heaven Hill* EP, released in late 1994 on the Burning Heart label from Sweden. The CD features "Pink Turns to Blue" (Sator), "Back from Somewhere" (Merryland), "Visionary" (Popsicle), "Don't Want to Know If You Are Lonely" (Fireside), and "The Girl Who Lives on Heaven Hill" (Ledfoot).

Also in 1994, the sadly overlooked noise-pop band Lotion included a song entitled "Gardening Your Wig" on their self-titled CD EP on the

Big Cat label in 1994, the song being a combination tribute to R.E.M.'s "Gardening at Night" and Hüsker Dü's "Flip Your Wig."

The Southern indie powerpopsters of Superdrag covered "Diane" on the B-side of their "N.A. Kicker" 7-inch in 1995. The same year, long-running Irish noise-rock band Therapy? also covered "Diane" for their fifth album, *Infernal Love*, released on A&M Records. The track became the third single from the album, complete with accompanying video, and reached the Top 10 in fifteen European countries, prompting the band to ask Hart to open their European tour. Interestingly, they also asked Hart if he would write a new version of the song with toned-down lyrical content, a request that Hart dutifully refused.

Also in 1995, indie rock royalty Sebadoh covered "What's Going On" on the official live bootleg . . . *In Tokyo*, while proto-emo melodic hardcore band Lifetime covered "It's Not Funny Anymore" on the band's *Hello Bastards* album (Jade Tree Records), and Revelation Records hardcore outfit Farside included "Hardly Getting Over It" as a hidden track on their self-titled CD EP.

As 1996 rolled around, the most interesting Hüsker nods came when the Posies included a genuine tribute entitled "Grant Hart" on the group's *Amazing Disgrace* album (Geffen). Then, powerpop legend Marshall Crenshaw covered Hart's solo "2541" on his *Miracle of Science* album (Razor & Tie). Then Anthrax included a cover of "Celebrated Summer" on their *Fueled* CD EP. The version is surprisingly faithful and not at all "thrashed-up" as one might expect. Australian indie-guitar act Screamfeeder covered "Keep Hanging On" on the band's *Gravity* EP in 1996. The song also found its way onto Screamfeeder's *Home Age* album in 1999.

In 1997, Italy's revered (and feared) crust-punk and grindcore community dominated a Hüsker tribute album titled *Land Speed Sonic*. The results were "Punch Drunk" and "The Girl Who Lives on Heaven Hill" (Cripple Bastards), "First of the Last Calls" and "In a Free Land" (Kina), "Ice Cold Ice" and "Flip Your Wig" (Lomas), "Too Much Spice" and "New Day Rising" (Shock Treatment), "I'm Not Interested" and "All Tensed Up" (Acredine), "Signals from Above" and "I'll Never Forget You" (Sottopressione), "Find Me" and "Celebrated Summer" (Punch Line), "Something I Learned Today" and "Everything Falls Apart" (Tempo Zero), and "I Apologize" and "Standing by the Sea" (Burning Defeat).

The following year, 1998, kept pace, offering a Hüsker cover by Dayton, Ohio, pop-punk band Sidecar ("Standing in the Rain") and more metal-love from Blackstar ("The Girl Who Lives on Heaven Hill"), a band that formed from the ashes of death-metal/grindcore legend Carcass. That year also saw covers from Heavens to Murgatroid ("Divide and Conquer") and Everready ("Diane"), and Face to Face covered Sugar's "Helpless." The decade closed with, among many other examples, a live version of the Posies' "Grant Hart" showing up on *Alive before the Iceberg* album.

As the new century commenced, exalted spazzcore band Charles Bronson covered "Punch Drunk" on its *Discography* double-CD release in 2000 (track 91 out of 117). On the far end of the punk rock spectrum, Green Day took a run at "Don't Want to Know If You Are Lonely" for a scrapped MTV pilot called *Influences*, in which hot bands of the day paid tribute to their biggest influences. The track showed up as bonus material on one or two of the many EPs accompanying the band's *Warning* album. Posies guitarist John Auer released a covers EP in 2001 that included a version of "Green Eyes." The venerable indie-rockers of Elf Power offered a fine version of "Never Talking to You Again" on their own covers EP in 2002, and that same year, the death-metal stalwarts of Entombed released a double CD of cover tunes that included their previously recorded (1998) version of "Something I Leaned Today."

The Foo Fighters included a live version of "Never Talking to You Again" on the *Low* CD single in 2003, and Jersey melodic hardcore band Ensign did "In a Free Land" for their covers album, also released in 2003. Sludgy metallic hardcore behemoth Anodyne covered "Beyond the Threshold" for the *Salo* EP, released in 2004, and that same year, the Poster Children covered "Divide and Conquer" on their *On the Offensive* EP. Also in 2004, Warp Records' top-shelf drone-pop outfit Gravenhurst offered "Diane" on their *Black Holes in the Sand* EP. Indie-dance band VHS or Beta recorded a genre-appropriate electronic version of "New Day Rising" as the B-side to their "The Melting Moon" 7-inch, released in 2005.

Recent years have provided a Russian-only Sugar tribute CD (released in a limited run of one hundred), Red House Painters/Sun Kil Moon front-man Mark Kozelek's version of "Celebrated Summer" on his *The Finally* solo LP, a cover of Sugar's "If I Can't Change Your Mind" by alt-rockers Train, and a Grant Hart two-band/two-song tribute 7-inch (the Maykings doing "Keep Hanging On" and Lorrie Matheson and the Brass Tacks covering "2541"), among other examples.

HÜSKER DID

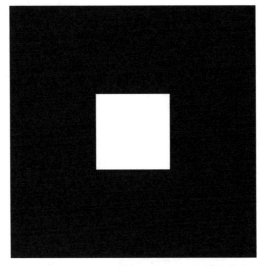

Appendixes

Hüsker Dü crammed a lot of releases into eight years of activity. In fact, by the time the group hit their stride in 1983 with the release of *Metal Circus*, they still had in them five more albums (one a double) and three 7-inch singles that they would release by January 1986. A comparable level of output and rapid stylistic progress had not been seen since the heavy-hitters of the mid- to late '60s. The first four or five years of Hüsker Dü's lifespan is punctuated by a confusing array of compilation appearances, whereas the Warners stint is notable for the saturation of promotional releases, usually in the form of 12-inch EPs but concluding with the "panic mode" promo release *The Warehouse Interviews*, a strange and uncomfortable listen served up as a double-LP set.

No matter how notable, notorious, or easy to attain, no unauthorized releases are listed below. And, as stated elsewhere in this book, the official status of Hüsker Dü's back catalog on SST is unknown. What is known, however, is that further unfounded or speculative information from either side of the fence—or worse, from writers who haven't even spoken with a source about the subject—is unneeded. Therefore, the inclusion of confirmed bootlegs and other releases of unknown authorization seemed like an unnecessary and possibly confusing gesture.

This being a book about Hüsker Dü, only Hüsker Dü releases are included in this discography. As a courtesy to the curious, the best ten post-Hüsker releases by Grant Hart, Bob Mould, and Greg Norton are listed, each with a brief synopsis, toward the end of this discography, along with other lists that might be helpful and fun for the prospective or current Hüsker Dü fan.

Please note: A huge and forever-gracious "thanks" goes out to Paul Hilcoff, creator of the Hüsker Dü Database, without which this discography would not have been possible. Though a few titles appear here that Paul has not included, much of this discography is a scaled-down and reshaped cousin to his exhaustive discography, which includes all of the post-Hüsker solo information that is excluded here. Visit Paul's discography at www.thirdav.com/hd_discog/00_intro.html.

APPENDIX I
Singles and EPs

TITLE: "Statues" b/w "Amusement"
FORMAT: 7" single
LABEL: Reflex Records
RELEASE DATE: January 1981
Probably re-pressed once or twice, since the $50 to $100 average asking price (as of 2010) and frequency at which copies pop up for sale would indicate more than 1,000 exist. All artwork and layout by Grant Hart. Now considered "Reflex A," though the sleeve carries no catalog number, indicating no future plans for Reflex existed at the time of release. Appears as bonus content on Rhino's 1993 CD reissue, *Everything Falls Apart and More.*

TITLE: *In a Free Land*
FORMAT: 7" three-song EP
LABEL: New Alliance Records
RELEASE DATE: May 1982
Many consider the title track Hüsker Dü's defining moment as a hard-core band. B-side comprises two shorter Hart-composed songs, "M.I.C." (as in "Military Industrial Complex") and "What Do I Want?" Also highly collectable, it commands around the same amount as "Statues" b/w "Amusement" but emerges less frequently. Only 2,500 were pressed, of which an unknown number allegedly disappeared while the band toured the West Coast. First Hüsker/Reflex release to feature the "731 Pontiac Place, Mendota Heights, MN," address that would serve as the band's mailing address until Reflex moved to the Nicollet office they would share with Twin/Tone.

TITLE: "Eight Miles High" b/w "Masochism World"
FORMATS: 7" single and later CD3
LABEL: SST
RELEASE DATE: April 1984
The best 7-inch to come out of the American underground in the 1980s? If not, it's certainly close. Mould never screamed like this . . . before or since. Reissued countless times on every color of vinyl under the sun. Very easy to find. Very essential.

TITLE: "Makes No Sense at All" b/w "Love Is All Around"
FORMATS: 7" single and later a CD3
LABEL: SST
RELEASE DATE: August 1985
This truly iconic Hüsker song actually made it onto classic rock radio for a short time. B-side is an earnest cover of the *Mary Tyler Moore* theme song.

TITLE: "Don't Want to Know If You Are Lonely"
FORMATS: 12" EP/maxi-single and 7" single
LABEL: Warner Bros.
RELEASE DATE: March 1986
The 12-inch is a three-song maxi-single with a live version of the Beatles' "Helter Skelter" (recorded live January 30, 1985, at First Avenue in Minneapolis) on which Soul Asylum's Dave Pirner can be heard providing extra vocals. Both versions have Mould's "All Work and No Play" on the B-side, but the 12-inch also has an extended 8:24 version with echo effects on guitar and vocals (twice the length of the edit on the 7-inch B-side).

TITLE: "Sorry Somehow"
FORMATS: 12" EP and double 7" single
LABEL: Warner Bros.
RELEASE DATE: Fall 1986
Second and final single from *Candy Apple Grey*. Both the 12-inch and the double 7-inch have the LP version of Mould's "All This I've Done for You" (following Hart's focus track on the 12-inch and as the B-side of the first 7-inch in the double-pack), as well as live versions of Hart's "Flexible Flyer" and Mould's "Celebrated Summer." Both live tracks were recorded at the Roxy Theatre in Hollywood on May 9, 1986, placing the release date in late '86. The 12-inch also has a fifth track, "Fattie," an uncharacteristically experimental and noisy drone piece credited to "Hart/Mould."

TITLE: "Could You Be the One?"
FORMATS: 12" EP/maxi-single and 7" single
LABEL: Warner Bros.
RELEASE DATE: January 1987
First of two focus singles from Hüsker Dü's second double album, *Warehouse: Songs and Stories*. Eleven months after the album's release date (also January 1987), the band would be broken up. B-side track on both formats is Hart's "Charity, Chastity, Prudence, and Hope," another track Warners had hopes for in terms of commercial success. The 12-inch features a third track that's not on any other release: "Everytime" is the first Greg Norton composition to be credited on a Hüsker Dü release since *Everything Falls Apart*.

TITLE: "Ice Cold Ice"
FORMATS: 12" EP and 7" single
LABEL: Warner Bros.
RELEASE DATE: Summer/Fall 1987

Final release by the active version of Hüsker Dü. Oddly, and perhaps telling of the band's internal climate, the 7-inch broke from the recently established pattern of featuring a B-side by the opposite songwriter (this B-side was Mould's unreleased "Gotta Lotta"). The 12-inch, however, did continue the approach of including unreleased live material, in this case, a medley of "The Wit and the Wisdom" and "What's Going On."

APPENDIX II

Proper Albums

For the purposes of albums, only U.S. labels and release dates are listed.

TITLE: *Land Speed Record*
LABEL: New Alliance Records
RELEASE DATE: January 1982 (U.S.)
Perhaps one of the most brutal hardcore albums released in 1982. The (very) poor sound quality accentuates the "blurred" nature of the performance, leading Terry Katzman to refer to the album as "the *Metal Machine Music* of hardcore." Dynamics are nowhere to be found, but repeated listening does bring out subtleties in the song structures and the performances. The CD version is divided into two tracks—one for each side of the vinyl record.

TITLE: *Everything Falls Apart*
LABEL: Reflex Records
RELEASE DATE: January 1983
The album (referred to by some as an EP or "mini album") that initiated the band's relationship with SST in-house producer Spot and Total Access Studios. Approximately 10,000 pressed, divided into two 5,000 runs. Vinyl copies regularly go for at least $30 as of 2010. An unknown number arrived from the plant unplayable due to serious warping, so beware of sealed copies! Retains the ferocity of *Land Speed Record* while featuring the band's first real "pop" moment with the title track.

TITLE: *Metal Circus*
LABEL: SST
RELEASE DATE: October 1983
This 12-inch EP is referred to both as an EP and an LP. Often regarded as Hüsker Dü's debut full-length for SST. The band's first bona fide classic.

TITLE: *Zen Arcade*
LABEL: SST
RELEASE DATE: July 1984
Double LP with gatefold sleeve that is widely considered the band's creative peak and is the first Hüsker Dü recording most fans are exposed to. Earlier pressings are on colored vinyl and are somewhat sought-after.

TITLE: *New Day Rising*
LABEL: SST
RELEASE DATE: January 1985
Mixed hot, trebly, and very dense. Avoid the current SST CD version for this very reason.

TITLE: *Flip Your Wig*
LABEL: SST
RELEASE DATE: August 1985
The release that broke the Hüskers in Europe.

TITLE: *Candy Apple Grey*
LABEL: Warner Bros.
RELEASE DATE: March 1986

Debut for Warner Bros. The band began recording immediately after signing with the label in October 1986 and also self-produced, a freedom practically unheard of for a major-label debut. An excellent effort featuring as its first single Hart's "Don't Want to Know If You Are Lonely," which, like Mould's "Makes No Sense at All" before it, pushed the band in front of newer and bigger audiences. The song was a respectable college radio hit and continues to be a go-to choice when Warners and Rhino assemble compilations like the *Left of the Dial* boxed set. A follow-up single, "Sorry Somehow" (also Hart's), was released in fall 1986. The first (and last) Hüsker Dü album to prominently feature acoustic instrumentation and balladry.

TITLE: *Warehouse: Songs and Stories*
LABEL: Warner Bros.
RELEASE DATE: January 1987

Hüsker Dü dissolved less than a year after the release of the band's final proper studio album. Two focus singles, "Could You Be the One" and "Ice Cold Ice," came from the album. Underground bands rarely have the opportunity or permission to release a double album this soon into a relationship with a major label. Twenty songs. Largely underrated and essential for the fan.

APPENDIX III
Compilation Appearances

TITLE: *Charred Remains*
FORMAT: Cassette
LABEL: Version Sound
RELEASE DATE: March 1982

The band contributed the *Land Speed Record* version of "Bricklayer" to this ultra-rare compilation. This era of first-wave American hardcore produced several cassette compilations that today pull unbelievably high collector prices, and this is no exception. Packaged in a file folder with photocopied pages for each band.

TITLE: *Barefoot & Pregnant*
FORMAT: Cassette
LABEL: Reflex Records
RELEASE DATE: Spring 1982

Contains outtake versions of "Target," "Signals from Above," and "Let's Lie." All three were recorded during the *In a Free Land* sessions. This is the second Reflex Records release (Reflex B; see Reflex Records Discography below). Reissued on CD by Terry Katzman in 1999 (Garage D'or Records).

TITLE: *Kitten*
FORMAT: Cassette
LABEL: Reflex Records
RELEASE DATE: 1982

Reflex C features live recordings from two nights in October 1982 at Goofy's Upper Deck in Minneapolis. Hüsker Dü's contribution is "It's Not Fair." Like *Barefoot & Pregnant*, *Kitten* offers a nice cross-section of the nascent Minneapolis/St. Paul hardcore punk and underground rock scene as it prepared to explode. Reissued on CD by Terry Katzman in 1999 (Garage D'or Records).

TITLE: *Code Blue*
FORMAT: Cassette
LABEL: Last Rites
RELEASE DATE: 1984

Another Midwestern cassette compilation that serious collectors of first-wave American hardcore would give their firstborn to own. The Hüsker Dü tracks are live from a soundboard recording of a 1982 gig in Tucson, Arizona (at the Backstage): "In a Free Land," "Target," and "It's Not Funny Anymore."

TITLE: *The Blasting Concept*
FORMAT: LP
LABEL: SST
RELEASE DATE: 1983

Raymond Pettibon's incendiary cover art (a nun being raped) caused problems for Twin Cities record retailers. Basically a promotional compilation for SST artists. Hüsker Dü is represented by its blazing "Real World."

TITLE: *Underground Hits #2*
FORMAT: Double LP
LABEL: Aggressive Rock Productionen
RELEASE DATE: Mid-1983

Hardcore compilation originally released on a West German label and reissued on CD in 1992. Hüsker tracks are "Deadly Skies" and "Lifeline." Also featured Meatmen, Adrenalin OD, Angry Samoans, and others.

TITLE: *Bang Zoom #6*
FORMAT: Cassette with 'zine
LABEL: Bang Zoom
RELEASE DATE: 1984

Features a recorded interview with Hüsker Dü and a live version of "Out on a Limb."

TITLE: *Department of Enjoyment*
FORMAT: Cassette with issue of *New Musical Express*
LABEL: *New Musical Express*
RELEASE DATE: May 12, 1984

The UK loved Hüsker Dü. To coincide with one of the band's several turns as *NME* golden boys, the magazine included an older and not very representative song ("Real World") on a cassette compilation that came free with that issue. Also featured the Smiths, Cocteau Twins, the Waterboys, Dr. John, and others.

TITLE: *A Diamond Hidden in the Mouth of a Corpse*
FORMAT: LP
LABEL: Giorno Poetry Systems Records
RELEASE DATE: 1985
Metal Circus outtake "Don't Change" rubs shoulders with contributions from Sonic Youth, Cabaret Voltaire, and others. Vinyl is common on eBay for around $10.

TITLE: *The Blasting Concept, Vol. 2*
FORMAT: LP
LABEL: SST
RELEASE DATE: 1986
Omnipresent SST bargain compilation featured one of Hüsker Dü's more powerful and representative tracks, "Erase Today," an outtake from the *New Day Rising* session.

TITLE: *The 7 Inch Wonders of the World*
FORMAT: Cassette
LABEL: SST
RELEASE DATE: 1986
Enjoyable collection of everything SST released on 7-inch up to 1986. Released on cassette-only format but was later reissued on CD in the 1990s (see Posthumous Releases). Hüsker Dü was represented by "Eight Miles High," "Masochism World," "Makes No Sense at All," and "Love Is All Around."

TITLE: *Smack My Crack*
FORMAT: LP and CD
LABEL: Giorno Poetry Systems Records
RELEASE YEAR: 1987
"Won't Change," a *Metal Circus* outtake, appears only on the CD version as a bonus track.

APPENDIX IV
Posthumous Releases

Beginning in 1989, SST began repackaging Hüsker Dü titles. Each full-length album was repackaged in the same format but on colored vinyl, with the addition of UPC barcodes and stickers on the shrink wrap stating the color of the vinyl. According to Grant Hart and Greg Norton, the band never received comps (free copies from the label designated for band members) or any sort of notification that the process was to take place. The colored represses promptly went out of print, only to be replaced by represses on regular black vinyl (no SST Hüsker Dü title on regular black vinyl has ever gone out of print). How many of these represses occurred is unknown, therefore it is impossible to determine accurate dates. Unscrupulous eBay sellers have a habit of listing the colored SST represses as "early" or "first" pressings when, in fact, all were pressed at least a year after the band broke up. What follows, then, is a list of authorized represses and reissues, and the reemergence of particular tracks via different compilations.

TITLE: *Duck and Cover*
LABEL: SST
RELEASE DATE: Summer 1990
Compilation of cover songs by a variety of SST artists and bands, many of which had broken up or left the label by the time this was conceived. Of questionable merit to anyone but the SST completist.

TITLE: *Never Mind the Mainstream: The Best of MTV's* 120 Minutes, *Vol. 2*
FORMAT: CD
LABEL: Rhino Records
RELEASE DATE: Late 1991
This was the second CD of a sold-separately two-CD set. "Could You Be the One?" would become one of a handful of Warners-era Hüsker songs to pop up repeatedly during the major-label alternative/grunge compilation cash-in campaign that lasted well into the mid-'90s.

TITLE: *SST Acoustic*
FORMATS: CD and cassette
LABEL: SST
RELEASE DATE: November 1991
The compilation cash-in was not the exclusive territory of the majors, as evidenced by this compilation of previously released (and perpetually in-print) acoustic tracks performed by current and former SST artists. "Never Talking to You Again" was wisely chosen to represent the Hüskers, and it should be noted that Grant Hart's "The Main" also shows up. It may be one of the more common SST titles to turn up in cutout bins, and the nation's largest online auction site always seems to have copies available.

TITLE: *Postmodern*
FORMAT: CD
LABEL: Arton
RELEASED: 1992
Israeli compilation of American and British underground/indie rock with a concentration on the mid- to late '80s. Features the studio version of "Don't Want to Know If You Are Lonely."

TITLE: *Everything Falls Apart and More*
FORMAT: CD
LABEL: Rhino Records
RELEASE DATE: January 1993

Ten-year anniversary CD-only reissue of the Hüskers' first studio album, plus a very nice selection of bonus tracks. This collection serves as a near-perfect snapshot of Hüsker Dü at the height of its powers as a hardcore band in the studio. Also notable for obvious hints that hardcore would soon be left behind (e.g., the now-classic title track). Bonus tracks include the *In a Free Land* three-song EP that preceded *Everything Falls Apart*; the debut single ("Statues" b/w "Amusement"); a previously unreleased and unedited version of "Statues" that clocks in at almost nine minutes; "Let's Go Die," a previously unreleased outtake from the Colin Mansfield "Statues" demos that was momentarily considered as the third song if the band's debut turned out to be a 10-inch; and the demo of "Do You Remember?" which proved that the guys were not immune to theme-song silliness (though the song is a serious and straight-up punk rock number). This release was also meant to shine some light on the respectable amount of material that was completed before the band ever signed to SST. Fantastic liner notes by Terry Katzman. Still somewhat common as a used CD.

TITLE: *Cash Cow: The Best of Giorno Poetry Systems 1965–1993*
FORMAT: CD
LABEL: Giorno Poetry Systems Records
RELEASE DATE: Early 1993

Includes the *Metal Circus* outtake "Won't Change." The CD booklet features the "last photo" of Hüsker Dü, taken in Lawrence, Kansas, on August 15, 1987.

TITLE: *Faster & Louder: Hardcore Punk, Vols. 1 & 2*
FORMATS: CD and cassette
LABEL: Rhino Records
RELEASE DATE: July 1993

Part of Rhino's extensive early-to-mid-'90s campaign to educate the alt-rock/grunge crowd on influential underground sounds that had a hand in shaping the topical movement of the day, one that was rapidly devolving into soulless pap. Volume 1 features the neither especially fast nor loud "Statues" edit from the *Everything Falls Apart and More* reissue; Vol. 2 includes the more appropriate "In a Free Land."

TITLE: *Rebellious Jukebox*
FORMAT: CD
LABEL: *Melody Maker*/Ablex Audio Video
RELEASE DATE: November 1993

CD compilation released by the U.K.'s *Melody Maker* magazine and named after the brilliant anchor song from The Fall's 1979 debut album. The Hüsker Dü track is the *Metal Circus* version of "Real World." A blazing hardcore workout is a strange choice to represent Hüsker Dü's take on post-punk when "Statues," "Amusement," or "Gravity" would have showcased the band's actual forays into the genre proper.

TITLE: *Grunge: The Alternative Compilation*
FORMAT: CD
LABEL: Warner Bros.
RELEASE DATE: 1993

This release from Warners' French bureau includes the *Warehouse* version of "You're a Soldier." The common denominator between all of the bands featured is Warners' access to its own back catalog, hence Jane's Addiction, Flaming Lips, Babes in Toyland, and the Red Hot Chili Peppers all apparently qualify as "grunge" (to be fair, Mudhoney and Mother Love Bone also were included).

TITLE: *The Living End*
FORMAT: CD
LABEL: Warner Bros.
RELEASE DATE: April 1994

This odd twenty-four-track live CD was released during Sugar's lifetime, which means there was an old fan/new fan interest in Hüsker Dü bubbling under the surface. Recorded in October 1987, the album comprises pieces of seven gigs sonically sewn together by soundman Lou Giordano to give the breadth of material needed to market the "set" as a career-spanning live album. In reality, the band was focusing on *Warehouse* most nights, and there were even gigs during the latter half of '87 that found the trio coming close to covering the entire album and little else.

With lengthy, liner notes by *Rolling Stone*'s David Fricke, this is not an essential album for the newcomer, but it does prove one very important fact about Hüsker Dü: Even when the personal/social climate within the band was at its worst, the Hüskers were able to flip a switch and give the audience—and themselves—an hour or more of what it was all about in the first place. In a 2008 interview with *SPIN*, Mould claimed to have never listened to this album.

TITLE: *The 7 Inch Wonders of the World*
FORMAT: CD
LABEL: SST
RELEASE DATE: 1995

See previous cassette-only release from the late '80s.

TITLE: *Shades Guitars Stripes & Stars*
FORMAT: CD
LABEL: Connoisseur Collection
RELEASE DATE: June 1996
CD from the UK that professed (via the liner notes and through the inclusion of bands like the Georgia Satellites, Jason & the Scorchers, Steve Earle, etc.) to be a survey of Americana, making Hüsker Dü's "Don't Want to Know If You Are Lonely" a puzzling choice.

TITLE: *Les Inrockuptibles: 10 Ans, 100 Chansons*
FORMAT: Six-CD boxed set
RELEASE DATE: 1997
Commemorating the tenth anniversary of *Les Inrockuptibles*, a French underground/indie-rock magazine. Again, Hart's "Don't Want to Know If You Are Lonely" is the lucky winner. Other bands/artists include the Boo Radleys, Nick Cave, the Jesus and Mary Chain, Waterboys, and Tindersticks.

TITLE: *Barefoot &Pregnant*
FORMAT: CD
LABEL: Reflex/Garage D'or
RELEASE DATE: August 1998
Nice reissue (still in print) of the 1982 cassette compilation originally released on Reflex. Features two Hüsker Dü tracks, and the booklet includes a previously unpublished photo of the Hüskers. Garage D'or is Terry Katzman's label, and he has gone on to reissue long-out-of-print or never-released material from the Suicide Commandos and the Suburbs as well.

TITLE: *Kitten*
FORMAT: CD
LABEL: Reflex/Garage D'or
RELEASE DATE: April 1999
Same reissue treatment as *Barefoot & Pregnant* (above), but features two Hüsker Dü tracks not on the original release: "Drug Party" and "Everything Falls Apart." Also of note are the great liner notes by Terry Katzman *and* Grant Hart, both of which have been reprinted below:

Before the rise of alternative rock and after the initial explosion of punk is where our second musical journey begins. *Kitten* was the third release on Reflex Records. Favorable reaction to our first Minneapolis compilation *Barefoot & Pregnant* (Reflex B) paved the way for this new collection. Since the label was run on a shoestring budget it was decided a cassette only project was the easy answer. It would feature Hüsker Dü, Man Sized Action, Riflesport and a host of hardcore bands central to the scene.

The seedy structure located downtown at 2nd and Glenwood was the site of many of the era's greatest shows. The Deck was basically a split-level workingman's bar/strip joint until 1982 rolled around. It was at that point when owner/manager Dan Cotlow hired a burly, friendly bouncer who loved hardcore punk. Enter Fred Gartner. Cotlow and Gartner made an arrangement; Cotlow would manage the strip joint downstairs, Gartner would utilize the "ladies rooms" upstairs as Goofy's Upper Deck, the palace of punk and hardcore.

The Deck's six-inch high stage played host to many traveling bands of the day. Most memorable were Black Flag, Minutemen, and the traveling hardcore circus known as B.Y.O. (Better Youth Organization) featuring Youth Brigade, Social Distortion and I believe Battalion of Saints. From an intimacy standpoint you couldn't get closer to the action than Goofy's. It was truly an in your face type of place.

Sadly, a punk rock club on the fringes of downtown, which doubled as a strip joint also, attracted the attention of the Minneapolis Police. In August a full-scale riot ensued when Final Conflict belted forth a white-hot set. After Mike Etoll, leader of the very bizarre Exmo-6-Desmo combo liberated a toilet from its mount sending it crashing to the concrete two floors below, the party was over. By that fall Goofy's Upper Deck was a punk memory, albeit a great one.

Herein lies a sound, an attitude and a presence peculiar to that time alone. Another audio snapshot more vital and urgent than many comps to follow. Close your eyes, feast your ears and ready yourself for a bone jangling experience. The decline of the mid-western civilization!

—Terry Katzman "18-Years-On"

The scenario was played out in a lot of cities at the time, early 1980s. Some bar is losing business. They get a pool table. That doesn't bring people in. They serve cheap drinks. That only brings in people with nothing to spend. Everything they try to get a clientele with only brings expenses. The management are desperate for ideas to bring people in the door. Finally, one day a kid walks in with a funny haircut and an interesting idea. "I'm looking for a place to have a few bands play . . . " In a week, the place is full every night and the bartender is selling more beer than ever. The owners hate the customers but love the money they bring with them. The playground called the Upper Deck was such a place. The city was about to buy the building and tear it down anyway, so why not sell a shitload of beer and run some insurance scams in the mean time. Although some great artists performed there, the place was a pigsty, owned by pigs, frequented by swine, written about by Sovine Existentialists trying to get their scene reports published in *The New York Rocker*. On an historical note, The Upper Deck has recently been acknowledged as the birthplace of the dumbing down of America. My suspicions are that the management choreographed the entire thing to make themselves look like the victims of the Freaky-Punk aggression. But wait . . . if you are listening to this disc for sounds of a real riot, Caveat Emptor! This live chestnut was recorded during an evening free of any insurrection or other civil disobedience, real or imagined.

—Grant Hart, 1999

TITLE: *Rage: More of the Songs Most Chosen by* Rage *Guest Programmers*
FORMAT: CD
LABEL: Virgin/EMI/ABC Music
RELEASE DATE: 1999

Rage is the Australian version of MTV's *120 Minutes*, having aired for the first time in 1987 as a music video program catering to the underground. In 1990 the show distanced itself from the growing worldwide pack of such shows by allowing guest artists to program entire episodes—up to forty videos for the several-hour program. The Hüskers were never asked to program an episode, but an unknown contemporary chose "Could You Be the One" for inclusion.

TITLE: *Gimme Indie Rock, Vol. 1*
FORMAT: Two-CD set
LABEL: K-Tel Records
RELEASE DATE: March 2000

K-Tel reemerged around Y2K with what would appear to be indie rock's death rattle, but the revamped compilation label was seemingly employed by at least a few decision-makers who were on the level. For one, the chosen Hüsker Dü track was "Pink Turns to Blue," a more-than-worthy but rare contender in the compilation sweepstakes. The promo one-sheet that accompanied the two-CD set contained the following not-so-out-of-touch passage: "Hüsker Dü, the Wipers, Pussy Galore, The Minutemen: these legendary bands passed stealth-like beneath the commercial radar of the waning '80s. They, and others like them, built a new infrastructure of labels, agents, and promoters which supported an underground network that would rise to occupy the mainstream for the better part of the '90s."

TITLE: *Doubleshot: Modern Rock*
FORMAT: Two-CD set
LABEL: K-Tel Records/Warner Bros.
RELEASE DATE: July 2000

Because *Gimme Indie Rock* was a surprise runaway success, this release came from Warners' Special Projects and used K-Tel in name alone for marketing purposes. "Could You Be the One" is the Hüsker inclusion, though the overall content of these two discs pales in comparison to the *Gimme Indie Rock* collection.

TITLE: *World's Greatest Air Guitar*
FORMAT: CD
LABEL: Hollywood
RELEASE DATE: June 2003

By far the weirdest compilation participation for Hüsker Dü. Imagining a bedroom air-guitar session to a Hüsker Dü song is not hard, but doing so after hearing a compilation full of Top 40 classic rock hits is a little strange. Choosing "Sorry Somehow" as the Hüsker track is downright absurd. Someone was having a laugh.

TITLE: *Newbury Comics: The Early Years, Vol. 2*
FORMAT: CD
LABEL: Rhino Records
RELEASE DATE: November 2003

CD compilation was put together for the twenty-fifth anniversary of the well-known East Coast record store chain to give an idea of the store's "Early Years" soundtrack. "Sorry Somehow" is once again the chosen Hüsker Dü track.

TITLE: *All That Rock*
FORMAT: CD
LABEL: Warner Music Australia
RELEASE DATE: 2003

Cash-grab comp of '80s indie, hard rock, and metal, for which "Hardly Getting Over It" seems like another head-scratcher, but exposure is exposure.

TITLE: *Left of the Dial: Dispatches from the '80s Underground*
FORMAT: Four-CD set
LABEL: Rhino Records
RELEASE DATE: October 2004

This well-intentioned but astronomically priced compilation was no doubt inspired by the attention and accolades that were being given to Michael Azerrad's *Our Band Could Be Your Life*. Because Warners is always in the shadow of any Rhino endeavor, the Hüsker contribution could only be one of a tiny selection of songs from *Candy Apple Grey* or *Warehouse*, and by this stage, no one will be shocked to learn that "Don't Want to Know If You Are Lonely" is that track.

TITLE: *The Bootlegs, Vol. 1: Celebrating 35 Years at First Avenue*
LABEL: SRO Productions
RELEASE DATE: November 2005

Thirty-five years are covered in a questionable manner, since the majority of the tracks date from the '90s or later and feature some usual suspects in the world of successful indie names. Only the Replacements and the Hüskers date from earlier, and the latter's "Books about UFOs" was conveniently filched from the band's most popular "bootleg" release, the *SPIN* concert of 1985.

TITLE: *All That Punk*
FORMAT: CD
LABEL: Warner Music Australia
RELEASE DATE: January 2006

Punk, punk-associated, mid-to-late-'80s indie, and '90s alterna-indie with the common thread being a past or present contract with Warners. And, yes, the Hüsker choice is "Don't Want to Know If You Are Lonely."

TITLE: *Live Featuring J. C.*
LABEL: Reflex
RELEASE DATE: July 2008

Three songs featuring Hüsker collaborator John Clegg, who passed away after a long battle with cancer on February 18, 2008. Clegg joins the band on saxophone for two versions of "Drug Party" and a recording of "What's Going On" that were culled from unreleased live tapes recorded at Duffy's and Goofy's Upper Deck in 1982 and 1983. Limited to five hundred copies and produced entirely by Hart, who also wrote the liner notes.

TITLE: *Candy Apple Grey*
FORMAT: LP
LABEL: Rhino Records
RELEASE DATE: March 2009

Announced only in trade publications, this was a 180-gram vinyl-only reissue of an album that continues to be very easy to obtain on original formats. Clearly Rhino had an eye on reissuing further titles in the back catalog until layoffs pretty much shelved any large-scale projects. No attempt was made to add hindsight reverence through new liner notes, and barring the heightened quality of the vinyl, there is but one difference between this and the original: the inclusion of a lyric insert instead of the original's printed inner sleeve. No bonus tracks, no promotion, and, therefore, no press. The perfect illustration of why the Hüskers need to spend two or three hours in the same room straightening out their back catalog and getting it into the proper hands for the deserved reissue treatment. Grant Hart did not know of this reissue's existence until eight months after its release.

APPENDIX V
Notable Promotional Titles

Like the preceding lists, this one excludes any post-Hüsker solo titles. Hüsker Dü and the Minutemen launched SST into the modern era of promotional releases when they necessitated abbreviated promo versions of the bands' respective double LPs—*Zen Arcade* and *Double Nickels on the Dime*—released on the same day in the summer of 1984. Before this, SST staff had used a black marker to write "Promo" or "Radio Copy" on the covers of regular commercially released titles before mailing them off to radio stations and magazines. Once Hüsker Dü was signed to Warners, the major made them very familiar with the promo release process. A label's promotional practices speak volumes about its confidence in a particular artist. Behind all of the "100 percent creative control" rhetoric used to successfully seduce Hüsker Dü was a very nervous major label.

TITLE: *Zen Arcade* Sampler
FORMAT: LP
LABEL: SST
RELEASE DATE: June 1984

Joe Carducci's method of promoting and sending out a double album to college radio. One must question, however, the positioning of "I'll Never Forget You" as the opening track, considering it is possibly the most intense and terrifying piece of music Mould has ever written. Following it with "The Biggest Lie" would make recipients believe the Hüskers had packed a double album with spine-tingling noisecore until track three, "Newest Industry," returns to the post-hardcore pop the band was then inventing and refining. The remaining side one tracks, in order, are "Whatever," "Somewhere," "Pink Turns to Blue," and "Turn on the News." Side two gives listeners "Eight Miles High," with the rest of the physical vinyl space used for band logo etchings. For collectors, this is the most sought-after of all Hüsker promo records, though a copy can be had for as low as $30. Appropriately, a seven-song sampler of the Minutemen's *Double Nickels on the Dime* entitled *Wheels of Fortune* was also pressed with a B-side of etchings.

TITLE: "Celebrated Summer" b/w "New Day Rising"
FORMAT: 7"
LABEL: SST
RELEASE DATE: December 1984

Issued to promote the upcoming full-length, *New Day Rising*, on which both songs appear. Like the *Zen Arcade* sampler, this was also pressed in an edition of five hundred. For some reason, it's two or three times as rare, commanding upward of $120. Its plain white sleeve is hand-stamped with the band logo and pertinent info.

TITLE: "Makes No Sense at All" b/w "Love Is All Around"
FORMAT: 12" single
LABEL: SST
RELEASE DATE: September 1985

A 12-inch version of the commercially released 7-inch single but with no artwork (only pertinent text on a white cover). Because of the larger grooves afforded by the 12-inch format, the sound is far superior to that of the 7-inch.

TITLE: *Candy Apple Grey* Advance
FORMAT: Cassette
LABEL: Warner Bros.
RELEASE DATE: February 1986

Far superior sound quality than the commercially released version. Either a different mix or a different mastering job that's EQ'd better, possibly for the purpose of radio play.

TITLE: *The March 1986 Guide*
FORMAT: Cassette
LABEL: Warner Bros.
RELEASE DATE: March 1986, presumably

Features "Don't Want to Know If You Are Lonely" and "Sorry Somehow" chopped up with interview snippets on the A-side along with other Warners artists getting the same treatment. Side two has an interview conducted at Nicollet Studios along with edited versions of "Crystal," "Don't Want to Know If You Are Lonely," "Sorry Somehow," "Hardly Getting Over It," "Eiffel Tower High," and "Dead Set on Destruction." Other Warners artists follow suit on this side as well. Slip design features an obscured photo of a woman holding a saxophone.

TITLE: "Sorry Somehow"
FORMAT: 12" single
LABEL: Warner Bros.
RELEASE DATE: Mid-1986

White-label promo with album version on each side. Oddly, such a release does not exist for the album's first single, "Don't Want to Know If You Are Lonely."

TITLE: "Flexible Flyer" b/w "Celebrated Summer"
FORMAT: 7"
LABEL: Warner Bros.
RELEASE DATE:Mid-1986

UK-only promo with the same live versions that turn up as the second 7-inch in the commercially released "Sorry Somehow" double-7-inch and on the equivalent 12-inch. White-label contains the typo "Produced by Bob Mould and Steve Hart."

TITLE: Warner Bros. Christmas Promo
FORMAT: Cassette
LABEL: Warner Bros.
RELEASE DATE: December 1986

Band members perform a one-minute a cappella version of "We Wish You a Merry Christmas." Includes picture insert.

TITLE: *The January 1987 Guide*
FORMAT: Cassette
LABEL: Warner Bros.
RELEASE DATE: December 1987
Features voice-over hype about Hüsker Dü and upcoming double-LP release *Warehouse: Songs and Stories*, which is edited into one-minute snippets of "Ice Cold Ice" and "Could You Be the One?" Features similar offerings from other Warners artists.

TITLE: *SST Godhead Storedude In-Store Play Device #5*
FORMAT: Cassette
LABEL: SST
RELEASE DATE: 1988
Features album version of "Don't Try to Call" along with tracks by other SST artists like Sonic Youth, Das Damen, Black Flag, and fIREHOSE.

TITLE: *Warehouse: Songs and Stories*
FORMAT: Double metal cassettes
LABEL: Warner Bros.
RELEASE DATE: Late 1986
Two metal cassette tapes in Dolby B. Essentially an audiophile version of the entire album. Also manufactured and distributed in the UK as one cassette.

TITLE: *Warehouse* Promo Sampler
FORMAT: 12"
LABEL: Warner Bros.
RELEASE DATE: December 1986
White-label promo with "Tell You Why Tomorrow," "Turn It Around," "Ice Cold Ice," "Could You Be the One?" and "You Can Live at Home."

TITLE: "Could You Be the One?"
FORMAT: 12"
LABEL: Warner Bros.
RELEASE DATE: December 1986 or January 1987
White-label promo with studio album versions on each side.

TITLE: The *Warehouse* Interview
FORMAT: Double-LP
LABEL: Warner Bros.
RELEASE DATE: January 1987, possibly

Several minutes of interview and a wider sampling of songs, including "Could You Be the One?" "You're a Soldier," "Ice Cold Ice," "Back from Somewhere," "Bed of Nails," "Too Much Spice," "Everytime," "Standing in the Rain," "She's a Woman (And Now He Is a Man)," "No Reservations," "Up in the Air," and "You Can Live at Home." Notable for the inclusion of Norton's "Everytime," which did not make the commercially released version of *Warehouse*.

TITLE: "She's a Woman (And Now He Is a Man)"
FORMAT:12"
Label:Warner Bros.
RELEASE DATE: Mid-1987
Contains title track plus "Ice Cold Ice," "Charity, Chastity, Prudence, and Hope," and "No Reservations."

TITLE: *Release 1: The Atlantic Group 1993*
FORMAT: Cassette
LABEL: Atlantic Records
RELEASE DATE: Late 1992
Promo sampler with Atlantic artists on side one and Rhino Records releases on side two. To promote Rhino's reissue of *Everything Falls Apart and More*, "In a Free Land" is included on side two.

TITLE: *The Living End*
FORMATS: CD and cassette
LABEL: Warner Bros.
RELEASE DATE: February 1994
Both formats contain entire seventy-seven-minute album. No inlay sheet for CD; cassette has photocopied sheet of paper folded to fit in case.

TITLE: *Do You Remember?*
FORMAT: CD
LABEL: Warner Bros.
RELEASE DATE: April 1994
Promo-only "best of" CD released to promote *The Living End*. Dips liberally into the SST catalog for album versions of eleven songs. Live version of "Hare Krsna" that was scrapped from *The Living End* can only be found on this CD and is more than eight minutes long.

TITLE: *Adventureland*
FORMAT: CD
LABEL: Hollywood Records
RELEASE DATE: Early 2009
Soundtrack for the movie is promo-only and therefore somewhat collectable. Hüsker track is "Don't Want to Know if You Are Lonely," which features prominently (approximately two minutes) in one scene.

APPENDIX VI
Miscellaneous

TITLE: *NME's Big Four*
FORMAT: 7" compilation
LABEL: *New Musical Express*
RELEASE DATE: February 1986
Four-band giveaway with issue of *NME* includes the Hüskers covering "Ticket to Ride." Also features songs by the Jesus and Mary Chain, Trouble Funk, and Tom Waits. The Hüskers were at their hottest in the UK at this time and garnered a lot of coverage in *NME*.

TITLE: *Leroy Steven's Favorite Recorded Scream*
FORMAT: LP
RELEASE DATE: Late 2009
To understand this release, we must refer to the creator's liner notes: "Between October 2008 and March 2009, I visited every record store in Manhattan and asked the employees for their favorite scream from recorded music. Side one of this record is a compilation of the screams; one from each song, edited together and arranged in the order they were submitted. Side two follows the same order as side one, but has ten second spaces between each of the audio tracks."

It's unclear which scream is from Hüsker Dü, let alone which song is represented. Includes 18x24-inch poster with map and record store information. Pressed in an edition of five hundred.

APPENDIX VII
Video

TITLE: *The Tour*
FORMAT: VHS
LABEL: SST
RELEASE DATE: 1986
Quasi-documentary of SST's "The Tour," a multi-band package tour featuring SWA, Saccharine Trust, Meat Puppets, Minutemen, and Hüsker Dü. The latter three bands rotated through the headlining slot. Twenty-five minutes of this eighty-minute VHS show the Hüskers blasting through eight songs at the Stone in San Francisco in March 1985. Members of the other bands join the Hüskers onstage for the closing cover of "Louie Louie," an obvious tribute or poke at Black Flag. Video was deleted from the SST catalog for unknown reasons, but

speculation leans toward the Meat Puppets' legal wrangling with the label to get control of their back catalog.

TITLE: *It's Clean, It Just Looks Dirty*
FORMAT: VHS
LABEL: Giorno Poetry Systems Records
RELEASE DATE: 1987

Five minutes of this sixty-minute video show Hüsker Dü performing "I Apologize" and "The Girl Who Lives on Heaven Hill" at First Avenue in Minneapolis on January 30, 1985. Basically a video companion to the LP/CD compilation.

TITLE: *Best of the Cutting Edge, Vol. 2*
FORMATS: VHS and LaserDisc
LABEL: IRS Records
RELEASE DATE: 1987

Standard "video magazine" format of the day features snippets of Hüsker interviews and live clips of "Something I Learned Today" and "Makes No Sense at All" shot at an unknown performance but dated October 1985.

TITLE: *Underground USA, Vol. 2*
FORMAT: VHS
LABEL: Videoflex/PFI
RELEASE DATE: 1989

Another video magazine. Features MTV-rotated video for "Don't Want to Know If You Are Lonely."

APPENDIX VIII
Reflex Records Discography

Reflex A	Hüsker Dü, "Statues" b/w "Amusement," 7" single, 1981
Reflex B	Various Artists, *Barefoot & Pregnant*, cassette compilation, 1982
Reflex C	Various Artists, *Kitten*, cassette compilation, 1982
Reflex D	Hüsker Dü, *Everything Falls Apart*, 12" LP, 1983
Reflex E	Rifle Sport, *Voice of Reason*, 12" LP, 1983
Reflex F	Man Sized Action, *Claustrophobia*, 12" LP, 1983
Reflex G	Final Conflict, self-titled 7" four-song EP, 1983
Reflex H	Otto's Chemical Lounge, self-titled 7" four-song EP, 1983
Reflex I	Ground Zero, self-titled 12" LP, 1984

Reflex J	Articles of Faith, *Give Thanks*, 12" LP, 1984
Reflex K	Man Sized Action, *Five-Story Garage*, 12" LP, 1984
Reflex L	Ground Zero, *Pink*, 12" LP, 1985
Reflex M	Minutemen, *Tour Spiel*, 7" four-song EP, 1985
no catalog letter	Hüsker Dü, *Live Featuring J. C.*, three-song CD, 2008

APPENDIX IX
For Beginners: Now What?

For the enthusiastic future Hüsker Dü fan, the band's discography can be a daunting one. For those who are simply curious and want to be sold on the band, there are releases that are not sufficiently representative of the band but are best appreciated after the top-shelf material is processed. The following list of ten releases proceeds from the best places to start through all titles that are essential for any newly minted fan.

1. *Flip Your Wig* (SST, 1985)
2. "Makes No Sense at All" b/w "Love Is All Around" (SST, 1985)
3. "Eight Miles High" b/w "Machismo World" (SST, 1984)
4. *Zen Arcade* (SST, 1984)
5. *New Day Rising* (SST, 1984)
6. *Candy Apple Grey* (Warner Bros., 1986)
7. *Metal Circus* (SST, 1983)
8. *Everything Falls Apart* (Reflex, 1983) or *Everything Falls Apart and More* (Rhino, 1993)
9. *Warehouse: Songs and Stories* (Warner Bros., 1987)
10. *Land Speed Record* (New Alliance, 1982)

APPENDIX X
Suggested Hüsker Dü Mixes

This Book in Fifty Songs: The Perfect Chronological Soundtrack
1. "Statues"
2. "All Tensed Up"
3. "Data Control"
4. "Everything Falls Apart"
5. "Gravity"
6. "In a Free Land"
7. "Real World"
8. "It's Not Funny Anymore"
9. "First of the Last Calls"
10. "Diane"
11. "Eight Miles High"
12. "Something I Learned Today"
13. "Pink Turns to Blue"

14. "Chartered Trips"
15. "Never Talking to You Again"
16. "Whatever"
17. "Newest Industry"
18. "New Day Rising"
19. "If I Told You"
20. "59 Times the Pain"
21. "Celebrated Summer"
22. "I Apologize"
23. "Books about UFOs"
24. "Erase Today"
25. "Makes No Sense at All"
26. "Love Is All Around"
27. "Green Eyes"
28. "Private Plane"
29. "Flexible Flyer"
30. "Divide and Conquer"
31. "Every Everything"
32. "Flip Your Wig"
33. "Keep Hanging On"
34. "The Wit and the Wisdom"
35. "Don't Want to Know If You Are Lonely"
36. "I Don't Know for Sure"
37. "Sorry Somehow"
38. "Hardly Getting Over It"
39. "No Promise Have I Made"
40. "Charity, Chastity, Prudence, and Hope"
41. "Ice Cold Ice"
42. "Back from Somewhere"
43. "Could You Be the One?"
44. "You Can Live at Home"
45. "It's Not Peculiar"
46. "No Reservations"
47. "She Floated Away"
48. "Too Much Spice"
49. "Up in the Air"
50. "She's a Woman (And Now He Is a Man)"

Mix for the Enthusiastically Curious Newcomer
1. "Makes No Sense at All"
2. "Pink Turns to Blue"
3. "Private Plane"
4. "It's Not Peculiar"
5. "Don't Want to Know If You Are Lonely"
6. "Chartered Trips"
7. "If I Told You"
8. "Ice Cold Ice"
9. "Erase Today"

10. "Eight Miles High"
11. "Something I Learned Today"
12. "Sorry Somehow"
13. "Everything Falls Apart"
14. "Diane"
15. "First of the Last Calls"
16. "Divide and Conquer"
17. "Love Is All Around"
18. "She Floated Away"
19. "If I Told You"
20. "I Apologize"
21. "Flexible Flyer"
22. "I Don't Know for Sure"

Mix of the Best Hardcore, Cathartic, or Generally Intense Moments
1. "The Biggest Lie"
2. "What Do I Want?"
3. "In a Free Land"
4. "All Tensed Up"
5. "Bricklayer"
6. "Punch Drunk"
7. "I'll Never Forget You"
8. "Eight Miles High"
9. "Something I Learned Today"
10. "Everything Falls Apart"
11. "Ultracore"
12. "Tired of Doing Things"
13. "Target"
14. "Beyond the Threshold"
15. "Obnoxious"
16. "Erase Today"
17. "First of the Last Calls"
18. "Won't Change"
19. "Writer's Cramp"
20. "Let's Go Die"
21. "If I Told You"
22. "59 Times the Pain"
23. "I Apologize"
24. "Signals from Above"
25. "Afraid of Being Wrong"

Mix for Those Apprehensive About or of Negative Opinion Regarding the Warner Bros. Era

1. "Don't Want to Know If You Are Lonely"
2. "It's Not Peculiar"
3. "She Floated Away"
4. "Ice Cold Ice"
5. "Sorry Somehow"
6. "No Reservations"
7. "You Can Live at Home"
8. "I Don't Know for Sure"
9. "Charity, Chastity, Prudence, and Hope"
10. "Back from Somewhere"
11. "Hardly Getting Over It"
12. "No Promise Have I Made"

Ten Best Post–Hüsker Dü Solo Works

1. Sugar, *Beaster* (Rykodisc/Creation, 1993)
2. Grant Hart, *Intolerance* (SST, 1989)
3. Bob Mould, *The Last Dog & Pony Show* (Rykodisc, 1998)
4. Sugar, *Besides* (with bonus live CD) (Rykodisc, 1995)
5. Nova Mob, *Last Days of Pompeii* (Rough Trade, 1991)
6. Bob Mould, *The Poison Years* (Virgin, 1994)
7. Grant Hart, *Hot Wax* (Con D'Or/MVD, 2009)
8. Gang Font feat. Interloper, self-titled (Thirsty Ear, 2007)
9. Grant Hart, *Good News for Modern Man* (Pachyderm, 1999)
10. Bob Mould Band, *Live at ATP 2008* (BMD09, 2010)

APPENDIX XI
Tributes

The following roughly chronological list of Hüsker Dü "tributes" includes songs with explicit, single-line mentions of the band (e.g., Sebadoh's "Gimme Indie Rock") and entire songs about the band or a band member (e.g., the Posies' "Grant Hart"). Given the vastness of indie rock and the number of local scenes around the world, absolute thoroughness would be impossible, but this list certainly covers the most prominent examples.

Replacements, "Somethin' to Dü"
Dead Milkmen, "The Thing That Only Eats Hippies"

Squirrel Bait, "Bob Mould and Those Pillowbiters" (early outtake on a free 7-inch included with the November 1987 issue of *The Pope* 'zine)

Masters of the Obvious/M.O.T.O. (Paul Caporino), "Candy Apple Wig"

Mold, "Bob Mould Hates Me"

Benalto, "Grant Hart"

The Posies, "Grant Hart"

Lotion, "Gardening Your Wig"

Furnaceface, "Ode to Grant Hart"

Splitsville, "Hüsker Dü"

Sebadoh, "Gimme Indie Rock"

KPOP, "Bob Mould"

Gutta Percha, "What About Bob Mould?"

Saturnine, "The History of Cleveland"

Anthemic Pop Wonder, "How Great Was Hüsker Dü!"

Wolf Colonial, "Jet Ski Accidents"

Bugs Multiply, "Thinking of Hüsker Dü"

Klimek, "For Grant Hart and Bob Mould"

Scott Bishop, "Kitten's Got Curves"

APPENDIX XII
Artists Who Have Covered Hüsker Dü Songs

The following artists have covered a Hüsker Dü song on a recording meant for commercial release or public distribution. Artists who have only covered solo or post-Hüsker songs by individual members have not been included. Like the tributes listed above, this listing comes very, very close to being comprehensive but cannot comfortably claim to be one hundred percent thorough. Still, as a collection of more than one hundred fifty artists and bands, it makes for a quick and easy confirmation that Hüsker Dü did indeed leave a lasting impression on a wide variety of creative minds, and continues to do so today more than ever:

2Bad, 20 Minute Loop, Acredine, Allison Ate, Alloy, Anodyne, Anthrax, Apple-O, Arcwelder, Balance, Balloon Guy, Bartt Richards, Baysix, Bellibone, Big Dipper, Big Drill Car, Big Trouble House, Blackstar, Blue Hippos, the Blue Up?, Bored, Boxhamsters, Braille Closet, Brzeszinski, Burning Defeat, Calhoun Conquer, Catherine Wheel, Charles Bronson, Coffin Break, Cripple Bastards, the Crowd Scene, Crummy Stuff, Cynical Spin, D.I., Deacon Blue, Die Art, Dogfight, Dottie Danger, Drunken Boat, Dylan Hicks & 3 Pesos, Elf Power, Engrained, Ensign, Entombed, Everready, Farside, Fireside, Floating Opera, Flour, Foo Fighters, Gigantor, God's Favorite Band, the Grannies, Gravenhurst, Green Day, Guz, Hammerhead, the Hang Ups, Heavens to Murgatroid, Heidi Berry, In June, Infestation of Ass, the Intentions, Janitor Joe, John Auer, Jolt, Jonas Jinx, Kerbdog, Kevin Keller, Killbilly, Kina, Ledfoot, Lies Incorporated/TVBC, Life Indicator, Lifetime, Lomas, Mark Davis, Mark Kozelek, the Maykings, Medfield M.A., Mega City Four, Merryland, the Mighty Mofos, Mink Stole, Mother Brothers, Motorpsycho, Muskellunge, My Own Worst Enemy, Neil Tergett, Nitrominds, NRA, Only Living Witness, Pansy Division, Peyton Place, Pig Meat, Political Asylum, Pollen Art, Popsicle, Poster Children, Potato Fritz, Pray TV, Prest Asbestus, the Pride, Pseudonymphs,

Punch Line, Radon, Richies, Richmond Fontaine, Ritmo Tribale, Robbie Lee, Robert Palmer, Rubbermaids, Salbando, Sator, Sciflyer, Screamfeeder, Sebadoh, Shock Treatment, Sick of It All, Sidecar, Sommerset, Sottopressione, Sport, Sportclub, Starbilly, Steve Shaw & Keith Lee, Strangemen, Superball '63, Superdrag, Teenage Larvae, Tempo Zero, Terry Hoax, Therapy?, Thomas Belhom, Treadmill Trackstar, Tres Kids, Trip Shakespeare, TVBC, Upset Noise, Vanilla Chainsaws, Vertigo, VHS or Beta, Vitesse, Walt Mink, Willie Wisely Trio, Wounded Knee, and ZuZu's Petals.

Finally, the annotated and comprehensive lists of tributes and cover versions would not have been possible without Paul Hilcoff's unbelievably helpful Hüsker Dü Database (www.thirdav.com). Paul's vast knowledge of all things underground rock, plus his unwavering loyalty to Hüsker Dü as a fan, are untouchable and increasingly rare qualities.

APPENDIX XIII
Heavily Influenced Contemporaries and Followers: A Quick and Cursory Reference List

FOO FIGHTERS: early, less metalloid, and more up-tempo material owes a major debt to late-period Hüskers, particularly Hart's *Candy Apple Grey* singles "Don't Want to Know If You Are Lonely" and "Sorry Somehow"

LEATHERFACE: singer/guitarist Frankie Stubbs' vocals are highly reminiscent of Bob Mould's, both in sound and phrasing; Stubbs' workhorse, hardscrabble pop-punk will appeal to anyone enamored with Hüsker Dü's post-hardcore efforts

LEMONHEADS: all albums through *It's a Shame About Ray*

LES THUGS: French pop-punk/melodic hardcore band's albums on Sub Pop owe a major debt to the Hüskers

NAKED RAYGUN/PEGBOY: all albums by either band; the former was a longer-running contemporary of the Hüskers, and the latter offshoot captured the Hüsker influence in a sublimely catchy fashion

THE PIXIES: early-'90s albums show more of a Hüsker influence than earlier work, though it's safe to assume that if one is a big Pixies fan, a healthy appreciation of Hüsker Dü is likely

SOUL ASYLUM: all albums through . . . *And the Horse They Rode in On*, especially *Made to Be Broken* and *Hang Time*

SQUIRREL BAIT: *Sun God* and *Skag Heaven* albums

SUPERCHUNK: self-titled, *No Pocky for Kitty*, and *On the Mouth* albums, plus the *Tossing Seeds* singles compilation

WEEZER: self-titled debut

269

See also Archers of Loaf, Arcwelder, Band of Susans Big Dipper, Buffalo Tom, Catherine Wheel, Green Day, Fluf, Guzzard, the Jesus and Mary Chain, Knapsack, Monsterland, New Radiant Storm King, Open Hand, Pond, Queens of the Stone Age, Swervedriver, Tar, Urge Overkill, and Walt Mink.

APPENDIX XIV
Complementary Texts

Readers who want to learn more about Hüsker Dü's musical and cultural periphery are encouraged to read the following:

Must-Read Books

ENTER NAOMI: SST, L.A., AND ALL THAT . . . BY JOE CARDUCCI (REDOUBT PRESS): As a historical document of SST, this book sits well with *Rock and the Pop Narcotic* by avoiding overlap, but it is still fragmented. The proper SST history will have to wait for the writer who's able to spend five years with Greg Ginn. As a biography and obituary for Naomi Peterson, the label's house photographer, this is a heartfelt and sad tribute to a deserving friend and colleague. Best read before *Rock and the Pop Narcotic*.

GET IN THE VAN BY HENRY ROLLINS (2.61.13): An autobiographical telling of Rollins' days with Black Flag that works by extension as a unique and insider biography of both the band and SST, circa 1981 to 1986. No matter what one's opinion might be when it comes to Rollins' spoken or written work, this is an essential read.

GOING UNDERGROUND: AMERICAN PUNK, 1979–1992 BY GEORGE HURCHALLA (ZUO PRESS): This wonderful and exhaustive account of the American punk and hardcore movement stands as one of the great triumphs of the self-publishing world, since Hurchalla self-funded and researched for more than six years. This one's essential as well.

OUR BAND COULD BE YOUR LIFE: SCENES FROM THE AMERICAN INDIE UNDERGROUND, 1981–1991 BY MICHAEL AZERRAD (LITTLE, BROWN): Essential, especially if one is young and in the process of forming a lifelong bond with great music. As of this writing, *Our Band . . .* contains the only biographical treatments of Minor Threat/Fugazi, Beat Happening, Butthole Surfers, Dinosaur Jr, Mission of Burma, Mudhoney, Minutemen, and Big Black.

RADIO SILENCE: A SELECTED VISUAL HISTORY OF AMERICAN HARDCORE MUSTIC BY NATHAN NEDOROSTEK AND ANTHONY PAPPALARDO (MTV PRESS): A tasteful, fascinating, and visually focused look at American hardcore from the beginning to the mid-1990s. Too scattershot to serve as a thorough biographical or annotated retelling, it's nonetheless a far more thoughtful and intelligent book than Steven Blush's often factually incorrect *American Hardcore*.

ROCK AND THE POP NARCOTIC: TESTAMENT FOR THE ELECTRIC CHURCH BY JOE CARDUCCI (REDOUBT PRESS): Quite possibly the most important rock 'n' roll book written in the past twenty-five years, this text would launch an appreciation of hard rock, heavy metal, and select underground bands (Hüskers included) that would develop into large-scale revivals and provide the groundwork for an astonishing amount of the rock criticism and reissue fervor that has occurred since the book's early-1990s publication. Essential is an understatement.

SPRAY PAINT THE WALLS: THE STORY OF BLACK FLAG BY STEVIE CHICK (OMNIBUS PRESS): The Sonic Youth biographer tackles Black Flag and succeeds, more or less. This one is hard to put down, even if the reader has heard many of the stories before.

TOUCH AND GO: THE COMPLETE HARDCORE PUNK ZINE '70–'83
BY TESCO VEE AND DAVE SIMSON, EDITED BY STEVE MILLER
(BAZILLION POINTS)

Important 'Zines of the Era

Each of the following 'zines was born of the early hardcore scene and lasted long enough to be a crucial piece of the developmental puzzle.

FLIPSIDE: Like *MRR* but sloppier and less stodgy. Archived at operationphoenix.com.

FORCED EXPOSURE: The Cadillac of hardcore 'zines grew into something great and influential before ceasing to exist in 1992. Allegedly, an archival book is in the works.

HONORABLE MENTIONS: *Conflict*, *Matter*, *Suburban Punk/Suburban Voice*, and *Ink Disease*. Some can be read in archival form at punkzinearchive.blogspot.com.

MAXIMUMROCKNROLL: Founded by Tim Yohannon and currently published by an assortment of dedicated souls, *MRR* is still kicking and still vital after all these years in direct opposition to perpetual backlash and financial hardships.

YOUR FLESH: A direct result of the Twin Cities' fertile early-'80s scene, Peter Davis' opinionated periodical subsequently became one of the longest-running 'zines of the past thirty years. Loads of archival content can be enjoyed by visiting *Your Flesh* in its current online incarnation, yourflesh.com.

For an almost-complete archive of Hüsker Dü press, be it glossy magazine or tiny Xerox job, please see Paul Hilcoff's archive page (part of his Hüsker Dü Database): thirdav.com/hddb.shtml. In addition, *SPIN* magazine has has dedicated a respectable amount of ink to Hüsker Dü, Bob Mould, and Grant Hart over the years. As of this writing, much of it can be found via Google's book search function.

ACKNOWLEDGMENTS

I wish there was a way to write "This book would not have been possible without the following people . . . " in a hard-hitting, superlative manner that accurately illustrates just how grateful I am for the selfless contributions of so many to this book, but there's not. Each person's contribution was unique, therefore it's impossible to articulate a universal "thanks" without falling short.

The majority of interviewed sources had no idea who I was at the onset of conversation. I have a special spark of gratitude for the people who trusted me when they didn't have to. The following list is not exclusive to interview subjects, since I have also included people who provided "behind-the-scenes" help, professional support and advice, side work (with the knowledge that I was deadline-challenged), lifesaving nudges in the right direction, and emotional fortitude:

Steve Albini, Patrick Amory, Mark Athitakis, David Barbe, Lori Barbero, Chris Benson, Jon Bream, Bill Bruce, Joe Carducci, Angie Carlson, Ian Christe, Clint Conley, Gerard Cosloy, Jim Crego, Bill Cuevas, Peter Davis, David Dunlap Jr., Santiago Durango, Ray Farrell, Anton Fier, Jon Fine, Heidi Freier, Eric Friedl, Matthew Fritch, Lou Giordano, David Grubbs, Grant Hart, Sara Hays, Tom Hazelmyer, Paul Hilcoff, George Hurchalla, Aadam Jacobs, Jeffrey Jensen, Peter Jesperson, Steve Kandell, Terry Katzman, Amy Kellner, Dave King, Mike LaVella, Jerry Labounta, Tony Maimone, Steve Manning, Colin Mansfield, David Markey, Joe McElheny, Bob Mehr, Eric Miller, Doug Mosurock, Greg Norton, Andy Nystrom, Chris Osgood, Henry Owings, Julie Panebianco, Austin L. Ray, Jeremy Sidener, Spot, Bill Stevenson, Steve Sutherland, Mike Watt, Sherman Wilmott, and Jon Wurster.

And thanks to my editor, Dennis Pernu, for putting up with my shit.

Finally, I must extend a special gesture of gratitude to Tom Scharpling; a deeply heartfelt salute to my mother, Mary F. Earles, who probably could have done without this whole mess; plus a loving thanks to my girlfriend, Jenny Hansom, who, despite logic, spent the past two years by my side.

SONG, LP AND EP INDEX

INDEX